NORFOLK ASSEMBLY

by the same author

★

HORACE WALPOLE

NORFOLK PORTRAITS

A NORFOLK GALLERY

COUNTRY NEIGHBOURHOOD
(Published by Faber & Faber)

★

THOMAS GRAY

MATTHEW PRIOR
(Published by the Cambridge University Press)

SIR WILLIAM PASTON
*from a painting by an unknown artist,
in the possession of the author*

Norfolk Assembly

by

R. W. KETTON-CREMER

FABER AND FABER LIMITED
24 Russell Square
London

First published in mcmlvii
by Faber and Faber Limited
24 Russell Square London W.C.1
Printed in Great Britain by
Western Printing Services Limited, Bristol

To
A. L. ROWSE

CONTENTS

9

ILLUSTRATIONS

PREFACE

This book is a collection of studies written at various times during the past eight years. Its scope is somewhat wider than that of its predecessors, *Norfolk Portraits* and *A Norfolk Gallery*, since one chapter deals with events of the sixteenth century, and another is a tribute to a contemporary of my own. In all three books, I have sought to achieve something of that 'synthesis of local and national history' advocated by Dr. A. L. Rowse long ago in the preface to *Tudor Cornwall*. That magnificent book first kindled in me the ambition to record, on however limited a scale, the history of my own county. The dedication of this volume is a small token of my gratitude to Dr. Rowse for the inspiration of his writings and the happiness of his friendship.

I have received much kindness and help from the owners of unpublished manuscripts. My thanks are due especially to the Dean and Chapter of Norwich, for permission to quote so freely from the diary of Dean Prideaux; to the Hon. Doris Harbord, for allowing me to make use of the papers and the 'household book' at Gunton, and to reproduce her portrait of Sir Thomas Browne; and to Mr. Gerald Yorke, for the use of the diary of Lady Beauchamp Proctor. Manuscripts in the British Museum, the Bodleian Library and the archives of the City of Norwich have also been consulted, and my use of them is acknowledged in the bibliography; but I would like to express here my thanks to the officials of those institutions for their assistance.

I am grateful to the editors of *The Times Literary Supplement*, *The Listener*, *The Eastern Daily Press* and *Norfolk Archæology* for permission to reprint certain material which first appeared in their pages. I would also like to thank the Earl of Ilchester, and Messrs. John Murray, for allowing me to quote passages from *Lord Hervey and his Friends* (1952);

Preface

and Messrs. Macmillan for permission to quote two stanzas from Thomas Hardy's poem *An Ancient to Ancients*.

For permission to reproduce certain illustrations my thanks are due to the Earl of Leicester, the Courtauld Institute of Art and the Norwich Museums Committee.

For help in various other ways I must thank Mrs. A. P. D. Penrose, Mrs. Ivo Hood, Mrs. St. George Saunders, Miss Sophia Mottram, Dr. W. O. Hassall, Mr. Philip Hepworth (City Librarian of Norwich), Mr. W. G. Hiscock and Mr. Francis Hawcroft.

R. W. K.-C.

Felbrigg Hall
  Norwich
March 1957

14

Part I

★

PEOPLE

SIR WILLIAM PASTON

I

At the opening of the seventeenth century the fortunes of the Pastons had reached their zenith. The early struggles of the family, so vividly described in the mass of medieval correspondence known as *The Paston Letters*, were only a distant memory. They had now been, for more than a hundred years, the undisputed masters of wide estates, living in opulence in their fine houses, influential in all the affairs of East Anglia. Their wealth had become proverbial. 'There was never a Paston poor, a Heydon a coward, or a Cornwallis a fool.'

At this time the patriarch of the family was Sir William Paston, who had been the head of his line for fifty years past. His portrait at the Grammar School at North Walsham, his own foundation, shows him in old age—dressed in black, bent and leaning on his staff, weary but benign. All his life he had lived at Paston, the family home in the village by the bleak and windswept seashore, where his ancestors had first risen from obscurity and whence their name was derived; or at Caister, the impressive castle close to Yarmouth, built by Sir John Fastolf in the fifteenth century, bequeathed by him to an earlier Paston, and thereafter held by the family against all the sieges and the lawsuits of rival claimants. Towards the close of his life Sir William had inherited Oxnead, the lovely Tudor house in the valley of the Bure, with its gardens and pleasure-grounds sloping down to the little river. Oxnead had been built by Clement Paston, an adventurous younger son, during his career as a soldier, a naval commander, and a courtier under two kings and two queens. After his death at the close of Queen Elizabeth's reign it had passed to his nephew Sir William, and was certainly the noblest of all his possessions.

B
17

The traditional prosperity of the Pastons was marred by a single bitter circumstance. Although there was never a Paston poor, there was always one who was a fool. Sooner or later, in every generation, at least one member of the family revealed this strain of mental instability. Proverbs and jests on the subject had long been current in Norfolk; and there was also a legend that long ago a Prior of Bromholme, worsted in a dispute about some land by an earlier Paston, had pronounced a curse upon his adversary and all his successors—'Sir, since you are thus inexorable and cruel to us and our brethren and house, you shall certainly from henceforth always have one of your family a fool, till it is become poor.'

Sir William Paston died in 1610 at the age of eighty-two. He was succeeded by his grandson Sir Edmund, who had lately married Katherine Knyvett of Ashwellthorpe; and their elder son William, the subject of this chapter, was born in the year of his father's succession to the estates. Sir Edmund was already a man of uncertain health. Some trouble with his leg used to keep him from active life for long periods at a time. Before long the affliction of the Pastons descended upon him also, and he grew incapable of paying much attention to the business of his estates. Fortunately his wife was a woman of exceptional powers. She managed his property with great ability, and her masterful rule extended over all his affairs. She received much help in these matters from the husbands of her sisters, and indeed from the whole ramifying Knyvett cousinship to which she belonged. The life of the widespread manors went prosperously forward; the Paston wealth continued its steady increase, year after year. And, most important of all, her elder son proved a promising and talented boy.

William Paston went to Cambridge, as a fellow-commoner of Corpus Christi College, at the age of fourteen. Many letters from his mother illuminate the three and a half years which he spent there, but only two of his replies to her have survived. In the first, as a lately-arrived freshman, he describes how he has played the surgeon and cured his tutor's sore finger. In the second, written early in 1625, he has been to the Court at Newmarket. There he saw Prince Charles and the Duke of

Buckingham, but the King was not well—he died, in fact, in the following month. Lady Paston's letters are intimate and delightful, filled with small jokes and pious admonitions and the most loving solicitude. William was to have a very reverend respect for the Master, and should on no account be too talkative in his presence. He was not to meddle with any of the townsmen, in earnest or in jest. He was always to be kind to the poor sizars. He must not exercise himself too violently at tennis, or eat too much fruit or pie-crust, or indulge in possetty curdy drinks. It was to be hoped that he hated the very smell of tobacco. All kinds of fine clothes were sent to him, beaver hats and silk stockings, a satin suit and a silver girdle; and quantities of delicacies, cakes and cheeses and boxes of marmalade. Especial provision was made against the austerities of Lent, but in that case a proper measure of caution had to be exercised. Outward observance must be kept up; the puddings and the sausages and the turkey pasty were 'to eate in your chamber, your good tutor and you together'.

Everyone liked William Paston at Cambridge. His tutor, the Rev. William Roberts, was devoted to him. The Master, Dr. Samuel Walsall, was greatly pleased by his conversation and good manners, and reassured Lady Paston on the question of his over-indulgence in tennis. 'There is not any exercise more wholsome,' he wrote, 'and not many more gentleman-like.' None the less, he drew up a new time-table 'to prevent daunger, and inconvenience, which might growe by the immoderate, or unseasonable use thereof'—exercise till somewhat past eight, breakfast till nine, study till eleven, recreation in the garden till one, study till somewhat past three, and exercise again until prayers. The young man followed this programme with diligence, and may indeed have deserved the praises of Thomas Fuller, a humble but admiring contemporary at Queens', who described him in after years as *invidendum decus Collegii Corporis Christi*. He read widely in several languages, and when he left Cambridge in the summer of 1627 he had become an extremely cultivated young man—'furnished with graces', as his mother had hoped in one of her letters, 'as a bee comes loaden to her hive'.

19

Early in 1629, less than two years after William Paston had returned home from Cambridge, his mother died and was buried in the chancel of Paston church. Her son raised to her memory a noble monument, the work of Nicholas Stone. Her effigy, a matronly figure carved in white marble, dressed in the pomp of ruff and veil, wide puffed sleeves and flowing gown, reclines beneath a double-arched canopy with a pediment above. The pallor of the statue is contrasted with the surrounding alabaster, the columns of marble veined in red and grey, the rich heraldic achievement supported by mourning figures; and on tables of black marble are inscribed her praises,

> *Whose vertue did all ill soe overswaye*
> *That her whole life was a comunion daye.*

From Stone's notebook it appears that he was paid the large sum of £340 for this monument, and he further recorded that while setting it up at Paston he was 'very extreordenerly entertayned thar'. It was the beginning of a long and intimate association between the celebrated sculptor and his young patron.

A few months after his mother's death William Paston married Lady Katherine Bertie, a daughter of Robert first Earl of Lindsey, a well-known soldier and a prominent figure at Court. Their betrothal is mentioned in one of the letters which that most likeable man, Paston's cousin Thomas Knyvett of Ashwellthorpe, addressed to his wife. Knyvett was the elder of the cousins by fourteen years, but his worldly affairs were in a very different posture. Although he might successfully have claimed the dormant barony of Berners, he was in fact a country gentleman of steadily declining estate. All his life he was fated to suffer disappointment and loss; yet his letters, recently published and perhaps not yet appreciated at their true worth, show him as unfailingly cheerful and sweet-tempered in all his troubles. When writing to his wife he usually referred to William Paston as 'our great cosin' or 'our great kinsman'. On this occasion he told Mrs. Knyvett in June 1629 that 'our great cosin is not yet married, nor will not be known when it shalbe, but it wilbe done very privatelye. Divers of his friends think he wooes very coldlye, he stayes soe little while with her when he goes.' The marriage took place towards the end of the year, and the young couple went to live at Oxnead. Sir Edmund remained at Paston, where he died three years afterwards. His monument, also the work of Nicholas Stone, stands in the church beside his wife's. It is altogether a simpler affair, lacking figures or heraldry, and with a modest urn in place of an effigy.

Hesitant though their wooing may have been, the short married life of William and Katherine Paston was a very happy one. A few years later, when the storms of the Civil War were desolating England, the sixteen-thirties appeared in retrospect as a golden decade, with 'so excellent a Composure throughout the whole Kingdom', in the words of Clarendon, 'that the like Peace, and Plenty, and universal Tranquility for ten years was never enjoy'd by any Nation'. Such would have been the view of William Paston and his wife. Both were opposed, by temperament and by family tradition, to the Puritan outlook in matters of church and state. They loved art and fine building and all the graces of life; and these were the years when the King was purchasing Mantegnas and Raphaels for his private collection, Van Dyck painting the Queen and her court, Rubens adorning the Banqueting House at Whitehall with those great canvases which displayed the power of monarchy driving rebellion and envy headlong to destruction. *Comus* was first performed on a Michaelmas night in the courtyard of Ludlow Castle. Falkland and his circle discussed philosophy and letters in the garden at Great Tew. Houses by Inigo Jones and his disciples rose in London and the countryside. In Norfolk something of this atmosphere was achieved at Oxnead. The place became renowned for its works of art, the extent and elaboration of its gardens, its hospitality and good cheer.

It has all vanished now. We can only attempt to reconstruct its beauties from the small remaining fragment of the house, the uncertain outlines of walks and avenues, and the entries in the account books of Nicholas Stone. The house itself stood on a rise of ground, and its gardens extended in a series of terraces down to the river. The Tudor splendours of the building were further enriched by some of Stone's choicest work—a magnificent chimney-piece which cost eighty pounds; a smaller chimney-piece in the banqueting-house (there is nothing to show whether this was a pavilion in the gardens or an apartment in the main building); a balcony with two doors and an architrave of Portland stone; a 'copper branch'—perhaps some sort of candelabrum?—166 pounds in weight; the heads of the twelve Caesars, bronzed; a great shield carved with the Paston arms. Stone also provided a number of statues —Venus and Cupid, Jupiter, Flora, a large figure of Cerberus on a pedestal, which is supposed to have been placed on the terrace in front of the south door—and an iron pergola of impressive dimensions, painted green and surmounted by eight gilded balls. All kinds of lesser ornaments for house and gardens are mentioned in his very miscellaneous bills—landscapes and figure paintings, picture-frames and a marble table, busts of Marcus Aurelius and Faustina, paving-stones and balustrades.

The fragment of an inventory, of uncertain date, gives some idea of the interior of Oxnead. It contained a few remarkable works of art, and a vast array of miscellaneous treasures and trinkets. Room after room glittered with Elizabethan display and Jacobean opulence—vessels of crystal and agate and cornelian and amber, fantastic shells set in silver and ivory, paintings in their richly carved frames, miniatures and enamels and plate and porcelain in endless variety. The hospitality of the house was gay and lavish. At the same time it was conducted with a refinement slightly disconcerting to old-fashioned neighbours, more accustomed in their own homes to strong ale and pewter than to fine wines and beautiful glassware. A Captain Robert Bacon is recorded in Sir Nicholas L'Estrange's book of jests as commenting from another point of view on the elegance of these entertainments. 'Revelling at Sir William Paston's, he had his sack served him in a curious Venice glass, but very much under the size he us'd to trade in. And after a long contemplation of his measure, "Sir William," sayes he, "if you value this glasse

OXNEAD

*from an engraving by John Smith after a drawing, reconstructing the house,
by John Adey Repton*

(as I beleeve you doe) tye a good long string to it, to draw him up againe, for, before God, I shall swallow him down at one time or other".'

All this happiness was cruelly broken before many years had passed. Lady Katherine had borne her husband three sons and two daughters: in the first week of 1637 she died at the birth of her sixth child. She was buried in Oxnead church, where a monument by Nicholas Stone was presently raised to her memory. Stone described it as a 'tomb for my Lady Katren his dear wyef'. He seldom included in his notebooks any such expressions of personal feeling, and it is clear that he knew Lady Katherine well and was grieved at her death. The most conspicuous feature of the monument is a bust in white marble against a background of black. It is unmistakably a portrait, and the youthful head is one of the most beautiful and moving of all his works.

The same note of personal sorrow is to be heard in a little volume of *Funerall Elegies*, published a few months later by Ralph Knevet, William Paston's poetical chaplain.[1] There are three of these elegies, addressed in the main to her sister Lady Elizabeth Bertie, who

> *late sweld up the streames of cristall* Bure,
> *With your more cristall teares, and rills more pure.*

They are not mere conventional expressions of grief. Knevet was an indifferent poet; but repeatedly, in his flood of verbiage, the sudden pathos of a few lines convinces the reader that the subject of Stone's haunting bust was a woman of exceptional sympathy and goodness. It was from the bottom of his heart that the chaplain mourned his patroness in the wintry weeks following her death, as he wandered in the frozen landscape round Oxnead,

> *When Hills, and Valleys, wrap't in sheets of Snow,*
> *Did pennance for their summer luxury.*

[1] The full title is *Funerall Elegies; Consecreated to the immortall memory, of the Right Honorable the Lady Katherine Paston, late wife to the truely noble, and heroicke, William Paston of Oxned Esquire*. At the close of the book are printed the epitaphs, Latin and English, on her monument in Oxnead church, which establishes them to be also of Knevet's composition.

In the year of his wife's death William Paston was obliged
to serve as High Sheriff of Norfolk. In 1638, as soon as he was
free of the duties of that office, he sought to assuage his grief
by a long period of foreign travel. He was accompanied by his
friend Thomas le Gros, son of Sir Charles le Gros of Crostwight, and by Ralph Knevet his chaplain. Nothing is known
of his journeyings until 31st July of that year, when he arrived
at Florence. Nicholas Stone's son and namesake had been
sight-seeing and drawing statuary in Florence for the past
month, and his diary gives several glimpses of his father's
patron and friend. Their first encounter took place on the day
after Paston's arrival: 'in the afternoone I mett Mr. Paston
hard by the temple of St. Michell, who being very courteous
said "Sometimes you must looke after me, for we must haue
many a walke together".' It is curious, and not wholly inap-
propriate, that the only remark of William Paston's that has
come down to us exactly as it was spoken should have been
these few friendly words to an obscure young sculptor.

Next day Stone waited on Paston, and accompanied him
while he looked for a lodging: eventually he hired an unfur-
nished house for three months, for the sum of twenty crowns.
They went sight-seeing together several times. At the Grand
Duke's gallery 'Mr. Paston profest he had not seene so many
rarytyes in one place in all his travells'. At Poggio Imperiale
he commissioned Stone to make fair drawings of the villa for
his collection. On another occasion he gave Stone a knife with
an agate haft, for the young man to present to 'Sʳ Bastian',
the keeper of the gallery, in return for his kindness while he
was drawing the statues there. Thomas le Gros set out for
England in September, and Paston went with him to Leghorn.
At the port he found a convenient ship which would take him
to Egypt, made a hasty redisposition of his plans, and returned to Florence for a few days to collect his baggage. Stone
much wanted to accompany him, but Paston 'thought itt no
wayes conuenient for me by reason of the losse of my time
and the great taxes that Christians pay entring Grand Cairo
and other parts of Egypt; but he told me he would doe me any

courtesy I would desire him for my father's sake or for my owne'.

So Stone, whose remittances from home had failed to arrive, borrowed some money for himself and his brother Henry, the future painter, who was also in Florence; and they dined with their kindly friend and helped him with his packing. On 21st September, 'being St. Matthew's Day, and a very rainy morning', Paston took coach for Leghorn, and thence sailed for Alexandria. He was attended by his three servants, whom Stone names as Mr. Bell, Mr. Seaker and Mr. Maxwell. The Reverend Ralph Knevet remained behind, 'hoping to meet Mr. Paston at Rome when itt shall please God he returnes, which he hopes to accomplish in six monthes'. A few days afterwards he and the Stones journeyed to Rome together. He does not appear to have enjoyed his time there. His unpublished poems, meritorious exercises in the manner of George Herbert, contain many disparaging references to cardinals, priests, the Vatican and so forth. One of them begins:

> *When I (at Rome) beheld poore people fall*
> *Before brasse, stone, and paper painted,*
> *Yea every mettall, and material,*
> *That canonized was, and Saynted,*
> *I wonder'd then, where the least sense did lye,*
> *Or in the Idoll, or the Votarye.*

Few of the young Englishmen who went abroad in the seventeenth century ever journeyed beyond the confines of Europe. Travel in the Turkish dominions was often dangerous, always uncomfortable and expensive. But for those whose curiosity led them to visit Egypt and the Holy Land the experience was unforgettable, and their adventures provided a wealth of conversation and reflection for the rest of their lives. Long afterwards William Paston caused the painter of his portrait to depict in one corner a little oriental landscape—a clouded sky, a group of pyramids and palms, a river on whose bank a crocodile devours a turbaned man while another hastens away with gestures of alarm. There were plenty of crocodiles in the Nile, besides the monster whose capture was so graphically described by William Lithgow a few years before;

but we shall never know what particular incident Paston
wished to commemorate in this way. Doubtless it was often
described at the Oxnead dinner-table, as was the phenomenal
rainstorm which he witnessed at Cairo. A few years later
Dr. Thomas Browne was able to assert in *Pseudodoxia Epidemica*, on Paston's 'honourable and ocular testimony', that it
is a Vulgar Error to suppose that it never rains in Egypt,
since during his sojourn there 'it rained in Grand Cairo
divers days together'.

Otherwise nothing is known about Paston's travels in the
east. Apparently he spent some time in the company of John
Greaves the astronomer, who mentions him—'my very noble
and worthy friend'—in his *Pyramidographia* as a witness to
the unwonted violence of the weather at that time. After
several weeks in Cairo he set out for the Holy Land, and
stayed for a while in Jerusalem. But his movements are obscure until Stone's diary records, in the following March, that
he had arrived safely at Rome with all his company. He
passed a month or so in sight-seeing with Stone, and making
a little excursion with him to Tivoli and Frascati. No doubt
he collected many rarities for the future adornment of
Oxnead. He left Rome in April on his way to Venice, and
reached England a few months later.

Back at Oxnead once more, with his latest treasures adorning its rooms, Paston resumed his open-handed and luxurious
hospitality. His cousin Thomas Knyvett stayed there in the
following February, and described the atmosphere of the
house, with an amused side-glance at his host's exotic reminiscences, in a letter to his wife. 'Dear Mustress: heer's no
parting without a glance of unkindness till Monday or Tues-
day, wherfore I have dispatcht this chimicall embassador to
let thee knowe that I am passing well, but what I shall returne
home I am a little doubtfull. One while we are Italians, another while Turks, by and by Egiptians, and eftsoones merry
Greeks, but all very well and handsome, the meene reduct'te
to a fine temper. I might spend another week and not see all
the rarityes. Indeed heer is a world of curiosityes and some
very rich ones, as cabinets and juells, but I must not forestall
my owne market, for if I enter into particulars I shall have

nothing to taulke of when I come home. . . . My cosin Paston presents his servis and commands me to crave your pardon for keeping of me.'

IV

By this time the golden decade was over, and everywhere the skies were darkening. Paston and Knyvett, as they talked and drank together at Oxnead, were uneasily conscious that their own views did not accord with the opinions of most of their neighbours. The feeling in Norfolk was strongly Puritan, and was growing more so with every month that passed. They were themselves anxious for peace and moderation in all things, but their private sympathies were with the King, the Church, the established order. At this stage, however, neither they nor anyone else anticipated the full violence of the conflict that lay ahead. The ominous year of 1640 advanced; the Short Parliament was elected, was dissolved, was succeeded in November by the Parliament destined to last through so many fateful years; but Paston continued without much perturbation to adorn his house and garden. Stone's account book shows large purchases of Purbeck marble and similar materials at this time. Statues of Jupiter and Hercules in Portland stone were sent down to Oxnead, and were followed next year by similar figures of Apollo, Juno and Diana.

In the summer of 1641 the King, who had created no new baronets in Norfolk for twelve years, suddenly bestowed that honour upon several of the leading gentlemen of the county. Although it was a distinction not always welcomed by its recipients, he probably had some hopes of strengthening loyal feeling in this corner of his realm at a time of uncertainty and strain. If so, he was to be disappointed later, when at least two of these newly-created baronets, Sir John Potts of Mannington and Sir John Palgrave of North Barningham, figured with great activity among his opponents. It is an indication of Paston's high standing in the county that he was the senior in this new creation, his patent bearing the date of 8th June 1641. It may have been about this time also that he married his second wife, Margaret Hewitt, a daughter of Sir Thomas Hewitt of Pishiobury in Hertfordshire.

People

The sympathies of the majority in Norfolk may be judged from the members who were returned to sit in the Long Parliament. The knights of the shire were both men of Puritan leanings, Sir John Potts of Mannington and Sir Edmund Mundeford of Feltwell. The five boroughs—Norwich, Great Yarmouth, King's Lynn, Thetford and Castle Rising—returned eight members who acted later against the King, and only two who supported him: Richard Catelyn of Kirby Cane, one of the members for Norwich, and Sir Robert Hatton, a courtier nominated for the little borough of Castle Rising. In Parliament, ten members against two; in the Norfolk towns and countryside, probably much the same predominance of Puritans over Royalists. Some of the borough members, moreover, were gentlemen of great local influence. Sir Thomas Wodehouse of Kimberley and Framlingham Gawdy of West Harling sat for Thetford; Sir John Holland of Quidenham was the other member for Castle Rising.

Opposition to these formidable and resolute neighbours was not easy for a man of Paston's temperament. Peaceable and moderate, anxious only to live quietly at his beautiful Oxnead, he deplored the contentiousness and ill-humour of the times. Why should he have to wrangle with Puritan squires about episcopal government and the prayer book, altar-rails and 'dopping worship' and the Popish injunctions of Bishop Wren? Whether he actively maintained High Church views, and had openly sympathized with the Laudian reforms of that courageous Bishop during his three stormy years at Norwich, remains uncertain; it is by no means impossible. But his general aim seems to have been the exercise of moderate measures, and the restoration of peace and good feeling to the Norfolk countryside.

It was a vain hope. Strafford was impeached and executed; Laud was imprisoned; the King made his fateful attempt to arrest the five members, and then withdrew from his capital city. The Puritan leaders, in Norfolk as elsewhere, rejoiced in the successes of their cause, and put increasing pressure upon everyone who was not yet openly on their side. This pressure was rendered almost intolerable to men of moderate views by an ordinance of Parliament for the mustering and training of the militia, which was at once countered by a proclamation from the King at York, forbidding his loyal subjects to carry out the directions of the ordinance. Most gentlemen of standing held commissions in the militia. Caught in this dilemma, Thomas Knyvett lamented to his wife that 'such is the sad condition of these times, as no man knowes howe to dispose himself, for nowe ther is so much declar'd as makes all officers in the kingdome Traytors of one side or other; neither are standers-by in any better condition.'

Already Parliament had cancelled the commissions of the existing Lords Lieutenant, and had replaced them by its own supporters. The new Lord Lieutenant of Norfolk was Robert Rich, second Earl of Warwick, and to him was entrusted the embodying of the militia under the new ordinance. He issued instructions to all militia officers to assume command of their companies; and Knyvett, who had gone to London, was one day confronted by Sir John Potts with a commission from Warwick to this effect. Nevertheless he determined 'to staye out of the way of my new masters till these first meetings be over'. Many others felt the same, among them Sir William Paston. He also came to London in May 1642, and told Knyvett that he had left Norfolk 'to avoid imployment'. In the search for some legal ground to justify this action he intended 'to be at the cost of the best councell in this towne in point of lawe, which he hath promised me privately I shall partake with him in'. His worries had a depressing effect on his spirits, once so convivial and gay; and Mrs. Knyvett learnt from her husband that the company of 'my great couzen, Sir William' was by no means 'so liquid as 't had wont to be'.

Paston decided in the end that it would be best to return to Norfolk. The situation was as yet obscure. He still saw some hopes of a settlement after the King had raised his standard at Nottingham in August, even after the indecisive battle of Edgehill a few weeks later. In that battle his first wife's father, the old Earl of Lindsey, had died of wounds, and her brother was made a prisoner. Deeply though his private sympathies were engaged, Paston hoped even now to exert some moderating influence in local affairs. It is possible that at first he may have succeeded in doing so. On 22nd September he attended a meeting of Deputy Lieutenants to arrange about the recruiting of men, the assembling of arms, and the collecting of money and plate for the defence of the county. Among his colleagues on this occasion were 'the four Sir Johns'—Hobart, Holland, Potts and Palgrave—who were so active on the side of the Parliament throughout the years to come; and one gentleman who shared his own Royalist sympathies, Sir Robert de Grey of Merton. During the next few days, meetings were held at Aylsham, Holt and Walsingham to receive subscriptions. On 8th October Paston attended such a meeting at Aylsham and subscribed £200, which was twice the sum volunteered even by the wealthiest of his Puritan neighbours. He also undertook to provide six horses fully furnished.

On 3rd December he was one of seven Deputy Lieutenants who signed a summons to the gentlemen of Norfolk to prepare the trained bands against 'divers forraigne forces', and to meet in Norwich on the 7th. These foreign forces were the troops which the Queen was assembling in Holland; their landing, expected somewhere on the east coast, was being eagerly awaited by Royalists throughout the country. In consequence the meeting at Norwich was a stormy one, and a violent clash of opinion took place between the Royalist and Parliamentarian elements among the assembled gentry. The Royalist sympathizers frankly said that 'if the Cavaliers were in the county, they should account them their friends'. The Parliamentarians were, of course, in a majority; and after much wrangling the leading Royalists, including Sir John Spelman, the son and heir of the great antiquary Sir Henry Spelman, and Hamon L'Estrange, the second son of Sir Hamon L'Estrange of Hunstanton, were 'commanded to depart the meeting'.

Nothing is known about Paston's own attitude on this occasion; but he seems to have determined soon afterwards that compromise was no longer possible, and that he must break loose from his Parliamentarian neighbours and openly declare for the King. He was markedly absent from the next important meeting of the Deputy Lieutenants, on 11th January 1643. On that day the momentous decision was taken that Norfolk should form part of the Eastern Association, the group of counties whose steadfast adherence to the Parliamentary cause was one of the deciding factors of the war. Shortly afterwards he was deprived of his militia command; and on 20th March Cromwell addressed a letter to the Chief Constables of the hundred of Holt, 'desiring them to give warning to all such in their hundred as found cuirassiers under the command of Sir William Paston, Baronet, to appear at Thetford on Monday the 27th instant, completed, to march away under command of Captain Robert Rich, for the defence of their county'. At some time during these months—it may have been quite soon after the controversial meeting at Norwich—he slipped across to Holland, and joined the group of Royalist sympathizers assembled there.

V

There is no record of what Paston did in Holland, or of what he had hoped to do. There were evidently good reasons why he withdrew to Rotterdam instead of making his way to the King's army at its Oxford headquarters. He had no military experience beyond the almost formal duties of a captain of militia in a decade of unruffled peace. His presence at Oxford, without the body of tenants and dependants which a gentleman from a northern or western county was able to bring in his train, would in no way have advanced the Royalist cause. King Charles was indulgent to those of his supporters whose estates lay in Parliamentarian counties, at the mercy of the local sequestration committees. The diarist John Evelyn, whose family property was in Surrey, 'finding it impossible to evade the doing very unhandsome things', obtained a licence from the King to travel abroad, and was engaged in a leisurely and protracted Grand Tour during the entire period of the Civil War. Paston, a considerably older man, at any rate took a stronger line than this. The assemblage at Rotterdam of Royalists from East Anglia was hardly accidental; and it must be supposed that they gathered there in connexion with some scheme of reinforcement or invasion of their own part of England. Their opponents soon knew all about it. On 14th June 1643, the House of Commons made an order that Sir

William Paston, and eleven other gentlemen from Norfolk and Suffolk, 'now residing at Rotterdam, and other parts beyond seas, doing ill offices against the Parliament, as this House is informed, shall be forthwith required to return into England within a month after notice left at their mansion houses, or otherwise all their estates, real and personal, shall be sequestered, and employed for the service of the Commonwealth'.

Paston and his companions ignored the summons. The situation in England at that moment looked more hopeful. Newcastle's army was driving down from the north into Lincolnshire, and it was thought that he would soon invade the counties of the Eastern Association. In August the town of King's Lynn declared for the King, and under the leadership of Sir Hamon L'Estrange held out for five weeks against Manchester's besieging forces. It may have been in connexion with this attempt that the Norfolk Royalists were holding themselves in readiness in Holland. But Lynn was effectively blockaded by the Parliamentary navy, and only one ship, with men and stores, was able to slip through. The town surrendered, and the grip of the Parliament on East Anglia was stronger than ever.

In the meantime the estates of the recalcitrant exiles had been duly sequestered. The rents of Paston's farms and the income from his manors were impounded. His wife, who had remained at Oxnead, was compelled to deliver up their magnificent plate. Some correspondence about this has survived. It appears that Lady Paston persuaded Sir John Potts, who was her neighbour at Mannington as well as one of the knights of the shire, to intercede with Manchester, then eagerly waiting for the plate to be coined into money for the payment of his troops. Eventually £1,100 worth of plate was surrendered. This represented a very large sum in the seventeenth century, and I am uncertain whether it reached Manchester entirely in plate or partly in cash. A certificate of protection was granted for what was left. 'I am glad', wrote Manchester to Potts, 'to have any occasion to expresse any respecte to persons of quallitye, and esteeme it a greater happiness to be understood as one thatt desires to win by

Sir William Paston

civillitye than by harshness. I have sent you the passe and protection accordinge to your desire, and shallbe ready to serve my Lady Paston.' Many years later, when Charles II paid a visit to Oxnead, Paston's son told the King that he would have been able to serve him far more richly in plate, 'had not a Blew Ribbon, that attended on His Majesty with a White Staff, plunder'd it from his Father by Trunksfull'. The reference was to Manchester, by then an elderly Lord Chamberlain in attendance on the monarch whose father he had defied and opposed thirty years before.

As the winter months passed by and the situation grew steadily worse, Paston felt that he had done his best and could now do no more. He and his family might well be reduced to penury, without affording the smallest help to the cause of the King. He too opened negotiations with Sir John Potts. On 15th February 1644, he addressed to him from Rotterdam a letter of surrender.

Much Honord Sir,

I doe infinitely acknowledge your manifold favors to me and my Pore wife, for which Sir I shall never forgett to be most thankfull. Sir I have a verie greate deale of reason to esteeme you my verie noble friende for your late advise to me, by George, to which Sir I assure you I am verie much inclinable, if you wilbe pleased to labor to sett me out a way, how I may make my Peace uppon reasonable Conditions with the Honorable House, and to be assured of my Lyberty, and estate, (payinge my proportions). I shold gladder visitt my owne country, than Oxford, and be subject to that authority under which I shall live, with fidelity and Honesty. Sir I have given George directions how your letters shall come to me, in which be pleased to give me the proceede of this my Binseness, and the most faythfull servis of your Servant shall never be wanting to express my selfe uppon all occasions

Sir
Your most faythfull and humble servant
WILL: PASTON.

A month later Paston was back in England, interviewing Parliamentarian grandees and appearing before their

Committees with a view to getting the sequestration removed from his estates. Several Norfolk Royalists were in London upon the same errand. Among them were Sir Robert de Grey of Merton, Sir Robert Kemp of Gissing, and Paston's cousin Thomas Knyvett. The last had been concerned in an attempted *coup* at Lowestoft early in the previous year, and was still in trouble for it. ' ''Tis pretty to heare the variety of all our fates since this time twelvmonth. . . . God healpe us, we have had all our shares,' wrote Knyvett to his wife. At the end of March he described how 'our great kinsman' and Sir Robert de Grey were referred to the Committee of the Covenant 'to consider what 'tis fit to allow them out of their own estates . . . this favore, for so it must be counted, was compast for them by a motion made by their friend Mr. Corbet.' Miles Corbet was one of the most rigid and intractable of the Parliamentarian doctrinaires, and especially hard upon his fellow-countrymen from Norfolk, as poor Knyvett had already found by experience. But Paston had other friends as well. It seems clear that the moderate Puritans, such as Sir John Potts, were anxious to have their important neighbour back amongst them once more, chastened and subdued by his experiences. Manchester likewise continued to use his influence in his favour. It was with an understandable touch of envy that Knyvett wrote in April: 'Sir William Paston, it seems, made a quick disspatch. I like those sudden consciences well, but I believe he hath reason to praye for my Lord Manchester's welfare as well as other folke.'

Paston's estates were finally discharged from sequestration, by an order of the House of Commons, on 3rd June 1644. I can find no record of the penalty exacted from him before the sequestration was removed; but the Parliamentarians were losing no opportunity of swelling their depleted funds, and it is most improbable that this rich delinquent was allowed to escape lightly. The annual value of his property had been estimated by the authorities as £5,595 8s. 0½d. Apart from the principal mulct, whatever it may have been, his entire income for almost twelve months had been forfeited while his estates were under sequestration, and his heavy losses in plate have already been described. Altogether the total penalty for his Royalist activities, ineffective though they had proved to be, must have amounted to a formidable sum; and the Paston fortunes seem never to have completely recovered in consequence.

Once he had achieved this costly reconciliation with the men in power, Paston found himself able to give some assistance to his other friends. He interceded with Corbet on behalf of Knyvett, who was in fresh disgrace with the authorities owing to the contents of some intercepted letters from his son, an outspoken young soldier serving in Holland. Before long he was able to leave London, and rejoined his wife at Oxnead. He was welcomed by his neighbours, and was obliged to resume, probably somewhat against his will, his old position in local affairs. As early as the October of 1644 his name begins to appear on various Parliamentarian committees, along with those Puritan names which had been there all the while. It is unlikely that he derived much satisfaction from serving as a Commissioner to raise money for the support of the Army in Ireland, for the raising and maintaining of Fairfax's 'New Model' Army, the maintenance of the Scottish Army under the Earl of Leven, and so forth. But situated as he now was, ever subject to the gentle neighbourly pressure of Potts and Hobart and the rest, he could hardly have done otherwise than conform.

VI

The war drifted slowly to its close. The King's captivity began, and ended only with his death. The Parliament was purged, and the nation was subjected to a long and agitating variety of experiments in government. Through all these years Sir William Paston remained quietly at Oxnead, nursing his broken fortunes and turning once more to art and literature for his consolation.

His buildings and garden adornments had ended abruptly at the outbreak of the troubles in 1642; and it is evidence of the confused state of his affairs that the unpaid balance of his account with Nicholas Stone, which in that year amounted to £24, was not settled until five years later. In 1652 he ordered five more 'heads' from John Stone, the youngest son of Nicholas, who was at this time carrying on what was left of the business with his only surviving brother Henry: but it was a sadly different order from the lavish commissions of earlier and happier years.

He must often have received visits from Dr. Thomas Browne, with whom he had many interests in common. Browne had published *Pseudodoxia Epidemica* in 1646, and was now turning his attention to problems of antiquarian speculation, such as provided the themes of *Urn Burial* and *The Garden of Cyrus*. Oxnead was situated in one of the more Romanized areas of Norfolk. Roman bricks are visible in the walls of the church; urns and pottery were (and still are) frequently discovered in the immediate neighbourhood. It is not surprising to read in the notes to *Urn Burial* that the contents of some urns unearthed close by at Buxton were added to the collection of 'the most worthy Sir William Paston'; and a few years after Sir William's death the discovery of what must have been a considerable Roman burial-ground, 'not much more than a furlong from Oxnead park', furnished Browne with the material for his tract entitled *Brampton Urns*.

Other writers besides Browne were entertained at Oxnead. The house could no longer offer the hospitality of the carefree thirties; but men of letters were still made welcome there, and the fire of learning was kept alight. Thomas Fuller spoke gratefully of Paston as 'the bountiful promoter of all my weak endeavours', dedicated a section of the *History of Cambridge* to him in a glowing Latin eulogy, and had much to say about the earlier Pastons in his *Worthies*. Edward Phillips, the Royalist nephew of Milton, wrote of 'the enlargednesse of your mind in making your House the Center of Hospitality to Strangers and Ingenious Persons' in the dedication of his dictionary, *A New World of Words*.

Indeed Paston became a great receiver of dedications, and our knowledge of his activities during this period of eclipse is mainly derived from them. William Coles, when inscribing his herbal *Adam in Eden* (1657) to this 'truly noble and perfect Lover of Learning', mentions his skill in medicine. 'In the laudable study of Physick', according to Coles, he had approved himself 'a good Patriot, as well as by those happy discoveries you have communicated to the World; but more especially in the Gout, which your Charity hath dispersed with so much successe and comfort to so many that have been afflicted with that painful disease.'

A different note is struck by Robert May, who dedicated *The Accomplisht Cook* collectively to two noblemen and three baronets, Paston among them, in whose service he had apparently been. Writing at the very beginning of 1660, he looked back wistfully to 'those times which I attended upon your Honours, those golden days of Peace and Hospitality, when you enjoy'd your own, so as to entertain and relieve others'. How far away they seemed, 'those Triumphs and magnificent Trophies of Cookery that have adorned your Tables', and how unlikely to be repeated! 'Hospitality, which was once a Relique of Gentry, and a known Cognizance to all ancient Houses, hath lost her Title through the unhappy and cruel Disturbances of the Times'. He could not know that the Restoration was now only a few months away, bringing better times for many, and not least for accomplished cooks.

But the most elaborate and informative of all these dedications was that of Edward Phillips in *A New World of Words* (1658). His dictionary, he says, 'could not have been more advantageously fortified against the various and uncertain suffrages of the World, than by being adopted into the Patronage of such a Person, whose accomplishment in the Arts and Ingenuities renders him capable to judge of what is written well or amisse in any of them'. He then proceeds to catalogue Paston's many qualifications for this task. 'Your admirable skill in Physick manifested in your frequent Cures of the most desperate Diseases, and those happy receits you have consecrated to the benefit of mankind; your exquisite knowledge in Husbandry and Horsemanship; your deep insight into the Mathematicks, as appears by your excellent choice of Jewels, and your rare fancy and invention in Carvings, Turnings, Paintings, and Annealings, in which the very Artists you have imployed have submitted to your polite judgement; your diligent search into the greater curiosities of Nature, wherein how much you have exceeded all others of

37

our Nation that have been famous in their Collections, your *Musaeum* abounding with an infinite variety of the most Choice and admired Rarities, can sufficiently testifie. . . .'

His collections have been long since scattered, his museum dispersed, and only a few of the works of art which adorned Oxnead are now identifiable. One of the most striking of these is his own portrait, by an unknown artist. Some authorities have suggested that it may be the work of Henry Stone, whom he had met in Florence long ago: if so, its date must be earlier than 1653, for Stone died in the summer of that year. Paston stands before a curtain, dressed in rich black with collar and sleeves of white. He wears long hair, a faint moustache, the smallest tuft of beard under the lower lip; his plump white hands grasp the folds of the cloak which enwraps his portly frame. His expression is grave, experienced, a little tired and worn, with heavy pouches under the eyes. And from the left-hand side of the picture the curtain has been withdrawn, to reveal the little scene with the crocodile which has already been described.

Later still, at the close of the Commonwealth, William Faithorne produced a pair of magnificent engravings of Paston and his wife. Paston's features closely resemble those in the portrait, but the moustache has grown longer and the face still fuller. Lady Paston is a rather mournful-looking woman of middle age, richly dressed and jewelled and with hair elaborately curled. The quality of both prints is superb, and it is not surprising that Horace Walpole regarded them as Faithorne's supreme achievement as an engraver.

VII

So he lived on through the years of the Commonwealth, with his pictures and antiquities, his museum and his mathematics and his remedies for the gout. Many of his former opponents must have disliked the progress of events as much as he did. The younger Sir John Hobart of Blickling, now his most important neighbour, was very much in the forefront of affairs, and even became a member of Cromwell's inglorious House of Lords. But several Norfolk veterans of the Long

Parliament, including the three surviving Sir Johns—Potts, Holland and Palgrave—had been among the victims of Pride's Purge, and were little more in favour of the drastic developments of the Commonwealth than their old Royalist opponents. Paston himself maintained some personal contact with Cromwell, and in 1655 was once more able to put in a good word with the Protector for his unfortunate kinsman Thomas Knyvett. His eldest son Robert, however, was strongly Royalist, and towards the end of the Commonwealth went abroad and spent much time at the courts of Charles II and the Queen Mother.

Unlike Knyvett and other former Royalists of his circle, Paston does not appear to have suffered any further financial loss or personal inconvenience during the Commonwealth years. But his efforts at retrenchment were of no avail. Perhaps his hospitality was still too lavish for his reduced means. Perhaps the temptation of adding to his collections was too frequent and too strong. Whatever the cause, he could not make good his losses; and he found it necessary to surrender one of the oldest portions of the family inheritance, the great castle at Caister and the lands around it. He had often borrowed money from William Crowe, a member of an old Yarmouth family who had moved to London and amassed a large fortune in the City. In 1659 he transferred his Caister property to Crowe, in payment of a debt of £6,500 which he was otherwise unable to settle. A few years later the new owner of Caister returned to end his days at his native Yarmouth, and directed in his will that he should be buried in Caister church. An attractive portrait-bust adorns his monument there, and suggests that the praises of his generous and amiable disposition in the long Latin epitaph may have been well founded.

Little more remains to be told about Sir William Paston. At the time of the Restoration he was only in his fiftieth year; but his health was already fast declining. The mysterious mental affliction of his family did not claim him as its victim. He had an only brother, Thomas, who lived to grow up and marry; and believers in the Paston curse observed that in this generation the prophecy was once again fulfilled, for Thomas had become insane before his early death. Sir William's three sons attained manhood, and one of them, his namesake died in Paris when on his travels in 1662. Another, John, has disappeared from view; but the eldest, Robert, figured with prominence from the outset of the new reign. He was elected to the Convention Parliament for Thetford, and to the Cavalier Parliament for Castle Rising. He was knighted by Charles II, married a rich merchant's ambitious daughter, and began to push his fortunes vigorously at Court.

To his heir Sir William seems to have left the furtherance of the family's affairs, and to have withdrawn himself into an almost complete retirement. On 22nd February 1663 he died. A few days afterwards he was buried at Oxnead, in the little church adorned by the bust of his first wife. But there is no monument to his own memory; and with his grandson the family and all its possessions collapsed in hopeless ruin.

CHARLES HARBORD

————————◉◦◦◦◦◦◦◦◉◦✦◦≈◦◉◦✦◦✦◦◉◦◦◦◦◦◦◦◦————————

I

Among the most dramatic paintings of their kind are the great canvases on which the Willem van de Veldes, father and son, depicted the naval battles between the English and the Dutch in the seventeenth century. The magnificent ships, the colour and gilding of the hulls, the scarlet waistcloths, the shot-torn sails and flags, the glow of fire, the billowing clouds of smoke, make compositions of confusing splendour. And the scale of these actions was immense, with the great navies furiously embattled across miles of sea.

> Borne each by other in a distant Line,
> The sea-built Forts in dreadful order move:
> So vast the noise, as if not Fleets did join,
> But Lands unfix'd, and floating Nations, strove.

In those memorable combats the men of Norfolk, the mariners from Yarmouth and Lynn and the little fishing and trading towns strung out along the coast, were playing their part. Of all the great sea-captains of those years, a particular lustre surrounds the three admirals, probably related in blood and intimately allied by environment and friendship, who appeared in quick succession from a group of coastal villages in the north of the county—Sir Christopher Myngs, Sir John Narborough and Sir Cloudesley Shovel. But we know little of the men who served with them, their subordinate officers, the masters and the boatswains and the seamen—the anonymous figures outlined in the van de Velde pictures against blazing woodwork or flaring sails, the huddled shapes clinging to a floating spar.

Just occasionally some memorial of one of them has survived, such as the tomb in Cley churchyard to James Greeve, 'who was an Assistant of Sir Cloudesley Shovel in burning

41

the Ships in the Port of Tripoly in Barbary, Jan. 14th, 1676, and for his good Service perform'd was made the Captain of the Ship called the Orange Tree of Algier, and in 1677 presented with a Medal of Gold by King Charles the 2nd.' Or we read the few remaining letters from Sir Thomas Browne to his younger son and namesake, in whose naval career he took such pride, and especially the letter in which the Norwich physician lovingly enumerates the tributes he had received upon his son's courage and ability—the approbation of the Earl of Sandwich, his Admiral; the cordial praise of his superior officers; the commendations of his moral character from the 'sober and learned chaplaine'; and, perhaps most flattering of all, the statement of Captain Fenne, 'a meere rough seaman', that in a moment of crisis 'if hee were to choose, hee would have your company before any hee knewe'. Yet here again oblivion descends on this gallant and distinguished young man, and we do not even know the date or the circumstances of his early death.

Thomas Browne was too modest to repeat Lord Sandwich's praise of his good conduct; and the Admiral's words were conveyed to the proud father through the kindness of a young member of his staff, Charles Harbord, a Norfolk friend and neighbour. A few years later Sandwich was to die at the battle of Solebay, in a manner which stirred the whole of England; and Harbord was to die at his side. Save for a few brief references in the diaries of Evelyn and Pepys, the name of Charles Harbord has faded from memory, one of those 'intolerably nameless names', thousands upon thousands through all our history, of forgotten men who died valiantly in their country's service. But a small packet of letters, still preserved by his family, has enabled me to put together the story of his life and his death.

II

The Harbords were a family of Welsh origin, established in Somerset from the early sixteenth century. They claimed kinship with the great house of Herbert, and were granted a variant of the Herbert coat of arms. One of them, Charles Harbord, became Surveyor-General to Charles I, and in the course of time to Charles II; he was knighted at Hampton Court in 1636. He married a lady from the Netherlands, Maria van Aelst, who bore him four sons—Philip, William, Charles and John—and three daughters. Shortly after the Restoration he bought an estate at Stanninghall in Norfolk; and a further connexion was made with Norfolk when his eldest son Philip married a local heiress, Anne Drury of Besthorpe, and established himself in that parish. Thenceforward the family all regarded Norfolk as their home.

Charles Harbord, the third son, was born on 10th May 1637[1] at The Moor or Moor Park in Rickmansworth, a house which his father rented for many years from Robert Carey, Earl of Monmouth. Nothing seems to be known about his upbringing and education, except that a part of his schooling took place in Holland, where Lady Harbord and her children spent much time with her own family during the unsettled years of the Civil War and the Commonwealth. He first makes his appearance in a rather tattered letter to his younger brother John, written from Saint Germains some time during 1660. This letter is mainly concerned with his health, and does not explain what he was doing in France at this time. He recounts to his 'most dear brother John' the details of a recent severe illness. For seven weeks he has been in 'a dayly dyinge condition', and is so altered that his family will not recognize him; but his strength is returning and he will start for England as soon as possible, 'for I fynde here no comfort in my Life and am at a vast charge. Pray God send us a good meetinge.'

Soon after his return to England he began his lifelong association with Lord Sandwich, and accompanied him during an eventful cruise in the summer and autumn of 1661. Sandwich was sent to demonstrate the qualities of English sea-power to Algiers and the other piratical strongholds of northern Africa. He was then ordered to take over Tangier, which had lately become a possession of the English crown

[1] The date of his birth is clearly written in his father's hand in a Prayer Book, and in his brother John's hand in a Bible, both of which are still at Gunton. There is evidently a mistake in the inscription on his monument in Westminster Abbey, which gives his age as thirty-two and not thirty-five at the time of his death.

as part of the dowry of Charles II's Queen, Catherine of Braganza; and finally he was to escort the new Queen on her voyage to England.

It is uncertain in what capacity Harbord attended Sandwich during this voyage; he probably acted as his companion and secretary, as he was to do in later years. A single letter to his father has found its way into the Bodleian Library, written on 10th January 1661–2 'from aboard the *Royall James* in Tanger Bay'. He looks forward to receiving letters from his family when he gets to Lisbon, and has sent them presents of chocolate and wine. 'I am most exceedingly beholden to my Lord Sandwich for his favour to me which I studie to deserve, and hope I shall alwayes behave my selfe as your Sonne. I pray present my humble dutie to my dear Mother, whom God send health and happynesse that you may live long in comfort together, my Love to all my Brothers and Sisters and friends, and graunt your blessing to

Sir

Your obedient Sonne

CHA: HARBORD.'

At the end of January 1662 the first Governor of Tangier, the Earl of Peterborough, arrived at the town; and shortly afterwards Sandwich left for Lisbon, and thence for England with the Queen. Harbord accompanied him to Lisbon, and went on to England in advance of him as a special messenger with letters for the King. Pepys met him at dinner at Lady Sandwich's house on 1st April, while he was in London on this duty. Later in 1662 he returned to Tangier, and served as an officer of the garrison under Lord Peterborough. He was given the rank of Captain and the command of a company of foot, and was much in the Governor's confidence. He also hoped to improve his slender fortunes by trading in the newly acquired colony.

All Harbord's other surviving letters are addressed to his brother John, and remain at Gunton Park in Norfolk, where John was in due course to establish himself and his line. The first was dated from Tangier on 7th November 1662; and since he had sprained his right wrist, it was dictated to his friend and companion William Holland—a younger son, presumably, of Sir John Holland of Quidenham in Norfolk—who had been a school-fellow of the two Harbords at Haarlem in 1651. The letter begins with reproaches to John for not having written for so long; news of the family at home was 'the greatest comfort I can reape in this place'. Otherwise all was well with him. 'I am (God be thancked) in good health, and his Excellency's great kindness to mee, together with my imployment, maks this place something comfortable.' He then turns to the possibilities of trade. 'Whilst I am heere, I would willingly make the best of my tyme I could, and therefore have written to Sir Charles [his father], brother Will, and brother Newman [a brother-in-law] to see if they can procure me three or four hundred pounds to venture for this place, the which I am confident will turne to a great advantage, being lay'd out in the Comoditis specified in the inclosed Invoyce.' The invoice contains a long list of 'very good commoditis that will turne to good account in this place', including strong beer, soap, candles, Suffolk and Cheshire cheese, spice, ribbon, canvas, thread, tobacco, drugget, cambric, holland and diaper. The letter concludes with a postscript to his old school-fellow from William Holland, mentioning that he is presently going to make a venture of his own into 'South Barbary'. An endorsement on a subsequent letter from Holland, in which he speaks again of his journey into South Barbary, tells us that 'he dyed under the hardship of this Expedition'.

Charles Harbord's next letter to John, written from the 'Upper Castle in Tangier' on 10th December, is again reproachful in tone. Several more ships had arrived, but they brought no letters from home; nor had he received a consignment of cloth 'which you promised to send mee and would have turned to good account'. He urges his brother to send out some part of the goods listed in the invoice enclosed in his last letter. Even though his father and other relations were not inclined to take part in the venture, there was enough of his own money in John's hands to purchase and dispatch a portion of the consignment. Apart from the anxieties over his letters and his goods, all was going well with him at Tangier.

'I have no great occasion of spending money here, being constantly at My Lord's table; his Excellency is so infinitely kynd to me that I am one of the Household. I command one of the best Compagnies in the Garrison, and we quarter and keep Guarde in the most honorablest posts.'

On 17th December he writes again. All is now well; a long letter has arrived from John, and so has his consignment of cloth and sundry other goods. 'My dearest I pray pardon mee if my last was a little sharpe, for I was exceeding troubled that so many shippes should arrive here without a word from you . . . lett me assure you it comforted me much that you still continue your old affections, my hart is still with you, and I doe perswade my selfe that by God's blessinge we shall meet again and live long together with comfort, which I pray God send.' Charles was sending his reply by Mr. John Gibbs, 'who was at sea with mee the last year, and now coming to Tangier, for his relation to Capt. Cuttinges who commanded ye *Royall James* under My Lord [Sandwich], I gave him leave to stay in my quarters'. Mr. Gibbs was a 'very ingenious man and very civile', and intended to return to Tangier. If he did so, John might send goods to any quantity in his charge; and Charles would arrange that 'he shall doe all my business of Trade, for I will not be seen in it, neither can a man be a marchant and a soldier and doe both well'.

After further discussion of his commercial ventures, Charles goes on to talk of conditions at Tangier. 'I have no great occasion of spendinge money here except I should take a ramble into Spayne, for here I have the Generall's table at command and am as one of his familie. Indeed I am exceedingly beholdinge to his Excellencie for his favours to mee. He is a very noble person who seekes nothinge but the King's service and the good of this place. I wish and shall studie to be as servicable to his Excellency as I can, and hope I shall return with health and honour. If the Mole be made and the Town fortified, and a peace with the Moors, this will be the best Garrison of the World. We dayly see our Enemies about the walls, and in the light nights abundance of all sorts of wild beasts. About three dayes since came in some Moors as if they would treat, so my selfe and another Captain and two

marchants that understood the language went 5 myles out of
the towne into Gaylan's camp where we delivered him the
Compliment from our Generall, then alighting from our horses
wee all satt upon the ground crosse legged lyke Taylers, but
after a long discourse wee tooke our leaves and I fear not much
will come of it he beeing so much brybed by the Spanyards.'
Ghailan was a neighbouring Moorish chieftain of considerable power, whose attitude was always a source of anxiety to
the garrison of Tangier.

The letter concludes with the affectionate good wishes that
invariably passed between these most devoted brothers. 'As
for my Mare I pray make the best of her for your selfe, and
the other in Norfolke when you goe there you may ryde her as
your own, or take her if you lyke her or anything else that I
have, all is most heartilie at your service. I shall alwayes, as
I have continually done, studie to doe you good. Now I must
take leave, recommending you to God's protection, who I
hope will send us a good meetinge, which is heartily desyred
by me who am and allways was

Dearest Brother

Yours

Cha: Harbord.'

III

This was the last of Charles Harbord's letters from Tangier.
He may have remained there for another year, and perhaps for
longer; but in 1664 an outbreak of war with the Dutch was
clearly approaching, and he returned to England and resumed
his attendance upon Lord Sandwich. One of the most attractive features of Sandwich's character was his power to engage
the loyal and devoted service of others. Harbord, only a little
older than his own sons, became his secretary at all times, his
lieutenant and bodyguard in war, the friend and companion of
his whole family in the years of peace.

Throughout the winter of 1664 and the early spring of
1665, Sandwich was at sea, prepared for any unexpected move
by the enemy. In April the entire fleet was assembled for
action, under its three Admirals—the Duke of York, Prince

47

Rupert and Lord Sandwich—and in May the Dutch fleet, under Admiral Opdam, came out of harbour. In the great engagement which followed on 3rd June, the Battle of Lowestoft, Sandwich played a decisive part, and was in fact responsible for the manœuvres which led to the victorious outcome of the battle. But the two royal Admirals received most of the credit and applause, and Sandwich was left with a sense of grievance that his services had not been properly appreciated.

Later in the year, however, he was given command of an expedition designed to intercept the Dutch East India fleet which, escorted by de Ruyter, was on its way home to Holland. De Ruyter and most of the ships evaded him, and reached Holland in safety. A party of East Indiamen took refuge in the neutral harbour of Bergen in Norway, and a squadron under Captain Teddiman was dispatched to enter the harbour and capture them. The attack, made under heavy fire from the Dutch ships and the Norwegian forts above the harbour, was carried out with great courage and determination; but eventually the English ships had to withdraw with over four hundred casualties. Sandwich's son, Sydney Montagu, and Charles Harbord were both members of this expedition, and one of Sandwich's nephews was killed at their side. In this engagement, also, young Thomas Browne particularly distinguished himself, and won those praises from Sandwich which Harbord made it his business to transmit to the old doctor at Norwich.

So far, it had been an unlucky cruise for Sandwich; but at the end of the summer, in two engagements, he captured a number of richly-laden East Indiamen and several of the men-of-war escorting them. This success, and the fabulous value of the prizes he had taken, revived his popularity and restored his self-confidence. Several of his officers were knighted by the King for their good service, and Charles Harbord was among them. But Sandwich made an unfortunate blunder about the distribution and disposal of prize goods from the captured ships, and gave his enemies a welcome opportunity to attack his reputation. Through his own negligence he was obliged to carry the blame for the dishonesty of others; and as a result he lost his influence at Court, and his prestige with the nation at large. On the last day of 1665 Pepys wrote in his diary:

'The great evil of this year, and the only one indeed, is the fall of my Lord Sandwich, whose mistake about the prizes hath undone him, I believe, as to interest at Court; though sent (for a little palliating it) Embassador into Spayne, which he is now fitting himself for. . . . Indeed, his miscarriage about the prize goods is not to be excused, to suffer a company of rogues to go away with ten times as much as himself, and the blame of all to be deservedly laid upon him.'

IV

Lord Sandwich's next employment, the Embassy to Spain, may well have been offered to him, as Pepys suggests, 'for a little palliating' of the damage which his reputation had sustained through this unfortunate business of the prize goods. But it was in itself a mission of importance and dignity. The resident Ambassador in Madrid, Sir Richard Fanshawe, had not been altogether successful in that position, especially in the conduct of a commercial treaty with Spain which was then under negotiation. In November 1665, therefore, Lord Sandwich was appointed Ambassador Extraordinary to the Court of Spain. He was instructed to complete the commercial treaty, to mediate a conclusion of the long-drawn hostilities between Spain and Portugal, and to oppose the progress of French diplomacy at Madrid by every means in his power.

Sandwich sailed for Spain from Portsmouth in the *Resolution* on 3rd March 1666. He was accompanied by his son Sydney Montagu and a large staff, which included Charles Harbord as his private secretary and William Godolphin as Secretary to the Embassy. On reaching Corunna they were obliged to perform a lengthy period of quarantine at a house near the neighbouring village of Burgos. On 23rd April Charles Harbord addressed a lively letter to 'my Lovinge Brother Mr. John Harbord' from 'our Country House at Burgo some 4 myles from the Caronna'. He did not propose to say much about the voyage, as he had already described it fully in a letter to his father. 'The 3rd March wee sett sayle from Spitthead near Portsmouth in the *Resolution*, a 3rd rate of 60 brasse guns, and 4th and 5th rates attending us, the

Foresight and the *Oxford*. The first part of our voyage was so
smooth and pleasant as our Land gentlemen began to laugh at
the stories they had heard of the sea. But the latter 4 or 5 dayes
brought some to their prayers and promises of amendment of
life, but all to cast up their accounts, and at the ballance found
the seamen deserved very well and that there was no sport in
itt. The 12 March about noon after 5 dayes tumbling at sea
into stormy weather wee came safe to an anckor in the Bay of
the Groyne or Caronna in Galitia.'

The country house where they were living was 'a poor one,
yet pleasantly seated on the side of a hill near a river that offers
sallmons, soalls, mulletts, lampreys; and above the bridge,
store of trouts of which I have taken severall with a fly.' At
Easter he had been 'at Saintiago, where all the pilgrims resort
to worship St. James his bodie there buried, and where indeed
were such ceremonies as I had never seen before'. Now the
mules had arrived for their journey to Madrid, 120 of them
in all, and a litter for His Excellency: and they would start in
a few days. It was 330 miles to Madrid, and there was not a
good inn by the way. 'As for my health it is at the old rate,
grunting and groaning, but I fear the Gout more than a Consumption, and have very lately lett blood and taken physik to
prevent itt.'

There are messages to all the Norfolk neighbours. 'If this
fynds you at Stanninghall, pray present my humble service to
all my friends round about you—to Sir Robert Paston and
Mr. Le Grosse, Mr. Pecke and Mr. Adams, to both parsons,
and all at Timber Hill and Norwich and everywhere else that
inquire for mee; and pray lett my nagg and mayre be spared
as much as possible may be, for at furthest I hope I shall be at
home next Christmas but I cannot give any guesse at it.' Of
the neighbours whom he mentions, Sir Robert Paston, afterwards Earl of Yarmouth, lived at Oxnead, and Thomas le
Gros, to whom Sir Thomas Browne dedicated *Urn Burial*, at
Crostwight. Mr. Peck was the squire of Spixworth, and Mr.
Adams of Sprowston.

The letter ends on the usual affectionate note. 'I protest I
beginne dayly more and more to love my own Country, and
if once returned, shall nott upon easy terms stir abroad any

more, but live with you, that wee may injoy one another as wee have often promised, and shall not fayle on my side.

Now Dear Brother the great God who hath still preserved us and sent us so many a good meeting will do it again if it be his will. To him I recommend you, and rest

Dear Brother
Your truly affectionate Brother and
faithfull servant
CHA: HARBORD.'

Four days after this letter was written, the Ambassador and his train set out for Madrid, and arrived there after a leisurely progress on 18th May. The negotiations over the commercial treaty lasted for many months; but Sandwich's skill and firmness were eventually rewarded, and the treaty was signed in the following year. It was a great personal success for the Ambassador: his conduct was warmly approved in England and went far to restore his reputation. The treaty between Spain and Portugal took almost as long to negotiate, but again Sandwich brought matters to a successful conclusion, and he was present at its signature in Lisbon in February 1668. Charles Harbord accompanied him to Portugal, and wrote briefly to his brother John soon after their arrival. On the 22nd of the previous month, he says, 'we got safe to this port of Lisbon, for to make peace between this nation and Spayne, which is God be praysed effected to both sattisfactions, the generall good of Christendom and everlasting honour of his Excellency'. They would soon be returning to Madrid, and hoped to be in England by the beginning of July. 'I hope to meet your letters at Madrid to sattisfye me of your good health, my father's and my brothers' and sisters'. For my part, I am at the old rate, but much fear the Gout which makes me live as carefull as I can. His Excellency and Mr. Mountague are very well and continue their kyndnesses very firme to mee, as I shall my faithfull service to them.'

Harbord's hopes of seeing his family in July were not fulfilled, as Sandwich was instructed, before returning home at the conclusion of his embassy, to visit Tangier and report upon conditions there. He reached Tangier on 14th August, and remained a fortnight. It was probably during this visit, and not during his earlier sojourn at Tangier, that Harbord made those drawings of the port and its fortifications which were later engraved by Danckerts, and which Pepys saw with admiration at Lord Sandwich's house in the following year. Harbord was a skilful draughtsman, and Sandwich had sent home many of his drawings of landscapes and buildings during their two years in Spain.

Sandwich sailed again from Tangier at the end of August and landed in England on 28th September 1668, thus concluding his long and successful embassy of two and a half years. He was well received by the King and Queen and by the chief ministers. As soon as possible he returned to his own house at Hinchingbrooke, with Harbord still accompanying him.

V

Little is known about Charles Harbord's life during the next three years. He did not marry; he does not seem ever to have possessed a house or estate of his own; only a single letter from these years has survived. He stayed occasionally in Norfolk with his brother John at Stanninghall, and with his youngest sister Katherine who had married Thomas Wright of Kilverstone near Thetford. But the greater part of his time was spent in the company of Lord Sandwich and his family.

As their friend and constant associate, he appears now and then in the diary of Samuel Pepys, who did not much care for him. Pepys had travelled far since the day when Lord Sandwich, loaded with honours at the Restoration and rightly expectant of more to come, had told his humble kinsman and secretary: 'We must have a little patience and we will rise together.' He had risen a great deal higher than Sandwich can ever have anticipated; and although he retained a proper sense of gratitude towards his old patron, their relationship was not always easy. Diligently and successfully pursuing his own career, Pepys often had occasion to deplore Sandwich's extravagance and his heedless way of life. He still played a part in his tangled affairs, and was sometimes obliged to lend him money; and he resented Sandwich's preoccupation with

Charles Harbord

Harbord and others, by comparison with whom he felt himself neglected and slighted. Late in 1668 he confided to his diary that he had small encouragement to wait on Lord Sandwich, 'because of the difficulty of seeing him, and the little he hath to say to me when I do see him, or to any body else, but his own idle people about him, Sir Charles Harbord, etc.' There was a difficult passage early in 1669, when the question arose of creating the office of a paymaster for the garrison of Tangier. Sandwich suggested Harbord's name to the Duke of York for the new office, without consulting Pepys, who as Treasurer of Tangier was obviously concerned in the matter. The Duke replied that Pepys's opinion should certainly be taken before anything was done; and in the end the pay-mastership was not established. Pepys was much gratified by the Duke's kindness, and felt uneasily that 'my Lord did go a little too far in this business, to move it so far, without consulting me'. Matters were eased again a few days later, when Pepys entertained Sandwich and two of his sons, together with Lord Peterborough, Sir William Godolphin and Charles Harbord, at a very successful dinner-party in his own house— 'the best of its kind, and the fullest of honour and content to me, that ever I had in my life: and shall not easily have so good again'. And in May he gave a farewell dinner, with Harbord as one of the guests, for Sandwich's son Sydney who was starting on his travels abroad. But some degree of cool-ness persisted between Sandwich and his former secretary. It has been pointed out that when Sandwich made his will a few months afterwards, he did not include among his executors the man who at one time had enjoyed his fullest confidence and the most intimate knowledge of his affairs; he did not even leave him any token of remembrance. And it may not be without significance that in the next decade, when Pepys was involved in the storm of political faction which culminated in the Popish Plot, his most persistent enemy and accuser was William Harbord, the brother of Charles and himself a mem-ber of the Sandwich circle.

That circle was joined about this time by a young man of great charm and talent named Clement Cotterell, the eldest son of Sir Charles Cotterell, Master of the Ceremonies. He

53

had been with Lord Sandwich in Spain during part of his embassy, and he accompanied Sydney Montagu throughout his tour of Europe. He was eleven years younger than Harbord, but they were soon on terms of close friendship. After his return from the Grand Tour, Cotterell joined Harbord in the faithful attendance on Sandwich to which his friend had already devoted so much of his life, and in which both were soon to die.

Harbord's last surviving letter was dated from a place called Tancker Hall on 13th April 1671. It related mainly to a coachman who had proved useless in London owing to his 'infirmitie and disabilitie of dryvinge a Coach', and whom he was returning to his brother John as being better suited to country occupations. 'If the Kinge comes not to Newmarkett as now it's thought he will not, nor into Norfolke this bout, I'll have my barbe at Hamstead, where I am lyke to be this summer, my Lord having taken a House there for himself and me, a very pritty one and near the Heath, which I hope will conduce very much towards my perfect recovery, which as yet I cannot procure. . . . My love to Brother Phill: and my Sister and to Nantie, and to those of Riborrow and Kilverston when you see them, and to all the rest of my friends with you.' The King did visit Norfolk that summer, mainly to inspect the port of Great Yarmouth in view of the approaching war against the Dutch. But Sandwich did not accompany him; and we do not know if Harbord felt it his duty to leave the quiet of Hampstead Heath and join in the enthusiastic welcome which his Norfolk subjects accorded to the royal pair.

VI

In 1670 Lord Sandwich had received the office of President of the Council for Foreign Plantations, which dealt with the administration of the English colonies in America and the West Indies. It was a dignified and important post; but he had little contact with the King or with the Cabal, the five men who really directed the policy of the country. He knew nothing of the circumstances which brought about the alliance with France and the opening of hostilities against the Dutch.

He knew nothing of the secret Treaty of Dover, although in 1670 it had been his duty, as Vice-Admiral of England and Admiral of the Narrow Seas, to convey Madame, the King's sister, from Dunkirk to Dover on the fateful occasion when she brought the Treaty to her brother. To his old friend John Evelyn, he made it no secret that 'he was utterly against the War from the beginning, and abhor'd the attacquing of the Smyrna fleete'—the unwarrantable attempt on a great Dutch merchant fleet which preceded the declaration of war. But as soon as hostilities began in the spring of 1672 he was recalled from his peaceful pursuits, and appointed Vice-Admiral to the Duke of York, the Commander of the fleet.

From the outset he was possessed by a sense of deep foreboding, of doom overshadowing both himself and his young companions. Long afterwards an unnamed friend recalled a group talking in a garden just before Sandwich went to sea for the last time. 'His Lordship then walking with his hands one upon the shoulder of Charles Harbord and the other upon Clem Cotterell's (for his greater ease, being then grown somewhat goutish and otherwise unwieldy) told the company that though he was then Vice-Admiral of England, and Admiral of the Narrow Seas, yet he knew no more of what was to be done that summer than any one of them, or any other that knew nothing of it. "This only I know," he said, "that I will die, and these two boys (meaning Harbord and Cotterell) will die with me."'

Besides his resentment at not being consulted on matters of policy, Sandwich had been wounded by the imputations of certain enemies against his personal courage. According to Evelyn both the Duke of Albemarle, who was now dead, and the hot-headed Lord Clifford, at this time a leading member of the Government, had given currency to suggestions of cowardice on his part, 'because in former Conflicts, being an able and experienc'd sea-man (which neither of them were) he allwayes brought off his Majesties ships, without losse, though not without as many markes of true Courage as the stoutest of them . . . my Lord Sandwich was prudent as well as valiant, and allways govern'd his affairs with successe, and little losse, he was for deliberation, and reason, they for action and slaughter without either.' But their whisperings had gained ground, and were very present in his mind when he said farewell to Evelyn a few days before he sailed. 'Going at Whitehall to take my leave of his Lordship (who had his Lodgings in the Privy Gardens) shaking me by the hand bid me God buy he should he thought see me no more, and I saw to my thinking something boading in his Countenance; no says he, they will not have me live: Had I lost a Fleete (meaning on his returne from Bergen, when he tooke the East Indian prize) I should have fared better; but be it as it please God; I must do I know not what, to save my reputation; something to this effect, he had hinted to me; but thus I tooke my leave.'

War was formally declared in March 1672, and on 21st April Sandwich hoisted his flag in the *Royal James*. He appointed Charles Harbord his First Lieutenant, and Clement Cotterell was on board the ship as a gentleman volunteer. The Duke of York was in command of the fleet, with Sandwich as his Vice-Admiral in command of the Blue Squadron. Early in May the English and French fleets joined forces in the Channel, and at the same time the Dutch fleet, under the command of de Ruyter, approached the Kentish shore. After a long period of manœuvring the opposing fleets came into contact off the Suffolk coast. The English and French were anchored in Southwold Bay or Solebay, and were lulled into a sense of false security by rumours that the Dutch had withdrawn towards Holland. Early on the morning of the 28th it was reported that they were close at hand, and preparations for battle were hurriedly made.

There is probably no truth in the story that at a council of war, shortly before the battle, Sandwich was taunted by the Duke of York for his caution and lack of enterprise. But the sense of fatality, the belief that he must redeem his reputation with his life, still lay heavy upon him. 'He dined in Mr. Digby's ship,' wrote Lord Mulgrave afterwards, 'the day before the battle, when nobody dreamt of fighting, and showed a gloomy discontent so contrary to his usual cheerful humour, that we even then all took notice of it, but much more afterwards.' And as he dressed in the summer dawn, and Valevin his secretary carefully arranged the ribbon of the

Garter across his breast and the collar and George about his neck, he spoke again of charges of cowardice, and said as he went on deck, 'Now, Val, I must be sacrificed.'

The Dutch bore swiftly down upon the English and French fleets, lying unprepared and in confused order close to the shore. The Blue Squadron, with Sandwich in command, lay nearest to the enemy and bore the brunt of the first attack. The battle began about seven o'clock on a calm sunny morning. The *Royal James* was engaged at that time by Admiral Van Ghent and his squadron, and was soon completely surrounded. One man-of-war after another poured their broadsides into her—'she never had less than three or four of their stoutest ships upon her'—and she beat off two fireships which were sent down upon her. At nine o'clock Sandwich dispatched pinnaces to Jordan, his Rear-Admiral, and Kempthorne, his Vice-Admiral, asking for their assistance. Shortly afterwards he was attacked by Captain Van Brakel in the *GrootHollandia*, which rammed the *Royal James* and was soon entangled with her rigging. By this time the casualties in the doomed flagship already amounted to three hundred men. Admiral Van Ghent then bore down upon her in his own flagship, the *Dolfijn*; and again her decks were raked by a succession of murderous broadsides.

At this stage Admiral Jordan and his squadron were seen approaching, and Sandwich believed that help was at hand; but through some unaccountable mistake, for which he was later much censured, Jordan sailed calmly past. Afterwards he said that he thought Sandwich's hard-pressed ships, obscured by the clouds of smoke and flashes of cannon, were those of the enemy; but to the survivors on the *Royal James* it seemed that he had deliberately deserted them. An eyewitness on shore took much the same view. 'I wished myself on [Jordan's ship] to have saved that brave Montagu,' he wrote, 'for he was in the wind of him, and might have come down to him. I saw the whole business, and was so near as I saw almost every broadside, and was in hearing and whistling of the shot.' Sandwich turned to Haddock, his captain, who was already wounded in the foot, and said quietly, 'We must do our best to defend ourselves alone.'

So the unequal battle continued. A shot from the *Royal James* killed Van Ghent, the opposing Admiral. A party of her sailors boarded the *Groot Hollandia* and cut away the tangle of rigging which held her to their own ship. Some of them were left behind on the Dutch vessel; but Clement Cotterell, who was the first to board her and pulled down her ensign with his own hand, managed to return to his Admiral's side. Freed from the ship which had impeded her movements for so long, the *Royal James* might still have had a chance of survival; but now yet another fireship bore down upon her, grappled with her and set her ablaze. Only a hundred men survived unwounded of the ship's complement of a thousand, and they could do nothing more. The flames roared and mounted, and the order was given for every man to save himself. Some leaped overboard; others crowded into a barge which sank beneath their weight. Captain Haddock, despite his wounded foot, swam for two miles and was rescued by another ship. One of Sandwich's pages stayed with his master until there were only ten men left on board. 'He moved my Lord to leap into the sea, knowing he could swim; but my Lord distrusting himself by reason of his fatness and unwieldiness said he would stay somewhat longer; but bade him to take care of himself, and soon kissed him and bade him farewell.' The boy managed to swim to safety. Harbord and Cotterell were both fine swimmers, but they remained with Sandwich until the last. By two o'clock in the afternoon the *Royal James* was burning furiously from end to end; and it is supposed that the Admiral and the little group around him flung themselves into the sea before the flames had reached them. By nightfall the flagship had burned down to the level of the waves, and drifted, a smouldering wreck, into the darkness.

VII

Elsewhere the battle had raged with almost equal fury. The English ships suffered heavy casualties and much damage; the French squadron, owing to a series of mistaken signals, never really came into action at all. In the afternoon the Dutch began to withdraw towards their own coasts, and the engagement was not renewed next day. For all its violence the battle proved indecisive, with the general advantage in favour of the Dutch. Evelyn, supervising the care of the wounded a few days later at the Nore, gazed sadly at the battered ships. 'The misse of my Lord Sandwich redoubled the losse to me, as well as the folly of hazarding so brave a fleete, and losing so many good men, for no provocation in the world but because the Hollander exceeded us in Industrie, and all things else but envy.' He recalled that farewell talk with the Admiral, his sense of doom, his bitterness at the slanders of his enemies. 'This it was which I am confident griev'd him, and made him enter like a Lion, and fight like one too, in the middst of the hottest service, where the stoutest of the rest, seeing him ingagd, and so many ships upon him, durst not, or would not, come into his succour, as some of them, whom I know, might have don. Thus this gallant Person perish'd to gratifie the pride and envy, of some I named.' Nor did Evelyn forget his friend's companions. 'Lost likewise with this brave man, was Sir Charles Cotterell's Sonn, whose Father was Master of the Ceremonies, and Sir Charles Harbord sonn of his Majesties Surveyor generall, two valiant, and most accomplish'd youths, full of virtue and Courage, and that might have saved themselves, but would perish with my Lord, whom they honor'd and loved above their owne lives.'

There was a long period of uncertainty before the fate of Sandwich and his friends was finally known. It was just conceivable that they might have been rescued by a Dutch ship. Eventually a ketch picked up the Admiral's body, bearing no marks of fire, swollen and gnawed by fishes, but recognizable by the Garter ribbon across his breast and the George and other jewels thrust into the pockets of his coat. The bodies of Harbord and Cotterell were never found.

The long days of uncertainty, and the gradual abandonment of hope, are described with pathos in three letters which old Sir Charles Harbord wrote at this time to his son John in Norfolk. In the first, written on 5th June, eight days after the battle, the anxious father is not wholly despondent. He had been 'in extream fear and sorrow for your brother and yourself, least you should have been in the ship with him, and soe

I might have lost you both, which would certainly have brought downe my head alsoe.' It is likely that John would have gone over from Stanninghall to visit Charles while the fleet was lying off the Suffolk coast; and he might have felt disposed, in the easygoing manner of that age, to join the ship for a time as a gentleman volunteer. But John, at least, was safe; and 'the last night your brother Will brought me news from Sir Joseph Williamson that in a letter of intelligence from Holland it was written that the Lieutenant of the Blew Admiral was alive in Holland taken up at sea, but no name of the person, which did but in parte relieve me'. His hopes were again a little raised when 'your sister Newman came to me this morning and told me Sir James Hayes, Prince Rupert's secretary, sent to assure her from the Prince that her brother was safe with the Prince of Orange, which I feare is too good if possible to be true at this tyme'.

But the next letter, dated 11th June, shows how these slender hopes were soon destroyed. 'Yours of 7 Junij came hither yesterday and putt me into fresh tears and great passion for your poore, but most worthy brother and friend. The Lieutenant that was saved was the third Lieutenant. It is now generally believed that your brother, who might have saved himself by swimming as well as any of those that did, and was much prest to it by my Lord, refused to leave him and continued with him and Mr. Cotterell and some others, praying upon their knees, till the fire tooke hold of them, and then they were soone suffocated and consumed. A greater scandell never was given by this nation, to suffer soe deserving a Vice-Admirall and soe many worthy gentlemen to perish for want of boates to save them, whereas the Dutch having but an ordinary ship on fire sent 16 boates to save the men and saved them all or most of them. This will make gentlemen lesse willing to serve the King, less bold in his service, and lesse carefull of the publique, which with the losse of such a sonne (as hath left few soe good men alive) makes me weary of living, and wish, if it had pleased God, I might have preserved his life with the losse of myne, the which might have been of more use to his King and Country than a thousand such as I am, but it hath pleased God to take him from me and leave me to bewayle my owne unhappiness, which I pray I shall doe to my last breath, for he deserved it at my hands.' The mourning to be distributed to the members of the family, their friends and servants is then discussed, and the opening of the will, which Sir Charles would not undertake 'until there be noe further hopes of his life, and how to doe it then I know not, finding my self ready to faint when I doe but think of it'. At the close of the letter comes a postscript: 'Mr. Fisher brings me news just now that my Lord of Sandwich his body is found with his George about him. If this be true then they did adventure to sea and were lost there, for it is not probable your brother if alive would not have written before this tyme. I am not comforted herewith. Holland is lost to the French, and soe shall we be ere long I feare.' It is clear that Sir Charles, like his friend Lord Sandwich, disapproved profoundly of the war in which his son had given his life.

The last of the three letters was written on 18th June. 'Now all my hopes are vanished and past hope.' Various survivors had been questioned, and it was certain that none 'of those that were left with my Lord of Sandwich upon the ship when these came off, that saved themselves by swimming, are found alive'. So Sir Charles had opened his son's will. 'It is soe pious and good that the perusing of it hath revived my sorrow for the losse of such a sonne as hath left the best reputation behind him of any man I have known; and I heare the King and Duke have exprest as much and more than I dare say.' A copy of the will had been sent to John, and only a few details are mentioned in his father's letter. It was evidently the kind of will that might have been expected from Charles Harbord, so simply and devotedly attached to his family and his friends. There were bequests to his brothers, sisters and brothers-in-law; and money was left to be laid out on gifts of remembrance—swords, gilt cups and covers, porringers and spoons—to a wide circle of friends, including Lord Sandwich's sons, Clement Cotterell, and 'poore Parson Dickinson'. He had asked to have a tomb erected for him in the Abbey Church of Westminster. 'His last expressions,' his father concludes, 'are soe religious and his end soe manly and courageous, and the neglect of saving them by sending them boates soe barbarous, that it breaks my heart to think of them. God preserve you and all good men.'

The grief-stricken fathers commemorated their sons by a single monument, a stately memorial of black and white marble, still to be seen in Westminster Abbey. It is surmounted by a broken pediment, enclosing a wreath of laurel and the inscription: 'To preserve and unite the Memory of two faithfull Friends, who lost their lives at Sea together.' Beneath are the interwoven initials of Charles Harbord and Clement Cotterell; and on two marble panels is related the story of their lives, their valour and their sacrifice.

HUMPHREY PRIDEAUX

I

Lytton Strachey, in his *Portrait in Miniature* of Mandell Creighton, observed that the great men of the Church of England have been less remarkable for pure piety than for scholarship or administrative energy. The generalization is not altogether a fair one; but it is certainly applicable to Humphrey Prideaux, Dean of Norwich, who was conspicuous among the churchmen of his day, as Bishop Creighton was to be two centuries later, in the fields of scholarship and of administration alike. He was a harsh, masterful, peremptory man. It is difficult to associate him in any way with the gentler virtues of his calling, with mysticism, deep spiritual experience, 'that most excellent gift of charity'. But as an organizer, a disciplinarian, a learned and persuasive apologist for his Church during some troublous years, he performed valuable service.

Disciplinarians are seldom very likeable, especially when they go to work with such obvious enjoyment as Prideaux. Even now, when almost three centuries have elapsed, his letters preserve for us the rough edge of his tongue, the contempt with which he viewed the majority of his fellow men. Yet if that series of angry and uncharitable letters had never been written, our knowledge of life in Oxford and Norwich in the later seventeenth century would be considerably the poorer. And when we consider his industry, his conscientiousness, his unremitting efforts to bring order out of confusion, and latterly his courage in the face of terrible physical disability, it is impossible not to respect and indeed to admire him.

People

II

Humphrey Prideaux was born on 3rd May 1648, the third son of a Cornish gentleman, Edmund Prideaux of Padstow, by his wife Bridget, daughter of John Moyle of Bake in the same county. His first schooling was at Liskeard and then at Bodmin. Later he passed three years as a King's Scholar at Westminster under the redoubtable Dr. Busby; and finally, at the age of twenty, he was admitted to a studentship at Christ Church, Oxford. There he took his degree as Bachelor of Arts in 1672, and became a Master of Arts three years later.

Throughout this period Christ Church was flourishing greatly under the rule of one of its greatest Deans, Dr. John Fell. New buildings were always in progress, culminating in the noble fabric of Tom Tower. Dr. Fell supervised the college, and the conduct and demeanour of all its members, with unremitting vigilance. During a memorable Vice-Chancellorship he had been able to extend his reforming influence over the University as a whole; and in particular he still kept the control of the University Press firmly in his own hands. This zeal for order and exactitude won the admiration of Humphrey Prideaux, and there can be no doubt that the young man modelled his own career to a considerable extent upon that of the Dean.

His other hero at Christ Church was the great orientalist Dr. Edward Pococke. He had already made some progress in the study of oriental languages; and in Dr. Pococke, who held the Professorships both of Arabic and of Hebrew, he found an admirably qualified instructor as well as a friend. The gentle dignified old man was always ready to impart his learning to others, or to recall his memories of the past. He had spent years at Aleppo and Constantinople, and during his travels had collected many of the manuscripts which formed Archbishop Laud's important legacy to the Bodleian. He had occupied Laud's chair of Arabic at Oxford since its foundation; and his association with the Archbishop, whom he had visited during his imprisonment in the Tower, had brought him some stormy passages during the Commonwealth years.

Prideaux never failed to speak of him with respect and gratitude, as 'the best friend I have in this place'.

Apart from Dr. Fell and Dr. Pococke, he seldom spoke well
of anybody. In 1674, when he was twenty-six years old, he
began a long correspondence with his friend John Ellis; and
in it he is revealed as a very censorious young man indeed. He
had little to say in favour of any of his colleagues at Christ
Church. They were 'dunces and knaves'. They preached
'most scandalous duncecall sermons'. Even the genial and
charming Henry Aldrich—classic, musician, architect, collector of books and prints, composer and singer of gay catches,
the best of good company—was rarely mentioned without a
sneer. But other colleges were of course a great deal worse.
Pembroke, just across the road, was 'the fittest colledge in
town for brutes'. The scholars of Magdalen and New College
were addicted to wearing pantaloons and periwigs and to
keeping dogs, 'to the notorious scandall of the University'.
Opposite Balliol was 'a dingy, horrid, scandalous alehouse, fit
for none but draymen and tinkers, and such as by goeing
there have made themselfes equally scandalous. Here the
Balliol men continually ly, and by perpetuall bubbeing add art
to their natural stupidity to make themselfes perfect sots.'
The depth of iniquity was achieved by certain Fellows of All
Souls, who engaged in the surreptitious printing at the University Press of *Aretine's Postures*, a set of indecent engravings
from designs by Giulio Romano, accompanied by a series of
sonnets, *De omnibus Veneris schematibus*, written for the purpose by Pietro Aretino. The Fellows were detected in this
enterprise by Dr. Fell, who impounded the plates and threatened their owners with expulsion. 'And I thinke they would
deserve it', Prideaux commented, 'were they of any other
colledge than All Souls; but there I will allow them to be
vertuous that are bawdy only in pictures.'

His correspondent Ellis was a contemporary who had left
Christ Church to enter the public service, and was destined to
hold a lifelong succession of minor political and secretarial
appointments. Prideaux had undertaken to keep him informed
about Oxford affairs, and could occasionally supply him with
details which might usefully be passed on to his official

E 65

superiors. But most of the correspondence, especially in its earlier years, consisted of private gossip. He described the quarrels and eccentricities of Anthony à Wood; and the stir in the academic world when the Duchess of Cleveland visited Oxford, and 'sate at least an hour in her coach that every body might see her', and entrusted her eldest son by the King, 'whom she confesseth to be a very kockish idle boy', to the care of Dr. Fell; and how two undergraduates in the London coach 'violated my ears with such horrid, dissolute, and profane discourse, as I scarce should have thought the divell himselfe dared either use or teach others, were it not that I was soe unfortunate as to have this miserable experience thereof'. The visit of Van Tromp to Oxford in 1675 was an occasion of particular interest. At a grand dinner with Dr. Fell he caused some confusion by demanding nothing but salt meat, and his appearance disappointed the undergraduates, who 'wondred to find him, whom they had found so famous in Gazets, to be at last but a drunkeing greazy Dutchman'. Subsequently Prideaux wrote that 'we got a greater victory over Van Tromp here than all your sea captaines in London, he confessing that he was more drunke here than anywhere else since he came into England, which I thinke very little to the honour of our University'. It is related elsewhere that the greatest victory of all was won at St. John's College, whence Van Tromp had to be brought back to his lodgings in a wheelbarrow.

Prideaux confided in Ellis and obviously valued his advice. Each stage of his career, and every step on his road to advancement, is therefore reflected in these letters. Like all the promising young men at Christ Church, he was peremptorily enlisted by the Dean into the service of the University Press. His first task, apart from the compiling of some notes upon Lucius Florus, was to edit 'a horrid foolish musty booke', the chronicle of John of Antioch, otherwise known as John Malalas. 'I wish I were rid of him,' he lamented; 'and if my opinion were to be harkned to, instead of goeing to the presse, he should be condemned back again to the rubbish from whence he was taken, and there ly till moths and rats have rid the world of such horrid and insufferable nonsense.'

Humphrey Prideaux

Eventually Dr. Fell did hearken to his opinion, and Malalas remained neglected until Humphrey Hody's edition was published at the Press in 1691. Instead, Prideaux was set to catalogue and annotate the inscriptions known as the Arundelian Marbles, which had been presented to the University a few years earlier by Lord Henry Howard, afterwards Duke of Norfolk, a grandson of the *virtuoso* Earl of Arundel who collected them. He undertook the work with some diffidence, complaining bitterly of the little time allowed him, and the inexorable demands of the Press for 'a sheet every week, whether he was ready or no'. He was able to comfort himself, as he told Ellis, with the reflection that 'it is out of the road, and therefore few will perceive where I walke not right'. Unfortunately the corrector of the press allowed the book to appear with innumerable misprints; and these, together with Prideaux's own errors, did considerable harm to his reputation as a scholar. He himself felt no pride and little interest in the book. Conscious that his bent was for oriental rather than for classical studies, he regarded it merely as a troublesome task imposed by Dr. Fell. And although its defects were immediately apparent to those few scholars who examined it closely, *Marmora Oxoniensia* was received, on its publication in 1676, with general approval. In the eyes of John Evelyn, who had been instrumental in persuading Lord Henry Howard to present the Arundelian Marbles to the University, Prideaux appeared 'a young man most learned in antiquities'. And the book secured him a valuable patron in the Lord Chancellor, Heneage Finch, afterwards Earl of Nottingham. He was sent to London to present a copy to the Lord Chancellor on behalf of the University; and his learning and ability so impressed the great man that he soon afterwards sent one of his sons to Christ Church under his care. Charles Finch took kindly to a life of learning, and in due course became a Fellow of All Souls, but died 'before he could make any appearance in the world'. His father was well pleased with his progress, and continued his favours to Prideaux. In 1679 he presented him to the Rectory of St. Clement's in Oxford. In 1680, when Parliament met briefly at Oxford, Prideaux acted as his chaplain. And in 1681, when one of the prebends in Norwich

67

Cathedral, which was in the gift of the Lord Chancellor, fell
vacant, the stall was bestowed upon him.

III

Norwich, in the later seventeenth century, was still one of
the richest and most populous cities in the land. High on its
mound, the great decaying castle dominated a maze of narrow
streets and the towers of close on forty churches, all crowded
within the circuit of the ancient walls. The river wound
among the houses and away to the port of Yarmouth, bearing
the cargoes of textiles—the bays and says, the bombazines
and the callimancoes—on which for centuries the wealth and
fame of the city had been founded. To a west-country man
Norwich must have appeared strangely remote, the capital of
an isolated province, the centre of its own small universe. It
retains something of the same air even today.

The Cathedral and its precincts occupied much of the
eastern quarter of the city, spreading over the low-lying
ground and down to the river bank. 'Our Close', wrote
Prideaux of the territory where he was one day to reign, 'is
as it were a town of itselfe apart from the city, separated from
it by walls and gates.' There were traces everywhere of the
destruction wrought by Puritan fanatics during the Civil War
a generation earlier. The Cathedral was full of broken stonework, shattered tombs, memorial slabs from which the
brasses had been torn away. Bishop Reynolds had rebuilt the
demolished chapel of his Palace, but much other damage was
as yet unrepaired.

Prideaux was installed as a prebendary of Norwich in the
summer of 1681. His stall had been previously occupied by
Dr. John Sharp, who had also started in life as chaplain and
tutor to the Finch family. The Lord Chancellor had lately
obtained the promotion of Dr. Sharp to the deanery of
Norwich; and a close alliance now developed between the
two beneficiaries of the Finch influence. They shared the same
active and reforming temper, and they found a great deal that
needed to be reformed. According to the Dean's biographer,
in order that 'he might inform himself completely of every

68

thing that was requisite to make him a *good governor*, he spent a great part of the following year in looking over the ledger-books, and making himself master of the state of their revenues, and the extent of his own rights and privileges'. In this task he was much assisted by Prideaux. And in various other ways the new Dean and the new prebendary came to figure prominently in the diocese of Norwich, especially since the Bishop, the talented and amiable Anthony Sparrow, was now disabled from active life by constant attacks of the stone.

Prideaux himself signalized his first year at Norwich by one minor but praiseworthy act of reformation. The tomb of the founder, Bishop Herbert de Losinga, which stood before the high altar of the Cathedral, had been virtually destroyed during the Civil War. On his own initiative Prideaux caused a new tomb to be erected in the same position, covered with a slab bearing a Latin inscription of his own composing, and adorned with the coats of arms of the Bishop, the Dean and the six prebendaries. This tomb was destroyed in its turn by a nineteenth-century Dean, who preserved only the inscribed slab, which he set into his grand new pavement of encaustic tiles, and the coats of arms, which he built into the gate-posts of a house in the Close.

The political situation in the city and the county was a matter of immediate interest to Prideaux. During the past three years, with their three successive Parliaments, the struggle between the Court and Country factions had been bitterly contested in Norfolk; and a petition over the two county seats, after the general election of 1679, had aroused an exceptional amount of ill-feeling. In his first letter to Ellis from Norwich, in the summer of 1681, Prideaux had remarked that 'this town I find devided into two factions, Whigs and Torys; the former are the more numerous, but the latter carry all before them as consisting of the governing part of the town, and both contend for their way with the utmost violence. I doe not believe any place can afford of either part more vehement votaries to it than this town.' It was just the same in the county. The Lord Lieutenant, Robert Paston first Earl of Yarmouth, a lifelong and passionate supporter of the King, was the leader of the Tory party. Sir John Hobart of

Blickling headed the Whigs. Between these two 'vehement votaries', and with his own considerable personal following, stood a representative of moderation, Horatio first Viscount Townshend. He had been deposed from the Lord Lieutenancy in favour of Lord Yarmouth some years before; but his reconciliation with the King, which now appeared possible, would alter the balance decisively in favour of the Court party. Prideaux strongly advocated the conciliation of Townshend in a long report on local politics which he sent to Ellis early in 1682, and which Ellis duly passed on to his official superior, Sir Joseph Williamson, the Secretary of State. Probably he sent other such reports to Ellis from time to time; and certainly the comments on local affairs in his private letters were always intended for transmission to higher authority at his friend's discretion.

For the next few years Prideaux's life was divided between his tutorial duties at Oxford and his periods of obligatory residence at Norwich. In 1676 Dr. Fell had been appointed Bishop of Oxford; and although he still remained Dean of Christ Church, he could spend less time upon the day-to-day administration of the college, and his mantle as a disciplinarian fell upon Prideaux. 'As a Tutor in the College,' we are told by his biographer, Prideaux was 'always very zealous and diligent in reforming such disorders and corruptions, as had from time to time crept into it; and made use of all opportunities in his power for suppressing them. This of course drew on him the ill-will of many of his Fellow Collegians, as must always happen to those, who endeavour at the Reformation of Discipline'. Most people, in fact, were alienated by his sharp tongue and his peremptory manner. He seems to have had few friends amongst his colleagues, apart from a few seniors such as Bishop Fell and Dr. Pococke; and something of his attitude towards the undergraduates may be guessed from a letter to the guardian of one of them, in which he describes a visit to London as the entering of 'the very jaws of Hell'.

His letters to Ellis reveal a growing distaste for Oxford. Although he had been appointed Dr. Busby's Hebrew Lecturer at Christ Church, he saw no likelihood that he would

succeed Dr. Pococke in the Professorship. The succession was
virtually assured to a relation of the Lord Treasurer; and in
any case his old friend and master was still in good health,
'and God long preserve him soe'. He was, moreover, losing
his enthusiasm for Hebrew studies, and published nothing
further of that nature except two tracts of Maimonides with
a Latin translation. His great patron Lord Chancellor Finch
died at the end of 1682; but he continued in the favour of his
successor in office, Sir Francis North, who early in 1683
bestowed upon him the excellent living of Bladon with Wood-
stock. In the same year his father died, leaving him 'a very
good younger brother's estate, whereby I may be enabled,
come what times there will, to support my selfe'. This inheritance, together with the income from his prebend and from
his new living, which could be served by a curate, led him to
consider severing his ties with Oxford altogether.

He took no final step, however, until the death of Charles II
early in 1685 altered the political scene and cast ominous
shadows ahead. Bishop Fell's health was declining fast, and
his death was only a matter of time. It could hardly be
doubted that the new King would appoint a Catholic as Dean
of Christ Church in his stead. In any event Oxford was clearly
destined to be the scene of violent religious conflict in the
years to come. Prideaux at last made up his mind that it was
time to depart; and his decision was influenced by a new and
unexpected factor. In July 1685 he wrote to Ellis: 'I have now
been long enough here to begin to be weary of a place where
now almost every one is my junior, and therefore have resolved to retire to my liveing and fix for good and all there;
and in order hereto I have hearkned to proposals that have
been made to me of marriage, and because they are such as
are very advantagious. I have already got soe far as the
sealeing of articles, whereby I have secured to myselfe
£3000; but after the death of the father and mother, whose
only child the gentlewoman is, I believe there will be at least
£1500 more. I little thought I should ever come to this; but
abundance of motives have overpowered me, and therefore I
have yielded to the circumstances of my present condition,
which would neither be convenient nor comfortable to me

without this resolution.' With typical self-reliance he ended his letter to his oldest friend: 'I doe not ask your advice herein, because it is too late for it; neither doe I your opinion, because you cannot judge of it without knoweing all my circumstances, which it would be too long for me now to tell you.'

Few men can have approached the married state with less enthusiasm. The match was at first entirely one of convenience, and 'I little thought I should ever come to this' accurately summed up his view of the relationship. There is no suggestion in his letters to Ellis of any personal regard for 'the gentlewoman I am to marry', or even a mention of her name. She was Bridget, the daughter of Anthony Bokenham of Helmingham, a Suffolk squire with ramifying family connexions all over East Anglia. Their marriage took place early in 1686, and proved entirely successful. Mrs. Prideaux remains a shadowy figure in her husband's background; but she won his chilly affections, and their years together were the happiest of his life.

From the time of his marriage Prideaux settled in Norfolk entirely. He felt no attachment to his native Cornwall, or to the home of his ancestors. 'My father's house lies on the north sea, and open to all the wind and weather from thence, which I am not willeing to endure,' he had written some years before. He was well content to be removed for ever from the west-country rain, the Atlantic gales, the roaring of the surf at Padstow. He thought Norfolk by contrast 'the pleasantest countrey in England, beeing all open and dry', and rejoiced in the clear invigorating air. He could scarcely find anything to grumble about: 'the only inconvenience', he wrote, 'is the want of good bread, but, this proceeding from a cause which any one may remedy that will, I beleive I shall not stick much at this'.

As a final severance of his ties with Oxford, he exchanged his livings in that diocese for the benefice of Saham Toney in Norfolk. At the public act of 1686 he proceeded to the degree of Doctor of Divinity. The same week brought the death of Bishop Fell, the old friend and preceptor to whom he owed so much. Prideaux was present at his funeral in the Cathedral, and left Oxford immediately afterwards. He never returned, even for a single day, during the rest of his long life.

IV

Prideaux was a man who greatly enjoyed the possession of power; but he was always content to exercise that power in a comparatively narrow sphere. Authority was not the less sweet to him because it was confined within the limits of a college or of a chapter. Security, stability and peace of mind ranked in his scale of values above wider and more dangerous ambitions. 'My thoughts,' he told Ellis shortly before he settled in Norfolk, 'are much averse from aspireing to high places. I see nothing but trouble and vexation in them, and therefore, to tell the whole of my heart, there is nothing which I doe soe much desire in this world as to be fixed in a station once for all, where I may have as little trouble as possible besides that which is the duty of my profession, and from whence I may noe more remove till I dy.'

As the reign of James II proceeded on its course, he was increasingly thankful for the step he had taken. At Oxford one college after another was embroiled in religious controversy. The new Dean of Christ Church was, as he had anticipated, a Papist. The Master of University College, Dr. Obadiah Walker, announced his conversion to the Catholic faith. The fellows of Magdalen resisted the King over the appointment of a new President, and were finally ejected in a body. These storms echoed but distantly in the tranquil air of Norwich. 'We live here remote from the center of affairs and in a great deal of quiet,' he wrote to Ellis late in 1686; and in 1688 his letters were still in the same strain. 'I have now lived here two years in great content, it beeing the most delightful city of any I have seen in England for a man to live in, especially in our district, which hath all sorts of conveniences to recommend it to our satisfaction.'

Nevertheless there were hints in these letters of his sense of an approaching crisis, and of the dilemma with which the Church of England must soon be confronted. The hints would probably have been stronger if Ellis, while himself remaining a Protestant, had not been connected with the Court through his brother, who had become a Benedictine many years before and was now chaplain to the King. For even in Norfolk the local Catholics, encouraged by the sympathies of their monarch, had been seeking to make new converts; and from the beginning Prideaux had taken a leading part in opposing them. Their spokesmen were a Jesuit, Father Thomas Acton, 'the chief Mass Priest of a Popish conventicle then set up in Norwich,' and a certain Webster, who before his conversion had been curate of St. Margaret's, King's Lynn. They made a point of stressing the invalidity of the orders of the Church of England; and Prideaux set himself to confute their arguments in sermons, letters and pamphlets. As usual, he did not withhold the rough edge of his tongue. Since Father Acton's services were held in a building which had once been used as a granary, he referred to his opponents whenever possible as 'the men of the granary'. And he further angered them, on an occasion when he happened to be the prebendary in residence, by refusing burial in the Cathedral to a recent convert of some importance in the city, insisting that he should be buried in the church or churchyard of the parish in which he died.

The crisis came in May 1688, with the King's instructions that the Declaration of Indulgence should be distributed by the Bishops to their clergy, and read during divine service in every church throughout the realm. The Bishop of Norwich at this time was William Lloyd, who had succeeded the invalid Bishop Sparrow two years before, and whom Prideaux rightly regarded as 'a very excellent person'. He was in full accord with Archbishop Sancroft in his opposition to the reading of the Declaration. But the Archbishop's letter summoning him to the momentous conference at Lambeth was delayed by a postmaster; and although he set out from Norwich directly he received it, he arrived too late to sign the petition which brought his seven fellow-Bishops to the Tower. He remained in London, acting as a link between his imprisoned brethren and their sympathizers; and he entrusted Prideaux with the distribution in the diocese of Norwich of the famous letter addressed to the clergy, sometimes attributed to Halifax, which was to prove so influential in dissuading them from reading the Declaration in their churches. It was a difficult and somewhat risky undertaking, and at one moment Prideaux was in serious danger of detection. The Bishop sent down two thousand copies of the *Letter*, which were conveyed to Norwich in the stage coach by an uncle of Mrs. Prideaux. On hearing of their arrival Prideaux hurried to the old gentleman's house, just in time to prevent a servant from opening the box in the presence of 'a lewd Physician, a spy for the Papists, and in all respects a profligate abandoned man'. Clearly it was suspected that something was on foot; but he soon thought of an ingenious way of circumventing those who were watching him. 'Having made up about a dozen packets with several of these letters inclosed in each of them, he superscribed them in feigned hands, to as many ministers in the City of Norwich; and sent a person, whom he knew he could trust, to Yarmouth, with directions to disperse them in several wherries, which came up every night from thence to Norwich; and this being faithfully executed, the letters were delivered the next morning as directed. Now as they were sent from Yarmouth, it was generally believed, that they came from Holland; and the Doctor, by this device, escaped all suspicion of having any hand in the affair. As to the rest, he sent them by the carriers, who go from Norwich every week, into all parts of the county, so that they were dispersed over the Diocese, without its being known, from whose hand they came, till all the danger was over'. So effective were the arguments in the *Letter* that out of twelve hundred parishes in the diocese, there were only four or five in which the Declaration was read.

A few months later the situation was entirely changed by the landing of the Prince of Orange and the flight of the King. Prideaux no longer need fear the denunciations of Popish spies. Instead he found himself, during the disorders which accompanied the Revolution, protecting supposed Catholics from the fury of the Norwich mob. Several houses of Papists in the city were attacked and looted, and the rioters then advanced upon the Close, where the occupants of certain houses were suspected of Catholic sympathies. 'But Dr. Prideaux having timely notice of their design, ordered the gates of the

Close to be shut up; and the inhabitants arming themselves for their defence, repulsed the rabble, who attacked them, to the number of five hundred men, and made them desist from their enterprize; upon which somebody crying out, "To the Bull!", they all went to the Bull, which was a tavern kept by a Papist in the city, and having plundered and gutted this house, finished their expedition.'

In December of this same eventful year Bishop Lloyd appointed Prideaux to the Archdeaconry of Suffolk, which had just fallen vacant. It was one of the last appointments which the Bishop was to make. Like Archbishop Sancroft and several others of his fellow prelates, he could not bring himself to take the oaths to the new monarchs, and was therefore suspended and finally deprived. For the remaining twenty years of his life he was one of the most active leaders of the non-juring Church. The new Archdeacon of Suffolk had himself at first regarded the advent of the Prince of Orange with considerable misgiving. He wrote to one of his sisters early in 1689 that after having expected, during the two late years of King James's reign, 'to be turned out of all', he now anticipated that fate even more under King William, 'oaths and tests being like to be put upon us, which I can never take'. But in the end, like the great majority of his fellow churchmen, he was able to reconcile the taking of the new oaths with his conscience, although he always regarded his old Bishop and other non-jurors with sympathy and respect. Once convinced of the rightness of the arguments in favour of the oaths, he became a fervent advocate for them; and so eloquent was his charge on this subject at his first visitation, that only three out of the three hundred clergy in his Archdeaconry refused to take them.

In 1689 the Dean of Norwich, his old friend Dr. Sharp, became Dean of Canterbury, and two years afterwards was appointed Archbishop of York. There had recently been some clouding of their friendship, and the misunderstanding was only cleared up by an exchange of letters some years later. In the course of this *éclaircissement*, Dr. Sharp was constrained to mention that 'I may have complained of the too great warmth of your temper, which now and then created uneasiness to me, and others of our society'. If the warmth of Prideaux's temper could disturb his relations with the congenial Dr. Sharp, it was not to be expected that he would look kindly upon Dr. Sharp's successor. This was Dr. Henry Fairfax, who had led the fellows of Magdalen in their resistance to King James, and now received the Deanery of Norwich as the reward of his courage and steadfastness. Unfortunately the rest of Dr. Fairfax's career was in lamentable contrast to his behaviour on that occasion. 'He is good for nothing but his pipe and his pot,' Prideaux wrote succinctly; and such seems really to have been the case. He found it so impossible to agree with the new Dean that he withdrew entirely to his country parsonage at Saham Toney, only coming to Norwich for his two months of residence in each year.

Twice a year, also, he visited his Archdeaconry of Suffolk. It was observed that 'for the first three years after the Revolution, he took upon himself the office of preaching at every place where he held his visitation, which was a caution then very necessary, for preventing such of the Clergy, as were not satisfied of the justice of the Revolution, from launching out on topicks, that might give offence to the Government, when it should come to their turn to preach'. In this, as in all matters of organization and discipline, he was not going to leave anything to chance. Those of his clergy who professed Jacobite sympathies were carefully watched. A particular source of trouble was the Rev. Thomas Alexander, who had been Lecturer to the Corporation of Ipswich until he was displaced at the Revolution. He had then obtained a small living in Ipswich, 'and was soe closely stuck to by the Jacobites, as beeing looked on a martyr for that cause, that he had almost undon the place in setteing the people togeather by the ears'. Some of his supporters were so influential that neither Prideaux nor the newly-appointed Bishop, Dr. John Moore, knew quite how to deal with him. Eventually, at the time of the abortive Jacobite conspiracy of 1692, he was arrested 'in a tinker's habit with a snapsack on his back' on some mysterious political errand in Essex. After he had spent some time in gaol the Bishop consented to intercede with the Government on his behalf, on condition that he left the diocese; and Prideaux was troubled with him no more.

Soon after Bishop Moore's appointment in 1691, and before he had arrived in Norwich for his installation, Prideaux sent him an indignant letter about the misdoings of Dean Fairfax. 'As to our Circumstances here you will best understand them when on the place, but in truth they are very unfortunate since our Dean by decay of parts hath in a great measure lost his understanding in businesse and yet retains his old inflexible obstinacy which makes him pursue his will (most an end fix'd by other men that encourage him) in things very absurd and with a ruffenesse of carriage not to be endured, whereby he hath broken us all in pieces. . . . I think him the unfittest man that possibly could be put in this place and that you will see when you are on the place. I have prevailed with the most exasperated of my Brethren to maintain all outward forms of decency towards him although it must be a peice of noe small selfedenyall to doe it. He hath seemed to maintain a fair correspondence with me since my resideing, and I have corresponded with him as fairly, but however unlesse he alters his conduct for the future I believe he must make a Chapter by himselfe, the Prebendarys will noe more come nigh him. Besides his conversation both here and at London is an exceeding great scandall to us which hath sunk his situation as low as the dirt and I am affraid some he has provoked will bring him upon the publick stage for it.' There was nothing that the Bishop or anyone else could do about it. The Dean continued on his unseemly path.

In this same year Dr. Pococke died, and Prideaux was after all offered the Professorship of Hebrew at Oxford. But it was now too late to think of moving again. 'I refused it,' he told Ellis, 'and that for two reasons: the first is, I nauseate that learning, and am resolved to loose noe more time upon it; and the second is, I nauseate Christ Church; and, further, if I should goe to Oxford again I must quit whatever I have here, and the advantage would scarce pay for the remove. But my main argument is, I have an unconquerable aversion to the place, and will never live more among such people who now have the prevailinge power there.' He preferred the seclusion of Saham, where he wrote and studied and enjoyed the company of a few congenial neighbours. One of these was an eminent non-juror, Sir Edward Atkyns, who had been Chief Baron of the Exchequer under the late King, and had retired to live at North Pickenham after refusing the oaths to his successor. Another was old Sir John Holland of Quidenham, an influential figure in Norfolk politics for several decades, and at his death in 1701 the last surviving member of the Long Parliament.

From Saham, and during his periods of residence at Norwich, he continued to deplore the iniquities of the Dean and his ally among the prebendaries, Nathaniel Hodges. He had long been on bad terms with Hodges, who was considerably senior to him in the Chapter, and with whom he had a prolonged dispute as to the stall in the Cathedral which properly appertained to his Archdeaconry of Suffolk. (This question was eventually submitted to the arbitration of the Bishop, who pronounced in Prideaux's favour.) His dislike of the Dean and of Hodges grew into an obsession, and he repeatedly spoke of them to Ellis with the most unclerical violence. The force and humour in the following description of the hated pair must not blind the reader to its probable exaggeration. 'We are here at a miserable passe with this horrid sot we have got for our Dean. He cannot sleep at night till dosed with drink, and therefore, when in bed, his man's businesse is to drink with him till he hath his dose; and it beeing his way to keep a man only for the time of his residence and then dismisse him, he hath spread his fame soe throughout the whole county that nothing is more scandalous; for his servants, whom he thus dismisseth, goeing into other familys tell all, especially one, a lewd fellow enough, beeing intertained by one Mr. Earle,[1] a drinkeing lewd gentleman of this county, to be his butler, gives there a most horrid account of his old master the Dean; and when the lewd ones there meet togeather to drinke, one of their cheife entertainments is to have the butler come in and tell all his storys of the Dean of Norwich, which represent him one of the greatest beasts in nature. And indeed his carriage in businesse represents him

[1] This was Erasmus Earle, the squire of Heydon.

79

as much a brute as his man can a beast, for he acts by noe rules of justice, honesty, civility, or good manners towards any one, but after an obstinate, self-willed, irrational manner in all sorts of businesses, whereby he disoblidgeth every one that hath any thing to doe with him. He hath after a most unreasonable manner disoblidged every one of the prebendarys except Hodges, and nothing will satisfy him but to be an absolute king over us. He comes little to church and never to the sacrament, though we have a sacrament every Sunday; and as for a booke, he looks not into any from the beginning of the year to the end. His whole life is the pot and the pipe, and, goe to him when you will, you will find him walking about his room with a pipe in his mouth and a bottle of claret and a bottle of old strong beer (which in this county they call nog) upon the table, and every other turn he takes a glass of one or the other of them. If Hodges comes to him (for scarce any other doth), then he reads *Don Quixote*, while the other walkes about with his pipe as before, and this is noble entertainment between them. Certainly the preferments of the Church were never designed for such drones; and yet these two fellows have about £300 per annum each, and never did it a farthing's worth of service in their life, professeing nothing else but to live idlely and feed their bellys upon what they have. Hodges is indeed noe drinker as the other, for his body cannot bear it; but although nothing is more mean than he, either in his birth or his merit, yet nothing can be more proud and conceited. Once in a year he will offer to preach, but, his sermons beeing most on end the translation of his morall philosophy lectures at Oxford, as soon as the people see him in the pulpitt they all get out of church. . . .'

In December 1693, shortly after the date of this letter, the Dean retired to London, and seldom thereafter visited Norwich. His departure was a welcome event for Prideaux, who was becoming weary of his self-imposed exile at Saham Toney. He had not found the place so conducive to study as he had expected, and he and all his family—there were now two sons and a daughter—suffered constantly from the ague which was then common in that countryside. Early next year he settled once more at his house in the Close, where 'the whole business of the Cathedral fell again into his hands, and he was obliged to undertake the burden of it, to prevent all from running to confusion'. It was a burden which he was very ready to assume. The affairs of the chapter were once again set in order. The behaviour of all the functionaries of the Cathedral was carefully watched. He paid especial attention to the condition of the fabric itself, having it minutely inspected every spring and ensuring that all necessary repairs were completed by Michaelmas—exercising, in fact, a degree of precaution which probably saved the spire from destruction during the unprecedented gale of 1703. Nor did he overlook the importance of maintaining good relations with the citizens of Norwich. 'Nothing is a more constant rule with me than never to meddle with their concerns, and indeed I very seldom goe among them,' he wrote. None the less, he kept a vigilant eye on everything that happened in the city; and he was able to tell Ellis, with sublime self-assurance, that 'I acknowledge I have as great a share of their respects as any of my profession perchance that hath ever lived among them'.

On his return to Norwich he resigned the living of Saham. Some of his friends could not see any necessity for this step; but as an archdeacon he had always discouraged non-residence on the part of his clergy, and was determined to set an example now. He accepted instead the much smaller living of Trowse, on the outskirts of Norwich, which he could serve in person. His duties there, and the business of the Cathedral, still allowed him plenty of time for study and authorship. Since leaving Oxford he had published only a few pamphlets; but he had long been contemplating a 'History of the Ruin of the Eastern Church between the years 602 and 936', and had indeed made some progress on it before he went to Saham. He had intended to describe, on a scale almost comparable to Gibbon's, the decay of the Byzantine empire during those three centuries, and the rise and spread of the Mahometan power. But first and foremost he was a clergyman; and he was much exercised at this time by the progress of Deism, a poison which had 'reached some places, where it is my particular Duty to prevent its Mischiefs; and infected some Persons, for whose Eternal Welfare, as well as Temporal, I have reason to be nearly concerned'. The giddy-headed young, in particular, were being misled by these fashionable doctrines, and 'confidently take upon them to call Christianity a Cheat, and an Imposture, without ever having considered what an Imposture is, or whether any of the Marks and Properties thereof can possibly agree with this Holy Religion, or no'. So he determined to give up his great historical project, and write instead a life of Mahomet, in order to show such people what religious imposture really means.

The book appeared early in 1697. Its full title was *The True Nature of Imposture Fully Display'd in the LIFE OF MAHOMET, with a Discourse annex'd, for the Vindicating of Christianity from this Charge: offered to the Consideration of the Deists of the present Age*. The biography was based upon a formidable array of authorities—Arabic works in profusion, and many treatises also in Hebrew and Chaldee, Greek and Latin. The discourse which followed was straightforward doctrinal argument, couched in the combative tones which Prideaux always employed. Whatever its effect on the deists may have been, the book was extremely well received by the learned world as a whole. It went into three editions within the year, and greatly enhanced Prideaux's reputation.

In 1700 some contagious sickness attacked his family. The children all recovered, but his wife died towards the close of the year. He lamented her loss deeply, and suffered anxieties over the upbringing of the children without the help of 'their dear Mother'. Naturally the question of a second marriage arose. He wrote to his sister a few months afterwards: 'I am mightyly pressed to marry again, with abundance of offers, and very valuable ones; but considering all circumstances, I shall think of making noe more changes till I make my great change of this life, as I hope, for a better. . . . Had it been convenient for me to take another wife, I should soon have determined my choice upon a gentlewoman, whom I have long known to be a very good and discreet woman, although not very beautyfull. Her father was Knight of the Bath at the Coronation of King Charles II, and of the antientest and most honourable family in this countrey. At his death he left an estate of about £1000 a year, which this gentlewoman, with

three other sisters, on the death of their elder brother, doth
now inherit. She is passed 40, and was never yet married.'
Neither she, nor any other of the good and discreet ladies of
Norfolk, was ever to alter his resolution.

In May 1702 the Dean died at last. Prideaux was appointed
to succeed him, and was installed in his new office on the 8th
of June, just twenty-one years after he first became one of the
Chapter of Norwich.

V

The Deanery of Norwich was the summit of Prideaux's
ambition. For the rest of his days he would rule in unquestioned authority over the little kingdom whose affairs he
understood so well. When Bishop Moore was translated to
Ely five years later, he could have been his successor for the
asking. Powerful friends urged him to make the necessary
application, and would have been assiduous in promoting it.
But he preferred to remain where he was, in that pleasant
sunny house beside the Cathedral, with the bells chiming the
hours and calling to worship, and the great spire soaring
above.

The objectionable Dr. Hodges had died in 1700, and with
the rest of the chapter he was on excellent terms. The same
could no longer be said of his relations with Bishop Moore,
or with the Bishop's Chancellor and son-in-law, Dr. Thomas
Tanner. Both were distinguished scholars and ardent biblio-
philes; but Prideaux, however zealous himself in the cause of
learning, was frequently in conflict with them over the respec-
tive jurisdictions of Bishopric and Chapter. He regarded them
as his adversaries, and had no good word to say for either.

He had made great advances towards setting the affairs of
the Cathedral in order during the absences of the late Dean,
but there was still much to be done. His predecessor had
appointed 'several obnoxious and scandalous persons' as
minor canons, choirmen and other functionaries. The removal
of these people, and their replacement by the best men he
could find, was his first aim. Leases of houses in the Close had
been granted to undesirable characters. The incumbents of

some of the chapter livings were not all that could be wished. Almost everything, in fact, needed to be tightened up; and almost everyone required to be admonished. He set to work with a will.

The extent of his reforms, and their effectiveness, may be judged from two volumes of his diary, hitherto entirely unpublished, which are preserved in the library of the Dean and Chapter of Norwich. The title-page of the earlier and fuller of these volumes reads: *Diarium Secundum Decani et Capituli Ecclesiae Cathedralis Sanctae et Individuae Trinitatis Norvici. Ab Anno 1703 usque ad Annum 1713.* The *Diarium Tertium* was carried on until the very end of his life. Unfortunately the first volume of all has disappeared, and we therefore do not know anything about his initial measures. But the surviving volumes, with their wealth of detail and their extreme outspokenness, provide a remarkable and perhaps a unique picture of an eighteenth-century chapter under a vigilant and irascible Dean. Everyone connected with the Cathedral, from the Lord Bishop himself down to the bedesmen and porters, makes an appearance sooner or later in their pages. Every kind of transaction is recorded—the appointment of new prebendaries, of minor canons, of schoolmasters and singing-men and vergers; the management of the houses and other buildings within the confines of the Close; the administration of the Chapter properties all over the county; the vexed question of the Parliamentary voting-rights of certain Cathedral functionaries, which they claimed by virtue of the houses attached to their offices; the ensuring that those functionaries whose rights were indubitable should vote as the Dean wished; and, of course, the interminable disputes with the Bishop and the Chancellor.

The tenants of the houses in the Close required, or anyhow received, careful supervision. There was trouble with Mrs. Pepper, who had been allowed to build a coach-house and promptly let it as a stone-cutter's shop, 'to the great disturbance of all the neighbourhood'. There might have been even more serious trouble with Mrs. Wood, the 'Apostate Papist' widow of the squire of Braconash, 'a famous Debauchee in his time', who wanted to come and lodge in the house

HUMPHREY PRIDEAUX
from an engraving by George Vertue
after a painting by Enoch Seeman

of a Mr. Clerk. 'This thing of getteing some Popish Gentlewoman into the Close hath been much laboured. The meaning
of it is they haveing Priests attending them if they could get
way for themselves to dwell in the Close, it would open a way
for their Priests to come in and endeavour to make a Harvest
for Rome among the Gentlewomen which live in the Close.'
Prideaux was having none of this. The leases of the houses in
the Close all contained a clause forbidding the tenants to
admit recusant persons to live with them. Mrs. Wood was
reported to be 'a very violent woman in her way and constantly keeps a Priest in her family'; so Mr. Clerk was held
firmly to the terms of his lease, and she was obliged to betake
herself elsewhere.

Delinquents were sternly dealt with, and their offences
recorded in the frankest detail. Mr. Pitcairn of Sedgeford, one
of the chapter livings, misconducted himself with one of his
own parishioners, and also with an ill woman at Wootton.
He and his brother, the rector of Wighton, were 'Confessors
for the Episcopall Church of Scotland, and for that reason
were forced to leave their Country; but this person hath very
ill maintained the Character of a person suffering for his
Religion, who hath so scandalously offended against the Dutys
of it'. He was eventually deprived. William Pleasants, one of
the lay clerks and master of the boys, was accused of
atheism and great wickedness of life. The charge of the boys
was taken away from him, not without good reason; but his
atheistical expressions, such as 'there is noe Heaven but a
quiet mind and no Hell but the Grave', were not conclusively
proved against him, and he was let off with a warning. The
most persistent offender, however, was Searles the Chapter
Clerk. Early in 1705 he was accused of being taken by the city
officers in a house of ill-fame, and at the same time had to be
admonished for failing to receive the sacrament for ten years
past. A few months later he was again caught in a similar
establishment, with a woman whom the officers 'put into a
cage, and there she was shown the next day (it being the
public Guild) to City and County in that public concourse for
Searles's whore'. Alderman Gardiner interceded for Searles,
since he needed his political support, but was soundly snubbed

by the Dean, who told him that 'the townspeople had nothing to do herein'. Eventually they got Searles to resign his post of Chapter Clerk, and appointed him porter instead, 'to keep him from starving, for he is a poor helplesse sottish wretch that is able to do nothing for him selfe'. He retained this office without further scandal till his death four years later.

Searles's predecessor had been one Cuddon, from whom the previous Dean, according to Prideaux, had accepted a bribe for his appointment to that office. 'He payd down the sayd 20 guineas upon a plate, and the sayd Dean Fairfax did tell them over and did accept and take the sayd summe.' It may or may not have been so. But amidst so much censoriousness, it is a relief to find Prideaux on one occasion using his powers of office for the benefit of a protégé of his own. In 1705 his coachman was too lavishly entertained at a house where the Dean was dining, and fell off the box on the way home. The horses took fright and ran away with the Dean sitting helpless inside the coach. Fortunately he recalled the sad fate of Bishop Grove of Chichester, who in a similar predicament had jumped out of the coach and was fatally injured by the rear wheel passing over him. So he remained where he was; and the horses were eventually stopped, after a headlong course of three miles, by a poor labourer named Aaron Alcock. Three years later Alcock was made a bedesman of the Cathedral. 'This person haveing stopped the Dean's Coach when the Horses run away with it on his Coachman's falleing out of the box, and thereby saved him from the danger which he might otherwise have run of his Life, the Dean for his reward procured this place for him.'

Throughout the later years of their association Prideaux had nothing but hard words for Bishop Moore, and his dislike was probably returned. Matters came to a head in 1705, when a tremendous dispute arose over the position of the Dean's and Vice-Dean's seats. On this subject the Bishop addressed to the Dean a letter of four and a half pages, to which the Dean replied with another of twenty-two pages. Eventually the Bishop gave way, but only, according to Prideaux, because he needed the Chapter's confirmation of two patents which he had granted to his own son. His Lordship, he noted sourly, 'would fain grasp anything for his brood. He would have don better to have taken the same care of their education that he doth to provide places for them afterwards, he being guilty herein of a very criminall neglect'. When the Bishop was translated to Ely two years later, Prideaux inserted in his diary (which, it must be remembered, he intended to transmit to his successors in his holy office) a most vindictive account of a prelate who was generally viewed with great respect. 'His father was an iron munger and a noted Tub preacher and all his relations were dissenters, only he followed the Church for the sake of the Bagg', and so forth at considerable length. Prideaux rejected all suggestions that he should make interest for the vacant see. Instead, he used his influence on behalf of his fellow prebendary Dr. Charles Trimnell, who was duly appointed. He and Trimnell were friends of long standing, and harmony reigned once more in the Close. At his installation the new Bishop 'payd all his fees which are customary due for the same, whereas his predecessor Bishop Moore payd none of them, but out of a stingy base temper sharked us of them'.

The increasing acrimony of the entries in Prideaux's diary may well have been due to the state of his health. He was suffering from stone in the bladder, and the disease grew ever more agonizing as the years went by. He was advised that in his case an operation would be extremely dangerous, and probably fatal. 'If soe,' he wrote to Ellis in July 1710, 'to put myselfe upon it is nothing lesse than selfe murder, and for that I cannot answer to God, who gave me my life; and therefore I must be content to bear my burden as it is, and it is heavy enough.' But his torments continued until death seemed inevitable within a few weeks; and then, in the hope of obtaining some temporary relief, he determined to undergo the operation. On 20th March 1711 he filled four pages of the diary, in a pitifully trembling hand, with various memoranda upon Cathedral affairs, 'to be directions to his Successor in case he should dy, which he earnestly desires he would be pleased to consider that the true interest of this Church may be duly and rightly carryed on.' On the 24th the operation took place, and this was likewise recorded in the diary. 'Dr.

Prideaux, Dean of this Church, was this day cut for the stone and a large rough stone was extracted out of him by Mr. Salter a surgeon of London, who came hither of purpose to perform this Operation, and it pleased God that the sayd Dean escaped this Operation with his life.'

VI

He escaped with his life, and at first all seemed to go well. Mr. Salter returned to London, leaving his patient in the hands of a young surgeon of Norwich named Pell, a pupil of his own in whom he had full confidence. But the months passed, and no progress was made; so that 'after he had been under the care of this surgeon a whole year, he seemed to be much further from a cure, than when he had first undertaken him; and during all this time the Dean had suffered as much pain and torment from him, as he had before from the stone itself'. Finally he journed to London, lying at full length in a litter, and was examined by Mr. Salter. The reader shall be spared the details of what had gone wrong. It is sufficient to say that, although Mr. Salter did his best, the Dean was condemned to inactivity and constant discomfort for the rest of his days.

But the pleasures of administration and study were still left to him. He began to assemble the material for the most ambitious of his literary works, the *Connection between the Old and the New Testaments*; and his management of Chapter affairs remained as vigorous as ever. He particularly enjoyed a prolonged battle with Nicholas Helwys, the squire of Morton, over the terms of a lease. Helwys was 'a very troublesome vexatious person, exceedingly quarrelsom and litigious'. Despite the 'huffeing quarrelsom messages' which he repeatedly sent, Mr. Helwys had met his match. He was reduced to asking for their differences to be submitted to arbitration; whereupon 'the Dean sent him word that noe man would refer it to any arbitration whether the Hat which he wears on his head is his own or noe, that the Dean and Chapter knew their rights and would maintain them'.

The dispute with Helwys was carried over into the concluding volume of the diary, and continued intermittently for years. It was not until 1719 that a final agreement was reached with this 'very overbearing rude man'. The entries in this volume are similar in theme and in temper to those in its predecessor. John Pleasants, one of the lay clerks, uttered rude and abusive words about the Dean, and was admonished for the same. Charles Tillett, a minor canon, was admonished for 'a Criminall and Adulterous Conversation' with Sarah Bayly, the wife of a waggoner. The admonition did no good; Tillett refused to give up his association with Mrs. Bayly, and resigned his place rather than stand his trial. 'He had the best voice in the Quire but having noe Harmony in his Conversation he was a scandal to the Church and it is to our advantage that we are rid of him.' There was trouble of a similar kind with another minor canon, Francis Folchier, who was also made to resign. He was a French Protestant, of a good family in Languedoc, and had come to Norwich a quarter of a century before. He had always appeared to be a man of blameless life; but Prideaux, sitting in state as 'one of His Majesty's Justices of the Peace for the Precinct of the Cathedrall Church of Norwich', heard depositions which left him in no doubt of his guilt.

Not all the entries in the last volume of the diary are concerned with disputes and delinquencies. There is a long tribute to Arthur Branthwayt of Hethel, steward to the Chapter, an able and upright lawyer who died in 1717. Branthwayt had been a staunch Tory, but was 'generally lamented by all of what party soever, and by none more than by the Dean and Prebendarys of this Church, to whom he had been a very true and faithfull friend and had served them very much to their advantage for above thirty years'. Prideaux at once bestowed the vacant office on his son Edmund, who was then a student at the Middle Temple. One wonders if he recalled those entries earlier in the diary in which he condemned Bishop Moore's solicitude for his own offspring.

A congenial task was imposed upon him in 1715, when Lord Townshend, the Secretary of State, invited him to draw up a scheme for the reformation of the Universities. Although he had not now set foot in Oxford for almost twenty years, and knew nothing of Cambridge except 'by enquiry and hearsay', he gladly undertook the task. He had no doubt at all that both Universities urgently needed to be reformed. 'If these fountains grow corrupt,' he told Lord Townshend, 'and instead of virtue, religion and learning, vice, impiety and ignorance gain the prevalency in them; then nothing but dirty and filthy streams will flow from thence, all over the island, and every part of it will be tainted and polluted with the corruptions thereof.' So he set to work, and produced under fifty-eight heads a scheme which would not only have reformed the Universities, but would infallibly have turned them upside down. Everyone at Oxford and Cambridge, from the Heads of Houses down to the humblest sizar, was expected to live henceforward by rules of impossible strictness. Comings and goings, devotions and studies, dress and diversions were elaborately regulated. Admonishments, penalties, deprivations, expulsions were dealt out unsparingly. Perhaps the most sensational of his proposals dealt with those dons who lived upon their Fellowships or Students' places, 'a dronish and slothful life, passing away their time idly and unprofitably, without endeavouring to qualify themselves for any public service, either in Church or State'. They were to be relegated to 'an Hospital, to be built in each of the said Universities, which shall be called DRONE HALL'; and there they were to subsist in discomfort upon twenty pounds a year apiece, to be paid by their colleges 'as a just mulct for their having bred up the said superannuated persons to be good for nothing'. Alas! Drone Hall remained (and still remains) unbuilt. Nor did any part of Prideaux's scheme advance further than Lord Townshend's files.

The first two volumes of the *Connection* were published in 1715, with a dedication to the second Earl of Nottingham, the son of Prideaux's old patron. In a characteristic preface he explained how he had been driven out of his pulpit, and disabled from the exercise of his profession, by 'the calamitous distemper of the stone, and the unfortunate management I fell under after being cut for it'. In these circumstances, and 'in order that I might not be altogether useless', he had undertaken his great work. Its full title was *The Old and the New Testament connected in the History of the Jews and Neighbouring*

Humphrey Prideaux

Nations, from the Declension of the Kingdoms of Israel and Judah to the Time of Christ. It was in fact a vast panoramic survey, the earlier volumes covering the captivities of Israel and Judah, the history of Babylon and Persia, the wars between Persians and Greeks, the conquests of Alexander and the conflicts among his successors. The narrative was constantly broken by digressions on disputed points of chronology, on Jewish religious customs, and indeed on any points which engaged the author's fancy or upon which he disagreed with other authorities. Although his health steadily deteriorated he wrote on indomitably, and completed the two remaining volumes three years later. In these he described the return of the Jews and the eventful history of the restored nation, the Maccabean revolt, the rise and dominance of the Roman power, and the endless vicissitudes of the eastern world until the birth of Jesus Christ.

The book was immensely popular, and passed into edition after edition. It securely established Prideaux's fame for generations to come. But it was the last work that he felt himself able to undertake. A form of paralysis had attacked his hands, and he could no longer hold his pen. In the preface to his two last volumes he reflected that 'it hath always been the comfort, as well as the Care of my Life, to make myself as serviceable as I could in all the Stations which I have been called to'. But now, through illness and age, 'I must spend the remainder of my Days in an useless State of Life, which to me will be the greatest Burden of it. But since it is from the Hand of God, I will comport myself with all Patience to submit hereto, till my great Change shall come, and God shall be pleased to call me out of this Life into a better.'

He had six more years to live—years of increasing bodily infirmity, but unbroken firmness of mind. He died on a Sunday evening, the 1st of November 1724; and was buried in the nave of the Cathedral which he had served so well, under a ledger-stone with an inscription which he had himself composed.

ACTON CREMER

'Out of monuments, names, words, proverbs, traditions, private records and evidences, fragments of stories, passages of books, and the like, we do save and recover somewhat from the deluge of time.' It is not really the historian's business to rescue from that deluge the hopelessly obscure, the deservedly forgotten; and perhaps I should make some apology for devoting a few pages to the shadowy figure of a distant relation of mine, Acton Cremer. He lived during the second half of the seventeenth century; and I feel an interest in him because he is the only member of the family, apart from myself, who has ever produced a book. He achieved only one book, and that was a translation of the work of another man. He experienced the pains rather than the pleasures of authorship, since his book was undertaken far from willingly, at the behest of one set in authority over him. Nevertheless, as a cousin and a fellow-writer I greet him across the centuries.

In Snettisham church in north-west Norfolk is the memorial brass of John Cremer, his wife, his six sons and one daughter. This John Cremer, who died full of years in 1610, was a typical member of a new class which rose during Queen Elizabeth's reign—the prosperous yeomen who worked hard, bargained hard, steadily increased their holdings of land, and whose heirs by the middle of the seventeenth century had attained the rank of gentry. His sons and grandsons became landowners in a wide ring of parishes east and south of the Wash—Snettisham, Ingoldisthorpe, Setch, North Runcton, West Winch, Heacham, Fring. Most of them married into families of similar standing in the immediate neighbourhood. But some of his descendants ventured further afield; and towards the middle of the seventeenth century one of these, Thomas Cremer, married a girl named Anne Acton of

Bockleton in Worcestershire, and settled at her home in that far-off countryside.

Acton Cremer was the second of their three sons. He was born in 1651, and was sent at an early age to Westminster School, then flourishing under the sway of Doctor Busby. Here he struck up a friendship with a somewhat older boy named Henry Aldrich. In due course they both made the usual progress of Busby's more promising pupils from Westminster to Christ Church.

They passed from one admirable preceptor to another. The Dean of Christ Church was Doctor John Fell, who since the Restoration had exercised over the great college that vigorous and dictatorial rule which won him the dislike of many and the admiration of all. Aldrich became one of his favourite young men, and before long was a leading figure at Christ Church. He was destined to succeed Doctor Fell as Dean; and he is still remembered at Oxford for his varied talents and his singularly attractive personality. Impressive examples of his skill as an architect recall his name—Peckwater, All Saints Church, the exquisite chapel of Trinity College. The music of his composition ranged from solemn anthems to the most frivolous of catches. He was a classic and a divine, 'a most universal scholar', and at the same time a lover of songs and tobacco and good liquor.

Acton Cremer matriculated at Christ Church in 1670, at the age of nineteen. He became a Bachelor of Arts four years later, and a Master of Arts in 1677. Little else is known about his academic career. Even the details of his friendship with Aldrich are obscure, since the latter directed that all his letters and papers should be destroyed after his death. But Doctor Fell thought highly of Cremer's abilities, and was much annoyed when this promising young scholar was discovered in his twenty-third year to be contemplating marriage. He had fallen in love with Elizabeth Penell, the daughter of a Worcestershire neighbour, Edward Penell of Woodstone.

An early and imprudent marriage might easily blight a hopeful academic career. In 1674 Cremer had only just become a Bachelor of Arts: indeed it is possible that he had not yet taken his degree. No Fellowship of a college, or Studentship of Christ Church, could be held by a married man. Doctor Fell decided to punish the amorous scholar, and give him ample cause for reflection on the folly of the step he was contemplating. He set him an imposition; and the imposition was no less a task than the translation, into English from the original Latin, of a learned treatise entitled *Lapponia,* an account of Lapland by Johann Scheffer, Professor of Law and Rhetoric in the University of Upsala, which had been published at Frankfurt in the previous year. The translation, if found worthy, would be printed at the press in the Sheldonian Theatre, whose working Doctor Fell supervised with an ilmost proprietorial interest.

The translation was duly made, and Doctor Fell was pleased with it. By a single exercise of his authority he had obtained a suitable production for his beloved press, and had checked— or so he might reasonably hope—the foolish aspirations of a headstrong young man. The book was licensed by the Vice-Chancellor, Doctor Ralph Bathurst, on 8th July 1674, and published 'At the Theater in Oxon' shortly afterwards. It was a slender folio of 150 pages, entitled The *History of Lapland, wherein are shewed the Original, Manners, Habits, Marriages, Conjurations &c. of that People.*

As Dr. R. W. Chapman has pointed out, the book was the first anthropological work to be issued from the Oxford Press. The engraved title-page was a curious and unconventional affair. It depicts three Laplanders with their boats, skis, tridents for spearing fish, and the other gear of their harsh existence, as well as some strange magical objects. The title itself is inscribed upon a reindeer-skin, complete with its antlers and hoofs. The text also was interspersed with some remarkable woodcut illustrations.

Scheffer's work was a closely detailed description of the Laplanders and the country in which they dwelt, their persons, habits and customs, their houses and clothes, their hunting and fishing and their domestic animals. He paid particular attention to their 'conjurations', their pagan beliefs and elaborate magical practices; and several mysterious objects of devotion and divination are reproduced in the accompanying woodcuts. Nevertheless, despite this anthropological interest,

it must have been a tiresome and unrewarding book to trans-
late, with all its tedious geographical particulars and long
lists of words and their meanings. I find no indication that
Acton Cremer carried out his task with any sort of enjoyment.
He wrote pleasantly enough, in the easy colloquial style of the
later seventeenth century; but one feels that he must have
been longing all the time to get away from the crude and ice-
bound existence of the Laplanders, and sing catches and
smoke his pipe in the jovial company of Henry Aldrich. At one
point perhaps, when he makes a valiant but not very successful
attempt to render some Lapp folk-songs into English verse,
there may be a fleeting allusion to his personal predicament.

> *A youth's desire is the desire of wind,*
> > *All his Essaies*
> > *Are long delaies,*
> *No issue can they find.*
> *Away, fond Counsellors, away,*
> > *No more advice obtrude.*
> > > *I'le rather prove*
> > > *The guidance of blind Love;*
> > *To follow you is certainly to stray:*
> > *One single Counsel tho unwise is good.*

According to the late Falconer Madan in his *Oxford Books*,
this stanza suggested Longfellow's lines

> *A boy's will is the wind's will,*
> > *And the thoughts of youth are long, long thoughts.*

It is a far cry from Acton Cremer's halting efforts to the
refrain of Longfellow's famous poem, and I do not know
where Madan found evidence of the connexion.

In any case Doctor Fell's remedy for a rash engagement
proved quite ineffective. Before two years had passed Acton
Cremer was married to Elizabeth Penell, and Christ Church
knew him no more. On 31st October 1676 a former colleague,
Humphrey Prideaux, mentioned in one of his letters to John
Ellis that 'Christ Church is now altogether become a stranger
to you, wee being al almost your juniors. Cremer and Keeling,
if you knew them, are lately cut of from us by marriage, and

the latter since by death. Cremer hath marryed very well, having above 2000 £ with his wife.' I suspect that Elizabeth Penell's ample dowry was due to the death of her brother Edward, a young lawyer of Lincoln's Inn, since she is described in a contemporary document as her father's only daughter and heiress.

Sustained by this very adequate fortune Acton Cremer and his wife settled down at Woodstone, and henceforward fade into complete obscurity. They had three sons and four daughters. He became Vicar of Clifton in 1687, and may have held other church preferment; but I know no details. He had died, comparatively young, by 1698. The sole remaining trace of my shadowy cousin occurs in a letter to a friend from Doctor George Smalridge, afterwards Bishop of Bristol, about the elections from Westminster to Christ Church in that year. 'There is one Cremer, godson to the Dean and son to a schoolfellow, fellow-student and intimate acquaintance of the Dean's, who, when he died, recommended this young child to the Dean's care and favour; so that, if there be any room for favour, that young man hath a very good title to it.' The Dean was of course Henry Aldrich; the young man was Acton Cremer's eldest son, christened Henry after his godfather; and he duly matriculated at Christ Church in the summer of 1698. After a creditable career at Oxford, no doubt rendered all the more agreeable by the sympathetic oversight of a very different Dean from Doctor Fell, he received preferment in Wales, and disappears from view as a Carmarthenshire vicar and a prebendary of St. David's Cathedral.

THE RECTOR OF FERSFIELD

(Written for the bicentenary of the death in 1752
of the Rev. Francis Blomefield, the historian of
Norfolk)

I

In comparison with some county historians Francis Blomefield is a shadowy and impersonal figure. The rich
humanity of such men as Lambarde of Kent and Carew of
Cornwall was not bestowed upon him. He cared nothing for
natural or architectural beauty. No gleam of poetry or
romance or historical imagination ever touched his sober
pages. His passion for antiquarian detail was unaccompanied
by any grace of style. Masterful and self-sufficient, he pressed
forward unremittingly with his laborious task, and died when
it was less than half-completed.

He is least remote from us, I think, in his own parish of
Fersfield. His church and rectory have not on the whole
undergone much change during the two hundred years which
have passed since he knew them. He would still recognize
many landmarks in the quiet prosperous countryside which
stretches for miles around his home—churches and farmhouses and barns, perhaps even trees. His eyes must surely
have rested upon that magnificent roadside beech at Roydon
on the way to Diss, if only as an unconsidered sapling; and
there must be other living links, in wood and hedgerow,
between the historian of Norfolk and the present day. The
houses with their clay walls washed in such various colours—
white, yellow, buff, orange, pink, cream; the steep thatched
roofs; the roads, with deep ditches beside them, winding
irresolutely through the level land; the wide commons, the
meadows thick with cowslips in spring, the elms full of noisy
rooks—the whole landscape cannot have greatly altered, even

though the fields have become larger, the hedges lower, the methods of cultivation so strangely different from anything he knew.

II

The Blomefields had been rooted for generations in the Fersfield soil. They were prosperous yeomen and minor gentry, *generosi* but never *armigeri*, although their antiquarian scion cheerfully assumed the arms of the Bromefildes of Kent, and set the chevron and the three sprigs of broom belonging to that family upon his parents' monument. At Fersfield they led the tranquil uneventful lives of their class, farming their land, taking a part in parish affairs, and marrying with families of the same rank in the same neighbourhood. Francis Blomefield did not overlook the fact that four generations of his immediate ancestors had all married heiresses or coheiresses. There was nothing very splendid about these matches; but each wife must have brought at least a farm or two, or a few hundred pounds in money, to enlarge the modest Blomefield fortunes. And since they were all heiresses, their arms were duly quartered with the sprigs of broom on the monument to his parents which the historian placed near the south door of the church: Agnes Jolly from the adjacent parish of Bressingham, Anne Muskett also of Bressingham, Elizabeth Peak of Thornham Magna just across the Suffolk border, and—from unusually far afield—his own mother Alice Batch of King's Lynn. In just the same way the rest of the Blomefields, all the brothers and sisters and uncles and aunts since Tudor times, had married into families of small gentry and clergy and merchants living at Bressingham and Fersfield itself, at Diss, Thetford, Kenninghall, Blo Norton, Redgrave, Flixton, Framlingham, half the towns and villages of south Norfolk and north Suffolk.

The same air of timelessness, of immobility within the East Anglian scene, clung also to their friends the Womacks, three of whom had been Rectors of Fersfield in continuous succession for ninety years, from 1595 until 1685. They remained undisturbed by the upheavals of Civil War and Commonwealth; there had only been a little trouble in 1659 when the

Reverend Arthur Womack, seeing the Restoration close at
hand, so far forgot his caution as to drink the King's health
and sing Royalist ditties with his churchwardens, and in consequence spent a few uncomfortable days in Ipswich gaol. After
1685 this dynasty of clerics sought their preferment elsewhere; but their links with Fersfield remained, and Francis
Blomefield and his younger brother Peter in due course chose
the daughters of the Reverend Laurence Womack, Rector of
Oxnead and Caister-by-Yarmouth, as their brides.

In 1708, when the future historian was a child of three, his
father bought from Lord Richardson the next presentation to
the living of Fersfield. The Reverend John Barker, a pious
and charitable man whom they all loved, died just about the
time when Francis Blomefield was ordained; and in the autumn
of 1729 the young cleric was installed in the church where so
many of his family had worshipped, and in the nearby rectory
which they had known so well.

III

The story of the writing of Blomefield's *History of Norfolk*
is well known—the patient assembling of material; the circu-
lars asking for information; the journeys to copy inscriptions
in churches, and the long days spent in dusty muniment-
rooms; the enormous and endless correspondence; the steady
unrelaxing toil year after year. Equally well known are the
circumstances of its production on his own press at his own
rectory, the printing of those slender parts in their grey paper
wrappers which were later assembled into the first great folio
volume. The whole enterprise was marked by his characteristic self-reliance, the confidence inherited from those generations of substantial yeomen who had farmed their own land at
Fersfield and called no man their master. 'I don't care one
farthing', he wrote on one occasion, 'if I print my work in a
manner to my own liking. I don't care twopence for all the
world except my subscribers, most of which are gentlemen in
my own way, whom I don't at all fear but I shall please. You
must understand I don't print (I thank God for it) for my
bread, having a comfortable subsistence independent of all

men, and therefore fear no loss of reputation.' That was always his attitude to the world, and he carried it beyond the bounds of prudence. He had set himself too formidable a task, and ran mysteriously into debt, and his great work was left to be finished after his death by other and less able hands.

But we are now considering Blomefield in his own church and parish, and hoping to learn more of him there. The church stands on a rise of ground close to the road, the exterior still much as it was in his own day, curiously high-shouldered in silhouette owing to the loftiness of the nave in proportion to its own length and to the little square tower. Within there have been several changes. The painted glass, which he recorded as having survived in quite considerable quantity, is now reduced to a few insignificant fragments. Roof and pulpit and pews were renewed in the nineteenth century. The pavement laid down by his predecessor Mr. Barker, and Elizabeth his wife, has been replaced by encaustic tiling. The 'new Sett of Clothes for the Desk and Pulpit, of Purple Velvet, with a neat Purple Cloth Carpet, wrought with Gold, and a Cushion for the Pulpit of the same, with Cushions to lay round the Altar Rails', all bestowed by the same generous pair, have long since vanished. But in the sanctuary a ledger stone of black marble, with finely carved armorial bearings, marks the historian's own resting-place; and many other features call him to mind. We can still see the monument which he erected to his parents; the stone commemorating his good churchwarden William Flowerdew, whom he buried 'between the Desk and the Chancell', now placed obscurely behind the font; the font itself, where he baptized his own children and so many other children besides; the fine Royal Arms of Queen Anne; the two medieval effigies upon which his careful antiquarian attentions were once lavished. These were the wooden figure of a knight in armour, and a stone figure clearly representing a lady but which he inexplicably supposed to be a priest. Traces of the original heraldic colouring satisfied him that both knight and 'priest' were members of the family of du Bois, lords of the manor of Fersfield and patrons of the church in the fourteenth century. He had the effigies carefully repaired, noting that their hollow interiors were full of burnt coals placed there to absorb the moisture; he repainted them in full and lively colours, and added inscriptions of his own composing; and when he came to print his *History of Norfolk* he had his own drawings of them—William du Bois, Priest, and Sir Robert du Bois, Knight—engraved as one of the few full-page illustrations in the book.

Across the road stands the rectory, with its little porch and steeply pitched gables, its cream-washed plaster walls and sunny low-ceilinged rooms. There have been some minor additions since Blomefield's time; but in general the house must be very like the house he knew. Apart from a few crumbling walls there is no trace of the older outbuildings, one of which contained his celebrated printing press. In the rooms which were the scene of his antiquarian labours and religious exercises and contented family life, something of his personality still lingers. I particularly remember an August afternoon when I was allowed, by the kindness of his successor, to examine in detail the parish registers and the church-wardens' and overseers' accounts which he kept throughout the years of his incumbency. For a couple of hours, as I read and transcribed what he had so carefully written, he was no longer a shadowy or an impersonal figure at all. He might almost have been present in the room.

IV

Stories have been circulated—and unfortunately they were given a wider currency by Walter Rye in the *Dictionary of National Biography*—that Blomefield in his later years neglected his parish and was absent from it for long periods at a time. Rye knew an old man, who in his youth had known an old woman, who asserted that the historian fell into extravagant habits, and wasted his substance in keeping a pack of hounds. Such gossip is usually on the same level as those legends of underground passages and headless horses which delight the compilers of guide-books and parish histories. It is all too true that Blomefield was in debt when he died; but the expenses of the *History*, the printing and the copying and the gathering of material, must have been more than sufficient to account for this. Even a superficial glance at the Fersfield registers and accounts will prove that he was an exemplary parish priest all his days. His researches of course necessitated occasional periods of residence in Norwich, and it appears from the registers of St. George Tombland that during the later seventeen-forties he sometimes officiated in that church. During the last few months of his life he seems to have lived more continuously in Norwich. His only other work, *Collectanea Cantabrigiensia*, was "Printed for the Author at his House in St Giles's Parish"; and he took over the tiny living of St Mary Coslany, whose value, according to his *History*, was no more than twenty pounds a year. But at Fersfield, from his institution in 1729 until less than three months before his death at the beginning of 1752, the entries in the registers are continuously in his hand, and every page is signed by him as rector. In one single instance alone, in the last year of his life, is there the smallest interposition of any other hand. The same applies to the accounts which he punctiliously wrote out each year for the churchwardens and overseers of the parish. There is nowhere the slightest suggestion of absence or neglect: in fact the evidence is all the other way.

Blomefield kept the registers with a historian's exactitude, together with an agreeably personal note where his own family and friends were concerned. He recorded with affectionate respect the virtues of his predecessor Mr. Barker—'vir fuit inter Probos et Pios semper numerandus, et ut vixit ita diem clausit extremum'. He described at some length his own institution and induction, and presently his marriage, although that ceremony actually took place in the parish church of Ashmanhaugh, where his brother-in-law was curate. He paid touching tributes to both his parents and to others of his relations. His father was 'a man of strict probity and integrity, of great Piety towards God, and Love to his Family, who practised what he declared, and declared what he practised, giving Example of Goodness to those that knew him, by whom he died much lamented, but by none more than by me Francis Blomefield, Priest, Rector of this Parish, his

Eldest Son.' His mother was 'a woman of well known religion and charity, pious, dutifull, loving and beloved, and by none more than by the mournfull scribe, F.B. her obedient son'. And to his churchwarden William Flowerdew he likewise rendered honour—'for his honesty and justice he lived, beloved by all; professing his strict adherence to the Church, and stedfastness in the faith, he died, universally lamented'. Such warm-hearted tributes are strikingly different from the cold and impersonal manner in which his own death was recorded by another hand—'Francis Blomefield Rect^r of this Parish departed this life on Thursday ye 11 Day of January 1752 & was buried in the Chancel on the South Side of the Alter on Saturday Evening Jan: ye 18th 1752.'

It was not in every parish that the incumbent was so good-natured as to write out the churchwardens' and overseers' accounts for the benefit of those functionaries, before they submitted them each year for the approval and signature of two local Justices of the Peace. But Blomefield, the harassed and over-worked historian, never failed to carry out this task. In the tall narrow ledger devoted to the churchwardens' accounts, everything is set down in his exquisitely clear hand —the details of parish finance, the money laid out on the Town Farm and the Town House, the rents which accrued from the Town Farm and the Town Patch and 'the piece in the meadow'; the repairs to the church roof and steeple, the whitening of the walls, 'placeing ye weather cock right', renewing the pales and gates of the churchyard; the dues at visitations and the liquor consumed at perambulations; wages to the clerk and sexton John Baker; payments for mending and washing the surplice; purchases ranging from 'a Common Prayer Book for the altar bound in red Turkey and neatly gilt' down to a sixpenny mop. In just the same way his writing fills the pages of the overseers' ledger, from the payment of Goody Buck's rent and the curing of Goodman Skirll's sickness in 1729, to the purchase of an apron for Swatman's child and a pair of breeches for Hubbard's child in 1751. Year after year the entries continue, revealing the steady unostentatious machinery of local administration as it functioned two hundred years ago—the careful management of the town stock, the levying of rates, the binding out of apprentices, the troubles over bastards and disputed settlements, payments for medicines and doctors' fees in illness, the purchase of blankets and firewood for the cold season, and of shoes and stockings and shirts and shifts and petticoats and waistcoats and caps for those in need.

There need, in short, be no doubt of Francis Blomefield's right to be numbered with those clerics of the Church of England who have combined a life of devoted parish duty with the pursuit of scholarship. There have been poets and philosophers among them, historians and antiquaries and translators, a great succession of classical scholars, and countless writers who have contributed to the splendid body of English devotional literature. They form an illustrious and varied company; and the Rector of Fersfield, the historian of Norfolk and the faithful shepherd of his flock, is worthy of his place among them.

ALEC PENROSE

(Alexander Peckover Doyle Penrose, 1896–1950)

I

We are living in an age of transition. Politicians and publicists are always reminding us of the fact, and it happens to be true. This transition may be to the general advantage, or it may not. It is too early to tell. But there can be no doubt at all that the process is endangering, and will continue to endanger, much that was valuable in the old order of things—a great inheritance of civilization, of tradition, of beauty in nature and in the works of man.

It was to ease this transition, and to preserve as much as possible of the amenities of the past for the enjoyment of the future, that Alec Penrose worked so hard for the last twenty years of his life. I only knew him during those years, when he was living in Norfolk at Bradenham Hall. There one would meet many friends of his Cambridge and London days; and they, like the paintings on the walls and the books on the shelves, brought to the Norfolk scene a waft of the air of Bloomsbury and King's. But Cambridge and London, though they influenced his life profoundly and though he loved them to the end, faded a little into the background once he had settled and struck root at Bradenham. The Norfolk country-side became his passion: not only his own estate, but the whole rich and varied county—city and seaport, town and village, mansion and cottage, farmland and woodland and heath and marsh and river and shore. Henceforward he worked for Norfolk with understanding and love, almost with a sense of dedication.

II

He came on both sides from ancient Quaker stock. The Penroses derived from Cornwall; his mother was one of the Peckovers of Wisbech, an old Puritan family of Norfolk whose

105

descendants had settled in that town as bankers and had risen there to opulence and title. He still possessed the certificate of discharge granted to 'Edmund Peckover, Gentillman' in 1655, after he had served under Fleetwood and other officers of the Commonwealth throughout the past nine years, 'dureing which time he behaved himself fathfulley and honestley as become a solgar'.

Both Alec's parents were members of the Society of Friends. His father, James Doyle Penrose, was a painter of repute; his mother was one of the daughters of the first and only Lord Peckover of Wisbech; he was the eldest of their four sons. His strictly Quaker upbringing and schooling were followed by service with the Friends' Ambulance Unit during the first World War. After the war he went up to King's, and was elected to a Fellowship in 1925. The theatre was in those years his absorbing interest. He designed sets and costumes for several productions, and his Fellowship dissertation took the form of a historical survey of scenic settings and effects on the English stage. Occasionally he appeared in Cambridge productions, and his performance as the Cardinal in the Marlowe Society's version of *The White Devil* is widely remembered. Both at Cambridge and in London he was much associated with that circle which is evidently fated to be known in English social history by the label of 'Bloomsbury'. Then, at the beginning of the nineteen-thirties, some deep and persistent strain of the countryman prevailed. He bought the house and estate of Bradenham, and went to live there with his wife Frances and their children.

Bradenham was a square red brick Georgian house of moderate size and admirable proportions, lying among its trees and meadows on a long gentle slope of the pleasant countryside between Dereham and Swaffham. Before long the whole estate bore the imprint of his discriminating care. Farms modernized, cottages rebuilt, fields newly drained, woods newly planted—he had always something fresh to show wherever one walked with him. In the house itself there was lavish hospitality for his friends both old and new. The Bloomsbury traditions of comfort and good living were well maintained in this far Norfolk backwater. There were long talks in the sunny garden, or in the shade of a great copper beech, or in the library upstairs, where the *incunabula* and illuminated manuscripts collected by his grandfather Lord Peckover kept company with the modern classics from Freud to Firbank. It was in every way a happy and a kindly house.

Alec had not lived long at Bradenham before there came an opportunity of carrying out what he had so much at heart— the saving of the countryside from desecration, the rescue of ancient buildings from decay, the adaptation of the old to serve the purposes of the new. In 1934 a Norfolk branch of the Council for the Preservation of Rural England was formed; he became its Honorary Secretary, and proved the mainstay of all its activities until the end of his life. He tackled the work with terrific energy and apparent enjoyment, with no hint that he might have preferred to be going to the theatre in London, or hunting with the West Norfolk, or looking after his own farm at Bradenham. Nothing was too trivial or too much trouble, and everything was undertaken with the same vigorous competence—lecturing, writing, photographing, organizing exhibitions, appearing at inquiries, coping with the most intractable problems, investigating the most boring complaints. It was my duty after his death to go through the files of his secretaryship; and I was astonished once again at the amount of hard and monotonous work that he had carried out, so quietly and with so little fuss, over all those years.

He did not allow those activities, however, to detract for one moment from his enjoyment of life. He took part in local government and administration of all kinds, and sat on endless councils and committees; but he still found plenty of time to hunt, to go to parties, to travel abroad, to drive very fast and rather alarmingly about the English countryside. I recall especially his year of office in 1947 as High Sheriff of Norfolk, how seriously he took his duties and at the same time how thoroughly he enjoyed them.

In public and private matters alike, he was guided by the deep-rooted conscientiousness of his Quaker forefathers. I remember so well his feelings about the Battle Area controversy in south-west Norfolk. Briefly, the military authorities had removed the inhabitants of certain Breckland villages early in the war, and had turned the district, with all its houses and churches and farms, into a Battle Training Area. But they had also given solemn and specific pledges to the inhabitants that when the war was over they would be reinstated in their former homes. In 1946, far from honouring these pledges, the authorities continued to use the area for training and were even seeking to extend it. There was much to be said for their action on military grounds, on financial grounds, on grounds of national expediency. In the eyes of most of us, I am afraid, it was a regrettable necessity. But Alec could not see it in that light. Promises had been given; promises must be kept. And he fought doggedly and persistently, if altogether in vain, year after year because injustice had been done and expediency could never palliate it.

He was a Liberal by deep conviction, hating compulsion, hating a rigid and unimaginative bureaucracy. He was the gentlest of men, but certain aspects of the bureaucratic mind, certain encroachments upon personal liberty, could move him to furious indignation. I remember his anger at the presence of certain Government departments, noted for the blend of obstructiveness and complacency with which they domineered over the East Anglian countryside, in the colleges of his beloved Cambridge. 'Nests of weasels' he called them; and I have never forgotten the phrase, so telling and yet so different from his accustomed kindliness of speech. It was natural, in view of his inherited traditions, that he should stand for Parliament as a Liberal in the general election of 1945. It was equally natural that after five years of government by doctrinaires he should warmly support the Conservatives in 1950. But he was not at heart a strong political partisan. He believed in human decency and, in the face of considerable discouragement, in the progress of the human race. He cherished the hope, which may yet prove to have been justified, that the new age will treat its inheritance from the past with understanding and gratitude.

III

It is not for me, one friend among so many, to analyse or even to discuss Alec Penrose's character. Integrity, generosity, tolerance, humour, the utmost kindness of heart—all those qualities were his, and we remember them with grateful affection. Nor shall we forget the determined courage with which he faced the illness which came so suddenly upon him in the autumn of 1949, and lasted until his death in the summer of 1950, at the age of fifty-four.

He might have been a philosopher, a mystic, a poet. He would sometimes speak of his religious convictions, which grew in strength and intensity during his later years; but I do not think he ever described in writing that journey of the spirit. And he was diffident about his poetry, which was admittedly uneven in quality, yet contained passages of haunting beauty, suffused with his sense of time and of the past.

> *How sleek grass grows about this funeral mound*
> *Where history so lightly passes*
> *That still the air exhales*
> *The horn's thin echo and the reek of torches*
> *Which flared upon a chieftain's obsequies,*
> *When pent in narrow darkness he was sealed,*
> *To crouch unmoving in the night of time,*
> *From wolf secure, safe from the knife of winter . . .*

His most tangible memorials are the buildings which he saved. For years he was the leading spirit of the Wisbech Society, whose members labour to defend the precious architectural heritage of that unique town. As a crowning achievement he was able to ensure that his mother's old home, Peckover House, with its dignified façade, its exquisite plasterwork, and the big secluded garden with its memories of his childhood, was consigned to the care of the National Trust. Unquestionably the finest building in Wisbech, the climax of all the beautiful houses along the North Brink, it stands safe from any threat of maltreatment, devoted to public and private uses of the most appropriate kind.

Most important of all, the intense preoccupation of the last years of his life, was the rescue of the Guildhall of Saint George at King's Lynn. This remarkable building, the shell of the largest medieval Guildhall now surviving in the kingdom, had been used as a theatre, a wine-store, all kinds of things, and had finally become a repository for stage scenery. With ever-growing dilapidation its eventual fate was still uncertain, but could hardly fail to be disastrous. He bought it, arranged for its complete repair and adaptation as a theatre and concert hall, and intended to place it in the keeping of the National Trust. When he died the work on the building was still unfinished, and the negotiations as to its future were not yet completed; but his widow carried all his wishes into effect. A year after his death, in the summer of 1951, the Guildhall of Saint George was opened by Her Majesty the Queen, now Queen Elizabeth the Queen Mother, during the week of the King's Lynn Festival. It is easy to forget the details of a ceremony once it is past; but those who were present will long remember the simple beauty of this occasion. After the opening there was a short recital of poetry and music. The last of the poems was by Thomas Hardy, *An Ancient to Ancients*; and as Leon Quartermaine read stanza after stanza, his lovely gentle voice seemed to me in some mysterious way to acquire an inflection of Alec's own.

> *We who met sunrise sanguine-souled,*
>   *Gentlemen,*
> *Are wearing weary. We are old;*
> *These younger press; we feel our rout*
> *Is imminent to Aïdes' den,—*
> *That evening shades are stretching out,*
>   *Gentlemen!*
>
> *And yet though ours be failing frames,*
>   *Gentlemen,*
> *So were some others' history names,*
> *Who trode their track light-limbed and fast*
> *As these youth, and not alien*
> *From enterprise, to their long last,*
>   *Gentlemen. . . .*

For a few moments it might have been the voice of Alec himself, musing, as he so often used to do, upon the perplexities of mutability and survival.

Part II

★

EVENTS

THE COMING OF THE
STRANGERS

I

Some day an important book will be written about the relations between East Anglia and the Low Countries. Throughout recorded history there has been a steady coming and going across the North Sea, and a constant interchange of ideas and techniques. In periods of trouble, whether civil or religious, the fugitives from either region have sought and found sanctuary in the other. In art and architecture, commerce and agriculture, the draining of marshland and the defence of their soil against the encroaching sea, in their textile industries most of all, the two communities were for centuries intimately linked.

The chapter which follows is mainly concerned with a single episode in this long association, the sudden influx of the 'strangers'—Dutchmen, Flemings and Walloons—into Norwich when Alva's persecution was raging in the Netherlands. It is an attempt to describe a mass immigration which left a lasting impress upon the city. A wealth of further detail, in the archives of Norwich and elsewhere, awaits some future researcher—perhaps the author of the unwritten book to which I have referred. In the meantime I hope this sketch may serve to recall a remarkable passage of East Anglian history.

II

The earliest and also the most enduring association between East Anglia and the Low Countries was in the field of textile manufacture. For much of the fourteenth century the city of Norwich, with its natural port of Great Yarmouth, served as one of the staple towns, through which the export

of English wool to the great manufacturing cities in Flanders—
Antwerp, Ghent, Bruges, Ypres—was compulsorily directed.
A network of trade arrangements grew up between the
English trading towns and their equivalents overseas, a pro-
fitable traffic symbolized by the figure of the Merchant in the
Canterbury Tales, well spoken, well mounted, well dressed and
conspicuous by his Flemish hat.

> *A Marchant was ther with a forked berd,*
> *In mottelee, and hye on horse he sat,*
> *Upon his head a Flaundrish bever hat;*
> *His botes clasped faire and fetisly.*
> *His resons he spak ful solempnely,*
> *Souninge alway th'encrees of his winning.*
> *He wolde the see were kept for any thing*
> *Bitwixe Middelburgh and Orewelle.*

Middelburgh was the important commercial town on the
island of Walcheren, and by Orwell it would seem that
Chaucer had Ipswich or possibly Harwich in mind. His merchant was clearly an East Anglian.

Symbol is replaced by actuality in certain magnificent
brasses at King's Lynn, which represent two commercial
magnates of the mid-fourteenth century, Adam de Walsoken
and Robert Braunche, together with their wives. Similar
brasses occur all over northern Europe, at Lübeck,
Stralsund, Thorn and elsewhere. Although at one time they
were supposed to be of German manufacture, opinion now
seems to have returned to the view that they were Flemish
in origin. They bear impressive witness to the state which
was kept by the great merchants of the age, alike in the
Hanseatic seaports and in the rich borough of Lynn. And at
the feet of the life-size figures are engraved the most charming little scenes of medieval life. On Walsoken's brass a
horseman carries his corn to be ground at the mill, huntsmen
are pursuing boar and deer, an important personage is borne
past in a litter. At the feet of Braunche and his two wives is
depicted a mayoral feast, with peacocks being served at the
board.

The Coming of the Strangers

Throughout this century the incomparable wool of England, from Yorkshire and the Cotswolds and the Norfolk sheepwalks, was exported to the Low Countries; and in return the Flemish textiles were imported in all their variety and excellence. Nevertheless the goods manufactured in East Anglia itself were by no means to be despised. Weaving was carried on in the crowded tenements of Norwich, and in towns and villages and isolated cottages throughout the countryside. The cloths of Aylsham and Worstead—the latter in particular —carried the names of two small Norfolk towns all over the land. But the aid of foreign technicians was also sought, and a certain number of Flemings and Dutchmen settled in Norwich and in the country districts of Norfolk. They were not always popular, and in times of disturbance were sometimes the victims of assault and even massacre. But there can be little doubt that their neighbours learnt much of their skill, and that on the whole the association was profitable to both sides.

Our forbears were likewise ready to avail themselves of the experience of the Netherlanders in draining and embanking. The same problems existed on both sides of the North Sea— vast stretches of fen and marshland, sluggish rivers and their mud-choked estuaries, and the endless battle against the tides along the low-lying coastlines. Dutch engineers were being employed in Norfolk at least from Tudor times. In the sixteenth century they are known to have carried out considerable works to the haven of Great Yarmouth; and as early as 1525 there was in east Norfolk a resident Dutch official bearing the title of 'dyke reeve'. He was Peter son of Peter, or Peter Peterson; and there is an inscription in the Dutch language to the memory of his wife in the church of Haddiscoe. Another Peter Peterson, the celebrated goldsmith and silversmith, so many of whose chalices survive in our churches today, was almost certainly of Dutch extraction also; but he was born in the parish of St. Andrew's, of parents already settled in the city, in the year 1518.

III

This steady but unspectacular intercourse between East Anglia and the Netherlands might well have continued indefinitely—a few merchants with their households established in Norwich and the ports, a sprinkling of immigrant artificers in town and countryside, and an occasional expert technician brought over to carry out specialist work. The Norwich subsidy rolls of the fifteenth and early sixteenth centuries seldom record more than ten or a dozen alien households. But early in Queen Elizabeth's reign the pressure of international politics brought about a very different situation.

It is unnecessary to describe the dynastic steps by which the Netherlands passed from Burgundian to Hapsburg dominion, and finally became an outlying portion of the world-empire of Charles the Fifth. The richest and most civilized communities in Europe, with their ancient traditions of independence, their vigour and their initiative, did not take kindly at any time to Spanish overlordship. And as the ideas of the Reformation spread ever more widely in those cities and provinces, one of the cruellest epochs in European history began. Philip the Second, succeeding to the Empire on his father's abdication in 1555, determined on the extirpation of the new heresies. He would bend this recalcitrant people to his will. When their resistance stiffened all attempts at moderation were laid aside, and a policy of total repression was adopted. Fanaticism was answered by fanaticism, the Inquisition by the Beggars and the Image Breakers. The southern provinces especially became a nightmare scene of massacres, reprisals, pillage and torture.

Refugees began to stream into England. Most of them crossed to the Kentish ports, and either settled there or made their way to London. There was not at first any large influx into Norwich. In 1561 nearly a score of families settled there, but during each of the next five years the newly arrived households were much less numerous. Then in the terrible year of 1567 the Duke of Alva was appointed Governor of the Low Countries, and was empowered to crush the rebellious provinces by ruthless military force. The stream of refugees became a flood; and in that year alone a wholly unprecedented total of 311 families found shelter in Norwich.

To some extent they came by invitation, and were assured of a welcome and, still more important, of gainful occupation.

The Coming of the Strangers

The textile trade of Norwich had long been declining, and the city was far from prosperous. New wares, new methods of manufacture, skilful and hard-working operatives were all urgently needed. In 1565 the Mayor and Aldermen, with the assistance of the Duke of Norfolk, had obtained a royal licence for 'thirty Douchemen of the Low Countreys of Flaunders', their households and servants, not exceeding ten in each family, to settle in Norwich. All were to be house-holders or master workmen; and all were 'to exercise the faculties of making bays, arras, sayes, tapstrey, mokadoes, staments, carsay, and such other outlandish commodities as hath not bene used to be made within this our Realme of England'. As there were not to be more than ten people in each family, the city authorities did not expect to receive more than 300 newcomers in all. The church of St. Mary at Tombland, which had been leased to the city by the Dean and Chapter for five hundred years, was assigned to the new-comers as their Hall for trade.

The names of the original thirty 'masters'—twenty-four Dutchmen and six Walloons—have been preserved. But the limits envisaged in the royal licence were vastly exceeded almost at once, owing to the influx which took place in 1567. A number of the 311 families which arrived in Norwich in that year were unconnected with any branch of the textile trade. Most of them, of course, included a due proportion of children, and some brought servants as well. In 1568 the Bishop of Norwich was required by the Archbishop of Canter-bury, acting on 'hir maiesties name and by hir commaunde-mente and aucthoritie', to make a detailed return of the whole body of the 'strangers', as they were already called. This document reveals that an entire new community had suddenly become established in Norwich, complete with its ministers of religion, its doctors, schoolmasters, merchants, shop-keepers, artificers and craftsmen of every description.

Although the strangers were usually described as Dutch-men, most of them came from the areas now included in Belgium or the northern frontiers of France. There was a sprinkling from Holland, Zealand and the other provinces comprised in the modern kingdom of the Netherlands; but

117

these provinces escaped many of the horrors which were being perpetrated further to the south. The vast majority of the settlers in Norwich were either Flemings from Flanders and Brabant, or Walloons from the French-speaking districts, from Lille, Namur, Valenciennes, Armentières, even a few stragglers from far down in Lorraine.

The greater part of them were engaged in some branch of the textile industry, as weavers, woolcombers, silkworkers, lacemakers, fullers or dyers. But virtually every trade was represented. There were tailors and shoemakers, carpenters and smiths, a jeweller, a cutler, a painter, a builder (*murorum exstructor*), two surgeons and a midwife. Those engaged in agriculture presumably settled in the countryside, though this Norwich list includes a solitary *agricola*. There were four booksellers and two printers. One of these, Albert Christian from Holland, has vanished from history: possibly he engaged in some other trade. The other, Antony de Solempne, who came from Brabant with his wife and two sons, set up his press in Norwich and produced the first books ever printed in the city. Virtually all his publications were in Dutch. They cannot have had an extensive sale, and it is perhaps significant that he was also given permission to trade in Rhenish wine. In addition there were ministers of religion, doctors of medicine, several schoolmasters, and a few persons of private fortune such as Petrus de Wols, *nobilis* from Flanders, who arrived with his wife and three sons, a manservant and three maids.

This return shows that in 1568 there were 1,132 Flemish-speaking strangers of all ages in Norwich, and 339 Walloons. In general the citizens made them very welcome. The sufferings which they had undergone, and which their compatriots at home were still enduring, won them the sympathy of a society in which Protestant feeling was intensely strong, and where the Marian persecutions of the previous decade were a vivid memory. Nevertheless the invasion was watched with a cautious eye both by the civic and the ecclesiastical authorities. The former were grateful for the impetus given to the city's trade, but were naturally afraid of undue competition. The latter, conscious that the Elizabethan settlement was still a young and tender plant, were determined that no outlandish religious doctrines, Anabaptism and the like, should be brought from overseas to molest it. Places of worship were allotted to the two new congregations. The Dutch were given Blackfriars Hall, the chancel of the great Dominican house which the city had acquired at the Reformation. Bishop Parkhurst granted the Walloons, who were fewer in number, the use of the chapel adjoining his palace. But the proceedings of both congregations were supervised with some care; and the Bishop's return of 1568 included a section devoted to those whose religious views were suspect or whose private morals deserved censure. The names are surprisingly few, and drunkenness rather than heresy would seem to have been the prevalent shortcoming. For example Jasper Aert, a carpenter, is recorded as being *ebrietati adeo addictus ut ad potatiunculos potius quam ad pietatem natus videatur*—so deeply addicted to drunkenness that he seems to have been born for potations rather than for piety.

IV

In the archives of the city of Ypres a small collection of letters has survived, written by some of these refugees in Norwich to their friends and relatives at home, almost all in this memorable year of 1567. Documents of the sixteenth century seldom throw much light upon the lives and emotions of the obscure; but these letters are full of personal and domestic detail of the most fascinating kind. Husbands write to their wives and children to their parents, comforting them, reassuring them, urging them to come over while there is yet time, and share in the peace and tolerance of their new home. 'Come as quickly as you can,' Clais Wevele tells his wife Tannekin, 'for I have no rest until you sit by me.' 'I have a gold coin,' writes Andries van de Haghe to his father. 'I would like to send it in the letter, but when you come to Norwich I will give it to you, for then you may have nothing in your pocket; when you come to Norwich you shall have gold.' Mayeken de Wert announces her safe arrival at Norwich, and begs her father and mother to join her, 'for the expense of the journey is easily gained, and God's service is

119

free there'. Pauwels de Coene sends his wife a barrel of herrings, which she is to sell to provide money for her voyage.

Everywhere there is a deep sense of relief from anxiety, and gratitude for the kindliness and hospitality of the Norwich citizens. Clais van Wervekin the hatmaker tells his wife that 'you would never believe how friendly the people are together, and the English are the same and quite loving to our nation. . . . Send my money and the three children. Come at once and do not be anxious. Know that I await you and doubt me not; send me Catelynken, Saerle and Tonyne.' And then domestic instructions: 'When you come, bring a dough trough, for there are none here. Bring also our long hooks to hang your linen cords on. Buy two little wooden dishes to make up half pounds of butter; for all Netherlanders and Flemings make their own butter, for here it is all pigs' fat.' Clement Baet, a maker of bays, writes to his wife that he was joyfully received at Norwich by his aunt Tanne and her husband, and many other friends. 'There is good trade in bays and I will look after a house as quickly as I can to get into business, for then it will be easy to make money. Bring all your and your daughter's clothing, for people go well clad here. . . . May God give you the same loving peace and riches as we have here at Norwich. It is very dear to hear the word of God peacefully.'

A delightful picture of the life of an industrious family is given by a boy called Gilles Navegeer in a letter to his grandmother. They had been in Norwich almost two years, 'where we are living in great quietness and peace, and the word of God is much preached amongst us'. His father, mother and sisters are all well. He had been learning bookbinding, but that was an unprofitable trade and he had lately taken to another—he does not tell his grandmother what it was. His father was employed in a threadtwist factory. His mother did *oude* work—perhaps some sort of embroidery? His brother Willeken was learning the trade of a cutler. His eldest sister Maeyken was working in a brewery run by a neighbour from Ypres. Another sister, also called Maeyken, spun thread. And his little sister Synken played all day.

For all their gratitude, the strangers were excellent men of

120

business; and having found this most promising new field, they proposed to exercise to the full their ability, industry and thrift. There is a suggestion of this when Leonard Keerlinck tells his brother-in-law that 'more can be bought at Norwich for a penny than for three at Ypres'; and a stronger suggestion when Jan de Haze writes that 'at Norwich we have a good time and make money from all'.

V

It has already been mentioned that the number of strangers of all ages and circumstances in Norwich, given in the Bishop's return of 1568, was 1,471, of whom 1,132 were described as Dutchmen and 339 as Walloons. As Alva's persecution intensified, and vast areas of the Low Countries were given over to civil war, the flood of refugees continued unabated. No later returns of their names and trades appear to have survived; but in 1569–70 they had increased to 2,866, and in 1571 they numbered 3,925—almost 4,000 in a city whose entire population at this time has been reckoned as less than 16,000.

The presence of this huge foreign community raised many problems, and the initial warmth of their welcome could hardly be maintained. At their first coming in 1565 a number of somewhat stringent regulations had been laid down for their behaviour and the control of their trade; and Thomas Whall, the Mayor in 1567, who particularly disliked these newcomers and was confronted by their first great influx during his year of office, succeeded in imposing additional restrictions upon them. But Whall's view was not shared by his successors. The Mayor of 1569, Robert Wood, assured Her Majesty's Council that 'all the compani of strangers we ar to confesse do lyve in good quiete and order, and travayle diligentlye to earne ther lyving'. The city was prepared to receive still more of them.

In 1570 the resentment against the strangers came to a head in a feeble and ill-organized conspiracy. It seems to have been as much an affair of the countryside as of the city. A group of malcontents, mostly of the minor gentry, planned to assemble on Midsummer Day at Harleston fair, and 'to have raised a number of men with sound of trumpet and beat of drum, and then to have declared the cause of their rising, namely, to expulse the strangers from the city and realm'. Such a course of action had alarming parallels with Kett's rebellion, which was still fresh in all men's minds; and oddly enough the conspiracy was betrayed by a member of the Kett family. On receiving his information the authorities acted promptly. The ringleaders were seized, and ten of them stood their trial for high treason at the next assizes. John Throgmorton of Norwich, gentleman, confessed himself to be the chief conspirator, 'and that none had deserved to die but himself, for that he had procured them'. He was condemned to be hanged, drawn and quartered, together with two other gentlemen, George Redman of Cringleford and Thomas Brooke of Rollesby. Five more suffered imprisonment and forfeiture of lands and goods.

The night before his execution, Thomas Brooke wrote a poem expressing resignation to his fate and confidence in the mercy of God. The lines have a decided resemblance to those written by other Elizabethans in his predicament; but there seems no reason to suppose that they are not genuine. The only printer in Norwich was still Antony de Solempne, the refugee from Brabant; and his productions had always been, and would continue to be, in the Dutch language. On this occasion alone a work in English was issued from his press, a single sheet containing eight verses, the last message of a man condemned to die for his ill-will to the community of which de Solempne was a member.

> *. . . What cawse ys then to quayle,*
> *I called am before*
> *To tast the Joyes which Christis bloode*
> *Hath bowght and layde in store . . .*

> *Who sende the Quene long lyfe,*
> *Much Joye and contries peace,*
> *Her Councell health, hyr fryndes good lucke,*
> *To all ther Joyes increase.*

The Coming of the Strangers

Thus puttyng uppe my greaues,
I grownde my lyfe on God,
And thanke hym with most humble hart
And mekelye kysse his rodde.

Despite this drastic vindication of the strangers, there was still an undercurrent of dissatisfaction in the city. There was much room for dispute over the sale and distribution of the Flemish and Walloon manufactures, and a constant fear of encroachment on English rights. Fresh negotiations were begun between the Corporation and the strangers, in which the Privy Council more than once found it necessary to take a hand. There was also dissension within the ranks of the Dutch congregation. The various ministers were at logger-heads, and the Bishop wrote in tones of exasperation about these refractory foreigners and the problems which they had brought into his diocese. Everything was put right in due course. Revised arrangements for the textile trade were settled to the reasonable satisfaction of both sides. The Bishop's authority in religious matters was decisively asserted; and the contending ministers were all removed from Norwich, the most troublesome of them, Theodore Rykewaert, becoming pastor of the Dutch church at Thetford.

Under the new arrangements the church of St. Mary at Tombland was used exclusively as their Hall by the Dutch, whose commodities were of the coarser kind—'bayes, Flemish cloths, Stamnett kersies, Flanders frezados, Spanish blankets, Hondschoote sayes and so forth'—and were known as the *Baytrie*. The more delicate manufactures of the Walloons—'moscadoes, carrells, grongrains, velvets, torteins and the like'— were described as the *Cangeantrie*, and were approved and sealed in another Hall. The products of both Halls prospered greatly, to the enhancement of Norwich in wealth and reputation. There were still occasional difficulties—the inclination of the Dutch to sell *aquavit* in the streets, and to frequent 'tiplinge howses' on Sundays and holy days; their habit of scouring and rinsing their bays in the river, 'lyke enoughe in this present tyme to conceave great plagues and other

dyseases incurable'; their objection to burning coal, to which
they were unaccustomed in their native land, and their exces-
sive consumption of wood and charcoal in consequence. But
in general the assimilation of the new community proceeded
with success. The freedom of the city was granted to its
members on easy terms, and they became increasingly identified with the everyday life of their neighbours.

In particular they exercised in Norwich their skill in raising
flowers, so that in the next century the gardens of the city and
the excellence of its gardeners were celebrated far and wide.
In the words of Thomas Fuller, 'the Dutch brought hither
with them, not only their profitable crafts, but pleasurable
curiosities'. They introduced the Florists' Feast which by the
reign of Charles I had become a yearly event, with its displays
of flowers diversified by the acting of specially written
masques and plays. Fuller spoke of their art in the cultivation
of tulips, 'feathered and variegated, with stripes of divers
colours', and asserted that 'the *Rose of Roses* (*Rosa Mundi*)
had its first being in this City'. As early as 1575 there was
established in Norwich a Dutch expert whose fame had spread
to the great houses of the neighbouring county. In that year
Sir Thomas Kytson summoned 'the Duchman gardner' to
Hengrave to view his orchards, gardens and walks, and gave
him three shillings and fourpence for his advice. Later he paid
him forty shillings 'for clypping the knotts, altering the alleys,
setting the grounde, finding herbs, and bordering the same'.

The complete acceptance of the strangers by their neighbours was shown by the part which they were invited to play
during the visit of Queen Elizabeth to Norwich in 1578. This
was the only occasion on which the Queen's summer progresses brought her into Norfolk, and a tremendous reception
was arranged for her in county and city. She arrived at
Norwich on the afternoon of 18th August. After being welcomed by the Mayor with an oration at Harford Bridge, she
entered the city by St. Stephen's Gate, and was greeted by a
series of pageants. The first of these was staged in St.
Stephen's Street, and was produced by 'the artizans strangers'.
On a long platform, adorned with pious and loyal mottoes,
was arranged a series of paintings 'artificially expressing to

sight' seven looms and their workmen, each engaged upon some branch of textile manufacture—worstead, dornix, mockado, lace, fringe and so forth. At one end of the platform stood eight little girls spinning worstead yarn; at the other end eight more children were knitting hose; 'in the myddest of the sayde stage stood a pretie boy richly apparelled, which represented the commonwealth of the citie; and all the reste of the stage was furnished with men which made the sayde severall workes, and before every man the worke indeede'. When the Queen arrived the boy greeted her in verse:

> *Most gracious Prince, undoubted Soveraigne Queene,*
> *Our only joy next God, and chiefe defence:*
> *In this small shewe our whole estate is seene;*
> *The welth we have, we finde proceede from thence . . .*

It was a paean upon the industry and frugality of the people of Norwich, and the city's advancing prosperity after the hard times at the outset of her reign:

> *So weake we were within this dozen yeare,*
> *As care did quench the courage of the best.*

It will be noticed that Bernard Goldingham, the poet who contrived the pageant and supplied the verses, did not actually give the strangers credit for the new state of affairs; but their share in it was tacitly acknowledged when they were invited to present this important feature of the city's welcome. The Queen was much pleased by the spectacle, and carefully viewed every feature of it before she moved onward to the other pageants awaiting her.

Three days later, as Her Majesty was riding out to hunt in Costessey park, she was greeted in the market place by the minister of the Dutch church, Hermanus Modet, who presented her with a richly wrought cup on behalf of the two foreign congregations. It was of silver gilt, in a green velvet case, and was engraved with the story of Joseph and his brethren. Within the cup was a serpent intricately coiled, and amidst its coils the figure of a dove. In a Latin oration the minister expressed the gratitude of his flock for the Queen's protection, and applied the story of Joseph to her own escape from the wiles of her wicked sister in days gone by. The cup was valued at £50; and before her departure the Queen bestowed £30 on the poor of the strangers' congregations. Of this sum £19 was allotted to Modet for distribution amongst the Dutch, and £11 went to Lodowyc Maupin, the minister of the Walloons.

The considered verdict of the civic authorities upon the strangers is to be found in a document among the State Papers. It is undated, but its title, *The Benefitte receyved by the Strangers in Norwich for the space of tenne years*, suggests that it must belong to the latter half of this decade. First and foremost, the strangers are praised for having brought a great body of trade to Norwich, by manufacturing a variety of stuffs which were not made there before, and by employing not only their own compatriots but also 'our owne people within the cittie, as also a grete nomber of people nere xx myles about the cittie to the grete relief of the porer sorte there'. Many decayed or ruinous houses in the city had been rebuilt and inhabited by them. Their work had given a great impetus to the general commerce of Norwich both at home and overseas. They contributed their full share to the national and civic expenditure. They had set an example of skill and industry to their neighbours, and in particular to the young people of Norwich. 'Item they digge and delve a number of acres of grounde, and do sowe flaxe and do make it out in lynnen clothe which sette many on worke. Item they digge and delve a grete quantitie of grounde for rootes which is a grete succor and sustenaunce for the pore bothe for them selves as for all others of citie and contrie.' They supported their own community without charge, begged of no man, and wholly maintained their own poor. To conclude, 'they for the most parte fear God and do diligently and labourously attende upon their severall occupacions, they obey all majistrates and all good lawes and ordynances, they lyve peacablie amonge them selves and towarde all men, and we thinke our Cittie happie to enjoye them.'

This glowing eulogy, which was more than once reinforced by others in similar terms, gives the generally accepted opinion of the strangers henceforward. Of course they had their black sheep—drunkards, fornicators, Sabbath-breakers, persons of lewd and ungodly life. They were not always amenable to civic discipline. There were people like Furmyn Vanwater, who 'for keping schoole contrary to order and being commannded to appear before Mr Mayour by the Conestable and refusing to come is therefore for his disobediens sett in the stocks with a paper on his head FOR DISOBEDYENCE'. But in general their good behaviour, their industry and their enterprise won golden opinions from all. At the beginning of the next century Michael Drayton, who found surprisingly little else to say in his *Poly-Olbion* about Norwich, bestowed upon them a long panegyric, to the disadvantage of his own more slothful compatriots. That famous city, he wrote,

> . . . *in her state doth stand*
> *With towns of high'st regard the fourth of all the land:*
> *That hospitable place to the industrious Dutch,*
> *Whose skill in making stuffs, and workmanship is such,*
> *(For refuge hither come) as they our aid deserve,*
> *By labour sore that live, whilst oft the English starve;*
> *On roots and pulse that feed, on beef and mutton spare,*
> *So frugally they live, not gluttons as we are.*

V

As the years passed, the number of the strangers continued to increase. Immigration from the Low Countries was greatly reduced in volume, especially after the northern provinces succeeded in establishing their independence, and the southern provinces were finally subjected. But the families of those already in Norwich multiplied exceedingly. Despite a formidable outbreak of plague during 1579 and 1580, in which 2,500 strangers are said to have died, their number is nevertheless recorded as 4,679 in 1583.

The two congregations, the Dutch in Blackfriars Hall and the Walloons in the Bishop's chapel, maintained their own services in their own tongues for many decades to come. But the wealthier strangers were often buried in the churches of the parishes in which they resided, as were their poorer compatriots in the densely-packed churchyards outside; and some interesting memorials and inscriptions have survived. In St. Mary Coslany is a monument to Martin van Kurnebeck, a Doctor of Arts and Medicine, and his wife Joanna. He died in 1578 and she a year afterwards. This memorial was erected by their executor Henry Jones, *in Cancellaris felicissimae Dominae Elizabethae Reginae Examinator;* and it is a little surprising that the inscription beneath their kneeling figures should contain the traditional Catholic formula *quorum animabus propicietur Deus,* which the Protestant enthusiasts of East Anglia had already expunged from so many earlier brasses. The floor of Blackfriars Hall used to be paved with epitaphs in Dutch; and there still remains on the wall a monument with inscriptions in Latin, Dutch and English, to Joannes Elison, pastor of the church from 1603 until 1639:

> *That worthy Elison, whose holy life and preaching*
> *Did equally advance with both his Dutch Flock teaching,*
> *Lies here in dust dissolv'd, whose loud sweet voice no more*
> *In this Church sounds, but now sings in that heavenly Chore.*

Pastor Elison and his wife, when visiting their son who returned to Holland and became a merchant in Amsterdam, were superbly painted by Rembrandt—most dignified figures in their black robes and stiff white ruffs, and in their way symbolic of the importance and esteem to which the strangers, once a community of harassed refugees, had now attained.

Slowly but inevitably the strangers became merged into the surrounding population, and their community lost its separate identity. The barriers of language were broken down. Some of the next generation remained bilingual, but the greater number preferred to use the speech of their English neighbours. There must likewise have been frequent intermarriages, although the investigation of these matters will always be hampered by the similarities between English and Netherland names, especially when they were written down by English clerks. The suffix *-son* is alone sufficient to cause endless confusion. In a list of the strangers at King's Lynn in 1572, the forty-four householders described as 'Dutchmen and not denizens' include people called Williamson, Johnson, Harrison, Thompson and Adamson, as well as such English-sounding names as Skipper, Colman, Bowen, Daniel, Joyce and Baker. Equally revealing is a 'certificate of the names and professions of all strangers borne, and of all such as are borne of parents strangers', which dates from 1622. Here we have Roger Symonds, Peter Colman, George Fox, Philip Andrews, James Porter, James Clarke and many more. James Hoste, who bought the Sandringham estate about 1686, was the grandson of Jacques Hoost, a merchant of Middelburgh who fled from Alva's persecution and re-established his business in London. As for the names which preserved a measure of their alien identity, many of them have figured to some extent in the life of Norwich in later centuries, and in several cases are still to be found in Norfolk today—Parmentier, Cockaday, de Hague, Phillipo, Provost, Goddart, Gilman, Fremault, Fromanteel, Vardigans, Goose, Williment, Ruymp. There can be few East Anglians, in city or town or perhaps even in the country-side, without some admixture of Dutch, Flemish or Walloon blood.[1]

The bonds between the eastern counties of England and the northern provinces of the Netherlands, now vigorously con-solidating their hard-won independence, were drawn ever closer as the seventeenth century advanced. The degree of personal contact, the extent to which the people of Norfolk and Suffolk visited Holland during this period, can be gauged from the recently published registers containing the names and other particulars of all travellers who embarked at Great Yarmouth during the years 1637–9. Men and women of every rank and condition were making the journey—tradesmen to sell their wares and collect their debts, craftsmen to learn the latest Dutch techniques, soldiers to take service in the armies of the States-General, girls to look for situations as maid-servants. Most of them, however, were ordinary folk of East Anglia out to enjoy a holiday abroad—'to see the country and to returne within a monthe'. And when, during the next two decades, civil war and arbitrary government were the fate of England, these holiday-makers were replaced by a succession

---

[1] As a result of the revocation of the Edict of Nantes in 1685, a considerable number of Huguenots settled in Norwich, including several families destined to play a part in the life of the city—Colombines, Martineaus, de Carles.

of refugees as the shifting tide of events dictated—Puritans, Royalists, Presbyterians, former Parliamentarians for whom the Cromwellian régime was too extreme, revolutionaries too extreme even for Cromwell, women and children whose menfolk belonged to all the contending factions.

The people of the Netherlands, in the course of those twenty years, had ample opportunity to repay the hospitality shown in Norwich and elsewhere to their own distressed kinsmen three-quarters of a century before. But the Civil War lies far outside the scope of this chapter, which was designed solely to tell the tale of that earlier migration. The Rev. William Bridge crossing the sea to set up his dissenting congregation in Rotterdam; Sir William Paston and his friends, 'residing at Rotterdam and doing ill offices to the Parliament', until the sequestration of their estates brought them home to make their peace as best they might; young Jack Knyvett, slipping across to Holland to join the royal forces mustering there, and getting his father into trouble over the outspokenness of his intercepted letters home; Charles Harbord and his brothers, passing their schooldays in peace and security among their mother's Dutch relations; Miles Corbet the regicide, kidnapped at Delft two years after the Restoration, smuggled back to England to stand his trial and to die at Tyburn—this is not the place for their stories. But it is curious to reflect that these and many other Norfolk exiles, holding such widely differing viewpoints amongst themselves, must alike have benefited from the instinctive sympathy which unites the peoples on the opposite shores of the North Sea, and which still enables the visiting East Anglian to feel that in the Netherlands he is less a stranger than a friend.

THE GREAT BLOWE

I

'Though we had Peace, yet 'twill be a great while ere
things be settled: Tho' the Wind lie, yet after a
Storm the Sea will work a great while.' Selden's
observations in his *Table Talk* were always much to the point.
The King had escaped from beleaguered Oxford and given
himself up to the Scottish army in 1646. The remaining
Royalist garrisons had surrendered in the course of that year.
Yet during the spring of 1648, in many parts of England,
popular opinion was still working exactly as Selden described
it, like a restless sea in the lull that follows a storm.

This was conspicuously so in Norwich, which still ranked
as the third city in the land. The second city, Bristol, had
experienced battle, siege and pestilence; but Norwich, deep
in the territory of the Eastern Association, remained wholly
unscathed throughout the war. That gave all the more opportunity for a reaction to develop against the victorious party.
The Army was quarrelling with the Parliament; the Presbyterians were at loggerheads with the Independents; and the
more sanguine of the Royalists were raising their heads once
more. The riot which convulsed Norwich in April 1648, and
which culminated in the gunpowder explosion known in
many contemporary records as 'the great blowe', was to
some extent the result of deliberate repression; but still more
it was the outcome of years of dissatisfaction and boredom.

In the sixteen-thirties, those far-off days before the war,
life in Norwich had not lacked colour and enjoyment even for
the humblest citizen. Guild Days were celebrated with
pageantry and stage-plays, the streets adorned with garlands
and streamers, Snap and Dick Fool raising laughter all along
the route of the procession. The Florists' Feasts took place
every year, flower-shows which were accompanied by elaborate

masques such as Ralph Knevet's *Rhodon and Iris,* and by prologues composed by poets of the quality of William Strode. Above all, Christmas was kept with the traditional mingling of reverence and gaiety, religious observance and family happiness. All this had long since been swept away. For the younger element in the city, the mass of apprentices just growing into manhood, it was a distant memory; but a memory which many of them liked to recall.

The Puritan clergy—John Collinges at St. Stephen's, Paul Rainham at St. Andrew's, the vociferous John Carter at St. Peter Mancroft—did their best to discourage such backward glances to days less austere. Carter in particular gave full rein to his eloquence. Four years earlier he had preached a celebrated sermon, *The Nail hit on the Head, and driven into the City and Cathedral Wall of Norwich,* in which he violently assailed the Mayor and Corporation for not having yet reduced the city to a sufficient state of gloom. At the Guild Day in 1647 he returned to the same theme, in *The Wheel turned by a Voice from the Throne of Glory.* The new Mayor, John Utting, was a man of moderate opinions, and in consequence was regarded with distrust by the more fanatical Puritans. *The Wheel* was openly directed at him and at those of his colleagues who shared his views. The magistrates were the wheels, and they should turn in accordance with the divine command. Yet they suffered fish to be sold in the streets on the Sabbath, and rebuked a godly minister who had dared to protest. 'Oh that these rusty and ill-shaped Wheels were filed, or oyled, or removed, and better put in their room!' Still worse, malignant clerics were reintroducing the old superstitions. 'O Wheels have you not eyes? Do you not see what abundance there are of these? Why do you let them lie so quietly? O Wheels! turn over them: either mend them, or remove them, or break them.' And as for the chief wheel, the unfortunate Mayor—'O Wheel! with all your weight, turn over Idolaters, Hereticks, Blasphemers, Schismaticks, Sabbath-breakers; suppress them, and make much of them that fear the Lord. . . . O Wheel! O Wheel! never leave turning, and turn all wheels to bring more faithful and able Ministers into the City. . . . O Wheel put on; to settle Church-government,

to settle the Union of Parishes, to procure Pastors for every
flock, to see the Sabbaths of the Lord sanctified. O Wheel
lift up God, lift up Christ into his Throne, and the Lord
will lift you up higher.' This remarkable outpouring was
published with a sub-ironical dedication to Utting, and a
note addressed 'To those Magistrates in the City of Norwich,
who were so highly offended, and exasperated at this Sermon'.
The Nail, for good measure, was reprinted at the same time.

Utting's sympathies seem indeed to have been tending
towards a cautious Royalism; and the publication of Carter's
sermons may have been part of a concerted campaign to dis-
credit him and his supporters. Certainly the suspicions of his
Puritan adversaries were not lessened when, towards the end
of the year, the apprentices of Norwich assembled in the
Castle Yard and petitioned him that the festival of Christmas
should be observed according to the ancient forms.

However warm his private sympathies may have been, it is
unlikely that the Mayor agreed to their request. At a time of
general tension, any such concession would have been unwise
and probably fraught with danger. Even so, the Puritan
faction presented him a few weeks later with a counter-
petition, urging 'a more speedy and thorough reformation'.
They complained that some of the ejected clergy had been
allowed to preach in the churches of Norwich, whilst their
own godly ministers were discouraged and slighted. In some
cases the Directory was being ignored, and the Prayer Book
and the old ceremonies were being brought back into use.
There were still images which had not been destroyed—a
crucifix on the Cathedral gate, another on the free-school, a
figure of Christ on St. George Tombland, and similar
abominations elsewhere. They demanded that the various
ordinances of Parliament for silencing ejected ministers, for
abolishing idolatry, and for defacing images should henceforward be strictly enforced. This document was signed, not
by a mob of unruly prentices, but by a considerable number of
substantial citizens. Nevertheless the Mayor disregarded it
entirely.

The Puritan leaders then took action. A party of them, including Thomas Ashwell, one of the Sheriffs, rode up to

London and laid their grievances before Parliament. On Saturday, 22nd April, a pursuivant arrived in Norwich, with orders to take the Mayor into custody and convey him to Westminster, there to answer the charges against him. A former Mayor, an elderly man of strong Puritan sympathies named Christopher Baret, was appointed to act as his deputy; and he and the Corporation were enjoined to take care 'that the orders and ordinances of Parliament be duly and punctually observed, and not slighted as formerly'.

II

A community such as Norwich possessed a deep sense of civic loyalty and pride. The Mayor represented, in the eyes of the citizens, the rights and privileges which they derived from their ancient charter. When they took their oaths as freemen they had sworn 'to support their Mayor and to keep him in the city during his year'; and they remembered that oath now. In 1642, at the outset of the Civil War, a Mayor of Royalist sympathies, William Gostlin, had been deprived of his office and for a time imprisoned. Deep feeling had been aroused then, even though opinion in Norwich had been weighted strongly on the other side. Now that a Royalist reaction was gathering strength, a repetition of the outrage caused still greater indignation. Many people of moderate views felt disposed to support Utting, in addition to those of Royalist sympathies or otherwise disaffected towards the Parliament. The apprentices were enthusiastically on his side, a body of tough and active young men with a natural intolerance of constituted authority, by no means a negligible factor in disturbed times.

As soon as the news of the Mayor's deposition reached Norwich, his sympathizers drew up a petition to Parliament, 'testifying his good government and behaviour'. They circulated it throughout the city, and obtained a great number of signatures. During Sunday, 23rd April, all sorts of rumours began to spread, and the people became restive. Groups started to shout abuse at the Puritan aldermen, and threatened to hang Sheriff Ashwell and the pursuivant upon the Castle mound. When it was reported that the Mayor was to be carried away secretly in the night, they locked all the city gates and took away the keys. Towards midnight a great multitude assembled in the Market Place, some of them with arms. A password, 'For God and King Charles', was given out; and a Royalist spokesman told them that 'if they suffered the Mayor to be carried away, they would have a governour put in (as was done at Lynn) and then all would be tried by martial law; and then we had as good be free of Catton, as free of the City, for freemen would have no freedom at all in any choice.'

The Mayor did everything possible to calm the tumult. He assured his well-wishers that there was no likelihood of his being taken away during the night, and begged them to disperse. But on Monday morning the people assembled once more, in still larger numbers and in a more threatening mood, in Chapel Field. Thence they moved to the Market Place, where the pursuivant was lodging at the King's Head; and when, about ten o'clock, it was rumoured that he was about to depart with the Mayor in his custody, they were with difficulty prevented from attacking the house. The Mayor in person tried to appease them. But they continued to shout that they would purge the Bench of Aldermen and the Common Council; that they would 'pluck the round heads out, and put such honest men in, as would go to Church and serve God'. Finally it was thought best for the pursuivant to leave the city unaccompanied by the Mayor. Some of the more responsible citizens managed to smuggle the terrified official out of his lodging, and escorted him a couple of miles beyond the gates, after which he made his way back to his masters at Westminster. The Mayor, although technically deposed from his office, continued his efforts to pacify the rioters.

But the situation was now getting completely out of hand. The crowd began to attack the houses of the leading Puritan aldermen, and especially that of Thomas Ashwell the Sheriff, whose information to Parliament had brought about the removal of the Mayor. They smashed Ashwell's windows, broke open the doors, and searched the house for arms—of which, since he was a captain of the militia, there was a considerable store. Some handed the arms out of the windows to their comrades; others drank the Sheriff's beer and devoured his brawn and his pies. They then attacked the houses of Thomas Kett, another of the party who had ridden to London to denounce the Mayor, and of a former Mayor and prominent Parliamentarian called Adrian Parmenter, whose wife's hasty distribution of food did not avert considerable damage. Other houses were entered, and the more purposeful of the insurgents collected and distributed all the arms they could find; but there was also a good deal of quite indiscriminate looting and destruction.

As the day wore on, the position grew still more serious. Many of the poorer citizens and apprentices had at first regarded the affair as a glorious day's holiday, as an opportunity to shout and halloo for King Charles and against the Roundheads, to break the windows and drink the strong beer of the powerful Puritan merchants whose rule they found so oppressive. But the authorities had already sent for help to the nearest military force, a body of cavalry stationed at East Dereham under the command of Colonel Charles Fleetwood: and word was brought to the rioters, about three o'clock in the afternoon, that the troopers were on their way. Fleetwood was away from Norfolk at the time; but his second-in-command had at once dispatched a troop of horse and a portion of another troop to Norwich. The news only served to stiffen the determination of the crowd, and they swore to resist the troopers at all costs.

They would need a far larger supply of arms than they had yet obtained; and there was in Norwich one ample store of arms, which they now resolved to capture. Not far from the church of St. Peter Mancroft, on the site of the present Bethel Hospital, there stood a large house which served as the headquarters of the County Committee and as its arsenal. It was known to contain a large supply of arms and ammunition of all descriptions; and its garrison numbered two or three men only, who were probably caretakers rather than guards, and can in any case have scarcely anticipated an attack from an angry mob. Nevertheless, when the crowd began to surge round the 'Committee House' these defenders bolted the doors and barred the windows; and one of them discharged a firearm through a window and killed a boy. This was the first loss of life, and it infuriated the rioters, who stormed their way into the building and began to remove the contents of the arsenal. Muskets, pistols, swords, pikes, armour and bandoliers were handed out to the jostling crowd in the street; and bundles of official documents were flung from the windows and trampled in the gutter.

At the height of the tumult round the Committee House, the first of the troopers came riding into the city. They were a small force by comparison with the angry crowd, who thought they could easily deal with them. The two parties, Royalist citizens and Parliamentarian troopers, joined in a confused mêlée up and down St. Stephen's and the neighbouring streets. Reinforcements arrived for the soldiers; more and more arms were looted from the Committee House, to replace the pitchforks and spits and other improvised weapons of the rioters.

The loading of seventeenth-century firearms was a cumbrous business, involving coils of 'match' and a good deal of loose gunpowder. The powder-barrels stored in the Committee House had been hastily broken open, and a proportion of their contents was dropped about the rooms. One of the mob afterwards described how he had filled his hat with gunpowder swept up from the stairs. Another rioter was seen 'very busy with a lantern in his hand'. It was inevitable that sooner or later the heat of such a lantern, or some even less adequately shielded flame, would come into contact with the scattered powder, and thence with the great powder-casks stored in the cellar. Suddenly, as the struggle continued to rage outside, the entire Committee House blew up with a tremendous explosion, killing a number of people and injuring many more, shattering the windows of several churches and innumerable houses, and showering débris all over the city.

III

The investigation of this affair occupied the magistrates of Norwich for many days afterwards; and the volume in which the depositions were taken down is still preserved amongst the city archives. All sorts of people were examined, in no particular order. Troopers, rioters and independent witnesses follow one another in bewildering succession; and it is difficult to make out, from these crabbed and crowded pages, the principle on which the magistrates committed certain individuals for trial and allowed others to go free. Some of the accused men may already have been regarded as notorious trouble-makers in the city. And after all the riot, in itself a sufficiently grave matter, had culminated in 'the great blowe' with its alarming toll of human lives. The ringleaders would now have to face the charge, not merely of riot and plundering, but of murder.

The general effect of this mass of depositions, to an investigator three hundred years after the event, is as confusing as the riot itself must have been to most of the witnesses and participants. Men and lads and even some women, who had joined in the fray with no thought of the serious developments that would ensue, are now desperately anxious to exculpate themselves. Indignant troopers are still sore from their bruises. There are hints of political prejudice, suggestions of malice between neighbours. Margaret Brady reports Richard Turrell as saying, when asked if the sermon were done, 'Noe, Church is done, but he thought Sermon wold never be done, and if Sermons were done it wold be a better world than it is' —deplorable sentiments in 1648, but with singularly little relevance to the question of the riot. Jonathan Lambe makes it clear that he is 'burthened in conscience', before he gives the evidence which will help to bring Henry Goward to the gallows. Samuel Wilkinson describes how Thomas Balden rushed past his house with a pitchfork in his hand, bawling against the 'troopinge rouges' who were riding into the city —'we will have the gates shut up and take them alive—now for these roundheadly rouges and whores!' Occasionally a deposition or a group of depositions will bring a particular episode into view, with its group of shouting and gesticulating actors; and then they relapse once more into the general turmoil.

One such episode, typical of many, is described in the

depositions of two of the troopers, John Cornelius and Thomas Skott. It involved a couple named John and Margaret Secker, and also a certain Martin Morley, a mason who was later to execute some remarkable mural monuments in the churches of Felbrigg and Foulden. Cornelius made no fewer than four depositions. In the first he stated that as he was riding down St. Stephen's Street 'one John Secker came forth with a watch bill and strooke violently att this informant therewith, and had not this informant warded off the blowe this informant doth veryly believe his head had bene cliven in peces'. In his second deposition he described how in the same street, near the house of Lady Frances Hobart—where the Assembly House now stands—a butcher named Worsley followed him 'with a great clubb in his hand', together with Risbrooke a watchmaker and Morley a mason. As the struggle swayed to and fro, 'the said Worsley with his clubb did strike down this informant's mare, and so he and his mare both fell, whereupon he the said Worsley together with the said Morley and Risbrooke haveinge staffs in their hands fell upon this informant and did beate him very much and had killed him had not releiff come in and rescued him'. The third deposition relates to an unsuccessful assault upon him by one William Pratt with a fork. The fourth brings Mrs. Secker into the picture—'the woman now present who confesse her selfe to be Margarett the wife of John Secker came runninge out with a speete and ran the same into the ribbes of his horse, her husband then beinge fightinge with him with a holbard'.

Nor was Cornelius the only victim of Mrs. Secker and her spit. Another trooper, Thomas Skott, deposed that he was 'charginge thorough the White Swanne backe lane, and when he came against the Lady Frances' gate he was dismounted by the ryoters, who presently after did gett up behind one Thomas Sissen his fellow trooper of Captain Sanckey's troope, and comeinge rideinge down against St. Stephen's church was boath of them beaten off their horse and was then wounded in several places by a little woman in a redd wastcoate with a speete in her hand, and beinge so wounded, beinge a door open at Thomas Toller's he would have gone in to have sheltered him selfe, but when he was goienge in the said

Thomas Toller and his wife did thrust out this informant and would not suffer him to remayne in their house, but thrust him out, and exposed him after he was wounded, and could not well goe, to the fury of the said ryoters.'

At her examination Mrs. Secker would not admit any of this. 'She sayth that upon Monday last in the after noone Goodwife Wilson and Sotherton's wife in St. Stephen's street cryed out for armes, whereupon this examinate brought a speete in her hand to the dore, and when she came there Martyn Morley mason took it out of her hand and did runne downe in the streete with it, but what he did she knowe not nor what further became of him or the speete, for she hath it not agayne. And she denyes that she did runne at any trooper or trooper's horse with her speete or any other weapon, or did hurt or wounde any trooper att all.'

In the same fashion Thomas Toller absolutely denied that he had turned the wounded trooper from his door. He had gone to work at John Peck's before five o'clock in the morning, and had continued working there until seven at night, 'except when he was sent to Ben Baker's in the White Lion lane to buy some bisketts to be sent into the country, and was not gone above a quarter of an hower but did not come amongst any of the mutinous company.' When he left off work he went to see the damage done by the explosion to St. Stephen's church, and the ruins of the Committee House, and then returned home; but by that time the riot was long since over. He had never refused shelter to any trooper, nor had any trooper sought it. At this point the deposition is much frayed and torn; but it would seem that some other trooper had accused Toller of wounding him, and had identified him by his hands, which were 'dyed with the colour of yarne'. There must have been many other men in the crowd whose hands bore the stains of their trade as dyers. Toller continued to maintain his innocence.

In the end not a single one of the people involved in this particular episode was committed for trial. In spite of the statements of Cornelius, the husband of Margaret Secker does not even seem to have been examined; nor was the wife of Thomas Toller; nor were Worsley, Morley and Risbrooke.

The Great Blowe

Probably they had all borne reasonably good characters hitherto, and were not the sort of people whom the magistrates wished to see punished. None of them was accused of plundering, and none had been seen on the premises of the Committee House. At all events their part in the riot was overlooked, and they sink once more into oblivion.

Very different was the treatment accorded to those considered by the authorities, rightly or wrongly, to be the ringleaders. One of these was a saddler named Henry Goward. Two men, Nathaniel Elmer and the conscience-burthened Jonathan Lambe, deposed that during the fatal afternoon they had heard Goward say 'It were a good turn to goe and blow up the Committee House upon the Roundheads'; and both had seen him prominent among the rioters. A little later Thomas Yonges heard Goward inviting the mob to advance on the Committee House and help themselves to the arms stored there. (Yonges was anxious to save his own skin; he had taken a pistol from the arsenal, but brought it away before the house was fired, and later gave it to Goodwife Baxter.) An inn-keeper's wife named Ursula Moore laid information that on the Sunday night, when she and her husband were in bed, Goward and other company, to the number of twenty, came to her door. They were making a great noise in the street, and bore halberds in their hands; 'and the said Goward did saye to her before she opened the doore, that they were watchmen for Kinge Charles and Mr Maior.' There was also a mysterious gentleman in a black suit, who asked the others not to disclose his name. They spent half-a-crown in drink at her house, and Goward paid the reckoning.

These appear to be the only references to Goward in the depositions. Further evidence may have been brought against him at his trial, although it seems most unlikely that he or anyone else deliberately planned the blowing-up of the Committee House. Whatever the facts of the case may have been, he was regarded as one of the chief fomenters of the riot, and in due course he was condemned and executed.

IV

Among the throng of excited apprentices, shouting up and down the streets for King Charles and confusion to the Roundheads, was a youth named Charles Porter. He was the son of the Rev. Edmund Porter, one of the former prebendaries of the Cathedral and rector of the parish of Hevingham. This once opulent cleric had been ejected from his preferments on account of his Royalist sympathies, and was no doubt living in considerable poverty. His son Charles, now apprenticed to a Norwich tradesman, lived to be a distinguished lawyer and Lord Chancellor of Ireland. He was a social and convivial personage—'his person was florid', according to Roger North, 'and his speech prompt and artificial'—and in later years he was fond of recounting to his dinner-table companions the part which he had played in this riot of long ago.

This was his version of the story as he related it to Roger North. 'He was the son of a prebend in Norwich and a 'prentice boy in the city in the rebellious times. When the Committee House was blown up, he was one that was very active in that rising, and after the soldiers came and dispersed the rout he, as a rat among joint-stools, shifted to and fro among the shambles and had forty pistols shot at him by the troopers that rode after him to kill him. In that distress he had the presence of mind to catch up a little child that, during the rout, was frightened and stood crying in the streets and, unobserved by the troopers, ran away with it. The people opened a way for him, saying, "Make room for the poor child". Thus he got off and, while search was made for him in the market-place and thereabouts, got into the Yarmouth ferry and at Yarmouth took ship and went into Holland, there being an opportunity of a ship then going off; and he was scarce out at sea before the pursuit came down after him; so narrowly he escaped hanging at that time. In Holland he trailed a pike and was in several actions as a common soldier. At length he kept a cavalier eating-house; but, his customers being needy, he soon broke and came for England, and being a genteel youth, was taken in among the Chancery clerks.'

The Great Blowe

The story is so vividly told that one hesitates to cast any doubt upon it. Charles Porter may indeed have met with the adventures which he describes. Yet it is curious that throughout the volume of depositions, in which the names of scores of the rioters occur, there appear to be no accusations whatever against him. If his part in the affair had been so conspicuous that it was necessary to pursue him to Yarmouth, surely his name might be expected to appear somewhere in the depositions. The volume does contain, however, the examination of an apprentice named Charles Porter; and he signs it in a clear and educated hand, the hand of a youth who had received good schooling. The great majority of the examinants either signed their evidence in a laborious scrawl or, still more often, affixed their marks. There may have been two apprentices named Charles Porter involved in the riot. They may both have been young men of good education. Nevertheless the coincidence does seem a little peculiar.

This Charles Porter had been observed to have a gun in his possession, and was under suspicion of having taken the gun from the Committee House. In his examination before the justices he explained his possession of the gun in this way: 'He sayth upon this daye fortnight his maister sent him to Thomas Barber of Magdalen Streete for mony, and the said Barber told this examinate that if he would buy a Carbyne he could helpe this examinate to a good penny worth, and there upon the said Barber went with this examinate to a soldier of Captayne Blissett's troope at the Bull who had the said Carbyne, and this examinate did buy it for eight shillings, and the said Barber told this examinate it was now a vacant time, he might kill pigions with it.' He did not carry the gun home, but sent it by a hostler to a person or place whose name is illegible. 'Upon Thursday last this examinate charged the same with powder, and as he was aboute to lett it off his maister came to the dore, and thereon he went and sett it in att Gibsons the Coblers.' This story was corroborated by Gibson's wife. Nothing is said in the examination about any part which Porter may have played in the riot; and it would seem that the justices were satisfied by his explanation about the gun. It is all very different from Lord Chancellor Porter's heroic reminiscences; and probably we shall never know whether there were two Charles Porters or one.

V

The destruction which resulted from the blowing-up of the Committee House was immense and widespread. Estimates of the number of deaths varies greatly. In the first excitement people talked of two or three hundred; but later an official report to Parliament put the total at about forty. Many others must have been injured. Considerable damage was done to the churches of St. Peter Mancroft and St. Stephen's, and to their windows in particular. At both the churchwardens' accounts show heavy payments to glaziers, masons and carpenters, and special parish rates had to be levied to meet them. At St. Peter Mancroft it was necessary to shore up the tracery of the great east window, and during the next few years it was entirely renewed. The work was entrusted to the mason Martin Morley, who had been implicated in the riot, and he received the substantial sum of £55. It is astonishing that so much of the medieval glass in the church survived these vicissitudes unharmed.

All over Norwich private householders mournfully surveyed their roofs, their windows, their ceilings—as their successors were to do in those same streets after the German air-raids three centuries later. Emergency measures were taken against the weather and the danger of thieves. Women and children were given shelter by neighbours whose houses had suffered less. The atmosphere is vividly preserved in two letters among the Tanner manuscripts in the Bodleian Library. The first was written, on the evening of the riot, by a prominent citizen named Joseph Payne to his brother-in-law Richard Bensly in London. It will be noticed how warmly he commends the Mayor for his conduct throughout the whole business.

Norwich 24° Aprilis 1648.

Brother our kind Loves remembered and to all good friends, thy letter I receyved with the inclosed, which before

I answer I must tell thee of the unhappiness befell our City this present day by an unruly multitude mett together to prevent our Mayor going to London who was sent for by a messenger from the Parliament. The Mayor used much diligence to preserve this messenger from daunger, which was done, and he gone safe and well towards London this morning. After this the multitude goeth to Shiriffe Ashwell, from thence to Mr. Kett's, so to Alderman Parmenter's where much mischiefe was done but no bloudshed, for the Mayor used what diligence he could to asswage theyr fury. The rout being gone from Mr Parmenter's the Mayor goeth to the Hall to consult with his brethren what course to take, then the people goeth to the Committy house (I mourne to tell you) where the Magazine of powder that was there was fyred, blew up the house where tis reported that at least 4 score are slayne and divers wounded, they are now pulling the mangled bodys out of the rubbish, at the very instant of this miserable accident cometh a troope of horse riding into the markett which then very easily disperst the rest. Sam Gosling is slayne by one of the troopers going in the street with his cloake on, as I heare. Further particulars I cannott tell yet. The breake of the ayre with the powder have blowne most of the glasse out of Mr Hobart's house and myne and out of the church, a great deale of damage done to the City, now at present blessed be our God the City is quiet and a watch sett of the trayned men to guard the City.

I pray go see my noble friend Mr John Hobart, his lodging is at Mrs Bagnall's house at the Flower de Luce court in Fleet Street, present my service to him and hir and his childrens' dutyes, tell him they be all very well but something affrighted with this daye's distraction, they shall lodge at my house untill I see the City a little setled, and at present we have stopped up his windowes with boards so well as we could, as soone as we can we shall get them mended, desyre him not to be troubled at any thing, what I can do for him or his I will.

Your loving brother
JOSEPH PAYNE.

To Mr Richard Bensly in Thridneedle Street.

Events

The second letter was written three days later by someone called Justinian Lewyn, who lived outside the walls of Norwich in the pleasant village of Heigham. It bears no address, but from internal evidence it was almost certainly addressed to the John Hobart mentioned in the previous letter.

Sir,

The Tumult is over, but the evill consequents thereof (I feare) are of longer date, for now an inquisition is on foote *nodum in scirpo querere* and God knowes what will bee the issue of itt. Much mischiefe came of the blowinge upp of the Committee House, and of larger extent than could easily have been imadgined, for your house in St Gregoryes had a share in it where most of the wyndows are much shattered—to the soe great affrightment of your little family, that thaye fledd for sanctuary (this night) to your neighbour Mr Payne, and the next morninge I fecht them to Heigham, where (I hope) thaye shall remayne in safety till your returne. Your house in St Gyles his parish fared much worse where your tennant (whom I understand woold not quitt possession by fayr means) is unhoused by this accident. I took care to board upp the windows of your louer roomes in your dwellinge house, and I heare that Dr Binge hath not been wantinge to you att the other, but taken order to preserve what tyle and glasse there could be saved. I purpose to inquire farther into itt, and doe earnestly intreat you to direct me wherein I maye doe you any service. And with mine and my wyfes best respects presented to my honnord Cozen and your selfe I beseech you to receive this truth, that I am

Sir

Your faythfull and obleidged friende

to love and serve you

JUST: LEWYN.

27° Aprilis 1648. *Heigham.*

A letter written to the Speaker of the House of Commons on the 4th of May by the Deputy Mayor, old Christopher Baret, has also survived. He takes the credit for the pursuivant's escape entirely to himself, and makes no mention of the Mayor's efforts to appease the tumult—indeed he contrives to insert several hints to the Mayor's disadvantage. At the time of the tumult Utting's mayoralty had only a few more weeks to run, and an ironmonger named Roger Mingay had already been chosen as his successor; but Baret and his supporters called an emergency meeting of the common council, which revoked Mingay's nomination and elected a more reliable Parliamentarian, Edmund Burman, in his stead. This was done by virtue of a special by-law, which had been much opposed by 'licentious and refractory persons'—in other words by the Royalist sympathizers in the corporation, who must now have been too subdued by the recent events to offer much protest. It is not surprising that the election went off, in Baret's words, 'with that quietness and peaceableness as was wonderful'—especially as a troop of horse had been drawn up outside.

Having described these manœuvres, Baret goes on to tell the Speaker of the particular solicitude shown by the Almighty, at the time of the explosion, towards the supporters of the dominant régime. 'Wee have, in the great sence of the Almighties goodnesse to this poore citty and his infinite deliverance of us, in a word Sir give leave abruptly to say, not an honest man slayne. In the blowinge up of the house ther wer 3 families in it consistinge of as I am informed 24 persons, divers neighbours next of many persons all overwhelmed in the same ruines, som lyinge above 4 houres buried are alive, all miraculously preserved, not one slayne, all the other deade, we heare not of one in the house escaped alive, above 40 persons already taken up, how many more shall [be] wee know not, besides broken shattered peices blown far and nigh, abundance. For this wee have appointed a day of Thanksgiving to Almighty.'

The phrasing and punctuation are somewhat vague, but the meaning is clear enough. And it is endorsed by some observations of the Rev. William Bridge, in a sermon preached before the House of Commons on 17th May. Mr. Bridge was that busy Puritan minister, once rector of St. George Tombland, who had fled to Holland in the days of Archbishop Laud, and of whom the King had written, in the margin of the Archbishop's report of his departure, 'Let him go, we are well rid of him'. He had, of course, come back again; and although his sermon was mainly devoted to an outpouring of thanksgiving for the Parliament's recent victory at St. Fagan's in Wales, his thoughts also returned to the city of his early days. 'Ye have heard,' he told the assembled Members of Parliament, 'ye have heard of the lamentation of Norwich. There was a generation of men that rose up and threatened to destroy the Godly Party there, but the Lord so ordered things in His Providence that those whom they threatened to destroy were preserved and the destroyers perished, nigh two or three hundred (if relations be right) blown up with powder or spoiled, and three godly families consisting of about twenty persons in severall rooms of the house that was blowne up were all preserved, and not a bone of them broken, whilst the other flew up into the aire, as spectacles of divine anger, as if God should speake from Heaven. These are the people whom I would have preserved, and those are the people that I would have punished.'

VI

Norwich had its own special day of thanksgiving for the safe deliverance of the city from this alarming conspiracy, as the authorities chose to regard it. The corporation attended at the Cathedral in full state, and listened to the eloquence of the Rev. John Carter in the morning and the Rev. John Collinges in the afternoon. Special peals were rung in the churches: at St. Peter Mancroft one Thomas Bubbins received 7s. 6d. 'for ringing on the thankcksgiveing day for the greate deliverance from the Blowe'. The sum of £250 was voted to the troopers, and a request was made that some of them should remain to ensure the city's safety. Colonel Fleetwood received the thanks of Parliament 'for the good service rendered by some of your regiment in the appeasing and suppression of the late tumult and insurrection in Norwich.'

John Utting, the delinquent Mayor, made his way to London, hopefully bearing with him the petition attesting his good conduct which his supporters had circulated and signed. But the second Civil War was about to break out in Kent and Essex; and the Parliament, faced by an uprising of great

potential danger, had no time to concern itself with the after-
math of a minor demonstration which had been successfully
quelled. It was ordered that Utting should be confined to his
house at Brandon Parva, on the borders of Suffolk; and nothing more was apparently done about him for many months
to come. His misdoings were investigated in the course of
1649, and in September of that year a committee reported to
the House upon his case. By that time Pride's Purge had
eliminated several local members who might have spoken on
his behalf, and he was treated with considerable severity. The
report put the worst construction on all his actions; he was
accused of organizing the petition in his own favour, encour-
aging the rioters, and ordering the gates to be shut against
the troopers. It was added, for good measure, that he had
embezzled some of the city funds. In all this he had been
greatly countenanced by Alderman John Tolye.

Now John Tolye was one of the most respected of all the
Norwich citizens. He had been twice Mayor, and had represented the city in the Short Parliament. Many of the depositions relating to the riot had been taken in his presence and
bear his signature. But his sympathies, like Utting's, were
with the King; and he was chosen for that reason, and perhaps
also because he was one of the richer citizens, to be Utting's
fellow-scapegoat. Parliament, on the strength of the committee's report, resolved that both were delinquents within
the ordinance of sequestration. They were sent for in custody,
and on 9th October were brought into the House by the
Serjeant-at-Arms. Utting was fined £500 and imprisoned in
the Fleet for six months; Tolye was fined £1,000 and imprisoned for three months; both were disabled from bearing
any office under the Commonwealth. Neither lived to see the
end of the Commonwealth, and no doubt they felt the effect
of these heavy fines to the end of their days. On Utting's tomb
at Brandon Parva were inscribed some lines which end:

Unto the Heavens thy Loyal Heart was Knowne
To have a Part with him whom God doth owne:
No faithfull Soule did ere take more delight,
God and his King and Contrye more to right.

Events

As for the rioters who had been committed to prison, they remained crowded together in the Castle throughout the stifling summer and the chilly autumn. In accordance with a disagreeable Puritan foible, they were purposely brought to trial upon Christmas Day. Nine were acquitted; twenty-four were fined £30 and sentenced to remain in prison until their fines were paid; eight were condemned to death. They were Christopher Hill, a brazier; Anthony Wilson, a blacksmith; William True, a dyer; Henry Goward, a saddler; Edward Gray, described as an 'oatmeal-maker'; two brothers, Thomas and John Bidwell, labourers; and Charles Emerson, whose occupation is not recorded. These eight men were hanged in the Castle Ditches on 2nd January 1649, in company with two old women convicted of witchcraft.

They were ordinary small tradesmen and artisans, who had blundered into an ill-conceived demonstration against the dominant power, the gloomy and self-righteous doctrinaires in whose control the country lay. They had engaged in looting and rioting; the murderous explosion at the Committee House was laid to their charge; and by the laws of the land they were justly condemned to die. But a little scrap of evidence, suggesting the sympathy with which some and perhaps many of their fellow-citizens regarded them, lies hidden in the parish register of the church of St. Lawrence. 'January 2nd 1648-9. Buried Charles Emerson, executed in the Castle Deekes as one of the praetended mutineeres when the then Committee house was blowne up with 80 barrels of powder.' The implications of words alter with centuries; but it seems probable that this use of 'praetended' means that the incumbent of St. Lawrence, even in that intolerant time, was confiding to the pages of the register his belief that Charles Emerson and his companions had not deserved so harsh a fate.

THE PHANTOM DUEL

Throughout the eighteenth century, and during the opening decades of the nineteenth, any personal disagreement might necessitate a resort to the pistol or the sword. 'It requires such a degree of passive valour', wrote Blackstone, 'to combat the dread of even undeserved contempt, arising from the false notions of honour too generally received in Europe, that the strongest prohibitions and penalties of the law will never be entirely effectual to eradicate this unhappy custom.' It is a tribute to English commonsense that duels in this country were not far more frequent, and that fatal duels were comparatively rare. Except for the occasional braggart and bully, and the hot-headed young man determined to prove his valour, the participants and their seconds usually acted with a good deal of circumspection. Honour, of course, had to be satisfied beyond any risk of criticism. Passions had sometimes risen too high, words had been spoken which were not to be retracted. But if matters could reasonably be adjusted without an encounter, the encounter did not take place. And if it had to take place, the seconds often found an honourable way of ending the proceedings at an early stage.

The disagreements—even that minute proportion of which some record has survived—could be violent enough. Quarrels might arise over every conceivable issue—politics, including the conduct of elections and the proprietorship or influence of boroughs; sport, with such fruitful fields for dispute as racing, betting, game-preserving; the subtleties of social *punctilio*; the whole vast area of personal relationships. The society 'subject to the rules of honour' was one whose members dominated their own private worlds, were not accustomed to be thwarted, and did not readily bear contradiction. Yet they would often display a surprising measure of reasonableness, moderation, even a willingness in the last resort to admit a mistake. There were, of course, some memorable duels. There were also some memorable quarrels which did not result in duels.

One such quarrel occurred in 1759, between Thomas Coke, first Earl of Leicester, and Colonel George Townshend, afterwards fourth Viscount and first Marquess Townshend. In this case there has survived, in defiance of all the evidence, a strangely persistent legend that a duel actually took place, in which Lord Leicester was fatally wounded. In the following pages I have sought to describe the circumstances of the quarrel, and to review the contemporary evidence, in support of my conviction that this duel was one of the many picturesque and dramatic episodes in English history which never happened at all.

II

Lord Leicester, the elder antagonist in the dispute, is now chiefly remembered as the creator of the noble house and domain of Holkham. He was a man of great wealth and very considerable influence. In his time he had figured in both Houses of Parliament, filling the office of Postmaster-General for a number of years, and had consistently upheld the Whig interest in the politics of his own county. The improvements which he carried out on his barren and windswept estates had been far from negligible, and in fact he deserves some of the credit as an agricultural pioneer which has gone to his great-nephew 'Coke of Norfolk'. But the planning, building and adornment of Holkham formed the central enterprise of his life.

His geniality, his love of sport, his hospitable and convivial manner of life blended agreeably with an enthusiasm for classical learning and a devotion to the most rigid standards of Palladian architecture. His old friend and neighbour Edward Spelman, in a charming passage in the dedication of his translation of Xenophon's *Anabasis*, recalled both aspects of his character from their early days. 'I remember', he wrote, 'when we were Foxhunters, and a long Day's Sport had rather

THOMAS COKE, 1ST EARL OF LEICESTER
from a bust by Sir Francis Chantrey
after a model by Louis François Roubiliac,
in the possession of the Earl of Leicester

tir'd, than satisfied us, we often pass'd the Evening in reading the ancient Authors; when the Beauty of the Language, the Strength, and Justice of their Thoughts for ever glowing with a noble Spirit of Liberty, made us forget not only the Pains, but the Pleasures of the Day.' In a more critical spirit Sir Charles Hanbury Williams, ever ready to mock at friend and foe alike, described him as

> . . . *the oddest character in town,*
> *A lover, statesman, connoisseur, buffoon.*

And he had other detractors, Horace Walpole prominent among them. But the impression gained from his private letters is of a very pleasant, kindly and warm-hearted man.

In 1753 his only son, after a career which lamentably belied his early promise, had died childless; and the whole vast inheritance of Holkham would pass to the son of his sister by a marriage of which he had disapproved. It was a tragic disappointment, and one which saddened all the closing years of his life. Yet it did not break his spirit, or alter the front which he presented to the world. In the eyes of Admiral Boscawen, who stayed with him in 1757, he was still 'the fat, laughing, joking peer' whose hospitality delighted all his friends. Although he had long since withdrawn from public affairs and lived almost entirely in Norfolk, he watched the current of events very closely from his retirement; and he saw no reason to keep his opinions to himself. When the Militia Bill was passed at an early stage of the Seven Years' War, and a part-time reserve force was duly raised in each county, he disapproved strongly both of the measure itself and of the way in which its provisions were carried out. He expressed his views with his usual forcefulness; and in due course they were reported to his neighbour George Townshend, who had been the chief promoter of the Bill and was now working feverishly to recruit and train the Norfolk Militia.

George Townshend was the elder son of the third Viscount, and grandson of the statesman and agricultural pioneer best known to fame as 'Turnip Townshend'. By the outbreak of the Seven Years' War he was an experienced soldier, having been in action at Dettingen and Fontenoy, Culloden and

Laffeldt. Horace Walpole, who was his cousin, described him
as 'a young man with much address, some humour, no knowledge, great fickleness, greater want of judgement, and with
still more disposition to ridicule'. There was a certain amount
of truth in this verdict. Townshend was hasty and hot-
tempered, resentful of authority and usually critical of his
superiors. His career had been marked by a series of quarrels
and disagreements; and his 'disposition to ridicule' showed
itself in his masterly caricatures, which amused and delighted
everyone except their subjects. For some years he had served
as *aide-de-camp* to the Duke of Cumberland; but his outspoken
criticism of the Duke's campaigns, and his wounding caricatures of the Duke's unwieldy person, had brought their association to an end. He then turned his attention to politics, and
had represented the county of Norfolk in Parliament since
1747. His younger brother and staunch supporter Charles,
a brilliant orator and future Chancellor of the Exchequer, was
member for Great Yarmouth. When George Townshend
carried his Militia Bill in 1757 he was thirty-three years of
age—a younger man than Lord Leicester by more than a
quarter of a century.

His activities in connexion with the Militia were entirely
to his credit. The nation had drifted, unprepared and ill-
armed, into the Seven Years' War, with a hard-pressed
Prussia as her sole ally. Disaster followed disaster; the
French appeared to be making vigorous preparations for
invasion; and by the summer of 1757 the situation seemed
almost desperate. Apart from the regular forces, which were
committed to operations in every corner of the globe, the only
troops available were the hastily-imported professional soldiers from Hanover and Hesse. Townshend's Militia Bill, in
which he was warmly supported by Pitt, gave English civil-
ians an opportunity to defend their own shores. The virtually
dormant militia system was revived throughout the country.
Each Lord Lieutenant was to command the militia of his
county, and recruiting was the responsibility of himself and
his Deputy Lieutenants. Each county was to provide a given
quota of men according to its population. The men were to be
chosen by ballot in each parish, and were to serve for three

years. Men chosen could provide substitutes or compound for a money payment, and there were various other exemptions. It was certainly a mild enough measure for a time of grave national crisis.

Nevertheless it met with considerable opposition, especially in the country districts. Many gentlemen, who had been loud in their denunciations of standing armies and German mercenaries, were distinctly reluctant to take any active part in raising and officering the new force. They were equally disinclined to allow the best of their servants and farm-workers to join it. There was a certain amount of opposition of this kind in Norfolk, where Townshend was devoting himself with furious energy to the task of organizing an exemplary body of troops. His own father, with whom he was on the worst of terms, made things as difficult as possible for him. Horace Walpole told one of his correspondents that Lord Townshend, 'who is not the least mad of your countrymen, attended by a parson, a barber, and his own servants, and in his own long hair, which he has let grow, raised a mob against the execution of the Bill, and has written a paper against it, which he has pasted up on the door of four churches near him'.

More serious was the opposition of Lord Leicester, who had taken a consistently hostile view of the scheme from its inception. A Whig of the old school, and faithful to the declining influence of the Duke of Newcastle, he regarded the Militia as an ineffective institution, unlikely to be of much real service in an emergency, and also as a dangerous institution, which might get into the hands of Tory country gentlemen with very alarming consequences. Instead of this makeshift body of soldiery, officered by amateurs and possibly controlled by Tories, he would have preferred to see the regular forces greatly enlarged. When Townshend's measure was before Parliament he wrote to the Duke of Devonshire that 'I shall send my proxy as usual to John Delawarr, with directions to oppose any clause of that foolish Bill'. In November 1758, in the last of all his letters to the Duke of Newcastle, he accused the Suffolk Militia of Jacobite tendencies, and remarked that in Norfolk, 'by what I have seen of the list, there are many if not most officers who never showed in peace

much zeal for this Government'. He assured the Duke that
'whatever you may hear, I must for the honour of my county
assure you it is not popular here, as I believe the next election
will show, notwithstanding newspaper puffs'. Then he appo-
sitely quoted Dryden's lines in *Cymon and Iphigenia*:

> *The country rings around with loud alarms,*
> *And raw in fields the rude Militia swarms;*
> *Mouths without hands maintained at vast expence,*
> *In peace a charge, in war of no defence.*
> *Stout once a month, they march a blust'ring band,*
> *And ever, but in times of need, at hand.*
> *Of seeming arms they make a short essay,*
> *Then hasten to be drunk, the business of the day.*

Leicester did not hesitate to make his views known in
Norfolk, and some of his witticisms about the Militia soon
came to Townshend's ears. It was reported, truly or falsely,
that he was holding up to public ridicule the force itself and
many of its officers, including the Lord Lieutenant, the third
Earl of Orford, who commanded it. Leicester and Townshend
were already on sufficiently bad terms. Although both would
have regarded themselves as Whigs, their political interests
in Norfolk had conflicted more than once since Townshend
became one of the members for the county, and of late years
their views on national issues had greatly diverged. More
recently still, they had disagreed on the subject of game. Since
his quarrel with his father Townshend had hired Cranmer
Hall, a house on the confines of the Holkham estate. He was
an enthusiastic fox-hunter, whereas Leicester liked to destroy
his foxes and preserve his pheasants. There had been rows
between keepers and huntsmen, letters of remonstrance,
appeals to the example of other neighbours, and a growing
ill-feeling. Leicester's rumoured insults to the Militia ex-
hausted Townshend's limited stock of patience. He was under
orders to join the expedition to Canada under the command
of Wolfe, and resolved to bring the matter to a head before he
sailed. On the 24th of January 1759 he dispatched a fulminat-
ing challenge to his elderly neighbour.

III

Copies of the challenge and of the resulting correspondence were much handed about in Norfolk, and several sets of the documents have survived. I have reproduced them below from copies which belonged to William Windham of Felbrigg, a close friend of Townshend and one of his leading associates in the organization of the local Militia. The letters are extremely discursive, and I have not thought it necessary to print some of their divagations and repetitions. The reader may rest assured that everything bearing on the challenge and its consequences has been retained.

The first document, the challenge itself, is printed in full. It should be explained that the Norfolk Militia was formed into two battalions, the Eastern and the Western, commanded respectively by the two Members of Parliament for the county, Sir Armine Wodehouse and George Townshend, with Lord Orford as Colonel in Chief. This young man had enthusiastically supported Townshend's efforts, and proved a most satisfactory commanding officer; but it would have been impossible for him, as Lord Lieutenant and the King's personal representative, to bring Lord Leicester to book for his aspersions on the Militia, even if he had desired to do so.

My Lord,

As I have been disappointed in the opportunity I much wished for to express myself publickly in the manner I think it becomes me to your Lordship upon your very unprovoked indecent and insolent behaviour towards a body of Gentlemen of respectable property rank and characters in this County for their spirited and generous engagements for the service of their Country; I cannot now (being called out of the Country upon the publick service) leave it without first demanding from your Lordship that satisfaction which I think I have a right to expect from you as you well know I being Colonel of one of those Battalions of Militia which you have been pleased so plentifully to abuse, consequently my Lord one of the first objects of your bitterness and ribaldry however ineffectual and contemptible. It is natural to expect the efforts of a malignant

157

mercenary renegade peer must be to obstruct the publick service and to blacken the characters of a set of Gentlemen who devote themselves from principle solely to the defence of their Country; yet when I my Lord consider the rank I have the honour and happiness to bear among them in this service, I shall not deny myself this opportunity to prove my respect towards my brother Officers at your expense if you have half the courage you have malice—perhaps at my own in some degree; but I fear that a man who lives and acts so much above all society as yourself will think himself responsible to nobody. However what I now propose to your Lordship is I assure you for your own conveniency, that you will give me a rendezvous with those weapons which I think puts most men very nearly on an equality: but lest you should they do not, I desire you will multiply them on your part as much as you please. We will each of us bring a friend or a servant as you like. This or an acknowledgement of the abuse and injustice you have done to the whole corps of Militia of this County I demand from you; and if you refuse it I shall, if it please God that I return from the service I am going upon, call upon you for it in a more publick manner whenever and wherever I meet you. I had myself in person made this demand at Holkham but apprehended I might have alarmed your Lady and servants.

Your Lordship may perhaps be inclined to impute this salutation to other acts of your ill usage of me as a neighbour, and to my discovering how much your private transactions about foxes and such things have been covered by a kind of superficial politeness of which you are so much the master and which when counteracted by real ill will is but mere treachery. These circumstances are of no more weight than your own publick declarations have given them, and serve only to distinguish how far a great man can act up to what he has expected from others; and when attended with promises they serve as well as greater objects to distinguish the gentleman from the tyrant and the honest man from the scoundrel.

I have, it's true, long foreborne your Lordship's repeated provocations; and whatever you may think of what I say or whatever you may determine upon, it's enough to convince you perhaps of a truth you have not yet heard, which is this that in a free Country (which I think this still remains) nor riches nor title nor even the privilege of years will authorise any man to play the tyrant; neither will it protect the insolence of any one man towards another, or prevent any gentleman from doing himself justice.

I am, as the friend and follower of real merit only, with the utmost contempt for the Right Honourable the Post Master General, his most obedient and humble Servant

GEO: TOWNSHEND.

My servant has orders to wait for answer and hope you will appoint time and place in your letter.
CRANMER,
January 24th 1759.

It is difficult to imagine a more wounding, a more insulting letter. It will presently be seen that at least one contemporary observer could only suppose that Townshend was drunk when he wrote it. But it must be remembered that for months on end he had been in a highly overwrought state. He had been straining every nerve to train and improve the force which was mainly his creation and in which he felt such pride. And as so often happens to the more vocal type of patriot during times of national crisis, he lost his sense of proportion. He could well have disregarded Leicester's reported words, as the ineffective sneers of a tiresome and obstructive old man. Instead, he allowed his anger to blaze forth in this flamboyant missive, and in consequence placed himself wholly in the wrong.

Leicester's reply was of great length, full of digressions, and in places almost wholly irrelevant to the matter in hand; but its general effect was to place the whole affair in a much more reasonable perspective. His tone was conciliatory without being undignified. He did not actually point out that Townshend, an experienced officer now in his middle thirties, was behaving like a hot-headed and ill-tempered boy; but by emphasizing the disparity between their age and physique, and the general haze of misunderstanding that had arisen

159

between them, he contrived to suggest that the whole dispute was unnecessary and indeed ridiculous.

Sir,

I received your letter which was wrote with so much warmth that I could not answer it in the manner I was desirous of doing, which was to endeavour to set you right in some misinformations I see you have had of me and mistaken constructions of my meaning any rudeness to you in my endeavouring to subvert the Militia Scheme, which you know I always thought of in a light quite otherwise than you do. I think if this Country was to trust to a Militia to defend it (though I have really as great an opinion of the courage both of the Officers and Private men as of any of the Army which is composed of such as them viz. their brothers and nearest relations) yet by what I have seen of exercising of soldiers, and the long time it takes to make them fit for service, I cannot think that men exercised but once a fortnight (as it seems to me to be directed by the Act, and that for only three years) can be such a defence as I should wish to see always kept up in this Nation to defend us. And therefore, as I have all along done, I endeavoured by talking to the few people I see to hinder it from being popular and to gain further strength from Parliament. Therefore I own I endeavoured to lessen the respect people might have of a Militia in general; and this I am persuaded of, that you who are so zealous for the libertys of this Country, will think every man has a right and ought to endeavour to prove what he thinks may be detrimental, as much as I really think you and everybody else has a right to support what they think right.

Thus far I flatter myself you have no reason to take ill of me and consequently that you do not. I acknowledge you would have very great reason to take it ill of me if I really had shown personal disregard to you or any one Gentleman because he was in your Battalion. So far from it, I am sure I never showed any to you; and as for your Officers I have never heard who the greatest part are. Some I don't know whose names I have heard; others I do know, honour and love. My old friend Herne who I was so intimately acquainted with (tho' now living so retired I have not seen for a vast while) I hear is one; Mr. Coldham, as pretty a young man as far as I know him as anybody, another; and many more both in your and the other Battalion, who I should be most exceedingly concerned to show the least slight to, and who, if I imagined they thought the things I have out against a national Militia in general as all tending as slights to them, I should not be easy til I had convinced them of the contrary, as I am now desirous to do to you that I never meant the least slight or disrespect to you therein. My saying I should always oppose the Militia, and the supporters of it, I hope you will no ways take as a slight meant on you any more than any Parliament man ought to do any opposition from those who differ with him in opinion, though they may have great personal regard for the man.'

At this point he harked back to the local politics of ten years before, when Townshend was first chosen to represent the county in Parliament. He explained how Townshend's father had 'broke correspondence with me' at that time, mainly owing to a disagreement between the leading partisans of the two families. 'This bred a coolness and want of visiting between us, and consequently I was ready to oppose your county interest, but with no other personal ill will to you. Things happened afterwards that brought us acquainted, and I was glad of it, in hopes that the old friendship that was between Raynham and Holkham might once more be cemented as it was in my good friend whom I truly loved, your Grandfather's time.' Unluckily their differences of political outlook, more especially over the Militia Bill, had maintained 'county oppositions' between them; 'but personal [oppositions] I never had the least idea of, as I have always been so used to live even in friendship in private life with those who I opposed in publick, that I did not think [political opposition] between people who live in the gay world was ever looked upon as private ill-usage. And as a proof of my thinking you took nothing personally ill of me, as I did not think I had given you any personal reason, I beg'd your excuse from formal visits, which are most regularly kept often where there is most personal dislike, and you very obligingly told me you should not mind them. The same thing I did to Lord Orford who I believe everyone knows I love and have I may in a manner say the tenderness of a Father for, his Father my best friend having desired me to be his guardian if Lord Orford died before his son came of age. This, Sir, I hope you will not think pride, which would indeed be sauciness and insolence in me or any man who should think himself above visiting men of your quality. This I am persuaded you don't impute to ill-neighbourhood, because an unwieldy old fellow can't run about as you young ones do.'

He then turned to the question of the game. 'As for private abetting killing foxes, that I solemnly deny and defy any one to prove, which is my reason my writing so long a letter to clear up other very false informations which I suppose you must have had, to occasion you writing so warm a letter. The foxes just about me you know I kill, and you even told me you did not take it ill; but I daresay you have been informed of ten, to one I killed—at least when I was a foxhunter, those informations were given to me.' On the other hand he had asked his tenants in Townshend's neighbourhood not to disturb the foxes there, and even to maintain coverts for them. He had likewise given orders that the game on the manors near Cranmer should be preserved for Townshend and his friends, and that his own keepers should not go there. 'You charge me with ill-neighbourhood on the reports of others.'

Then he reverted once more to the main subject of Townshend's displeasure. 'If you or any gentleman had told me they look on what I said of the Militia as reflecting on them I should have at once dropt it, for what I meant was not to displease no one man, but to prevent the popularity of the general scheme. I joked with Lord Orford about it at first, but he desired I would not to him, and I never after did. Lord Orford might as well take this as a personal offence to him as you do, but I would so soon bite my tongue off as say anything abusive on him. I assure you I had as little thought that anything I said should be personal against you or any other gentleman as against him who has equally a Commission in the Militia. I write a very long letter, but the affair is serious, and I take the liberty of an old man to clear up things to a young one who I remember quite a child at my friend your Grandfather's and the more so because I see you are very warm and I am sure by your letter you have had false information against me.

'It would grieve you much if, unexplained, things were to be carried to extremity, where you could get no honour by vanquishing a man older than your Father and grown quite unwieldy and unfit for such encounters by a long lazy and inactive life and entire disuse of sword or file, not having for this twenty years wore a sword that could be of any use, and for a pistol I never could hit a barn door with a gun, so it would be difficult for me to chose weapons; and I think to begin to turn duellist in my grand climacterick would be a greater proof of indiscreet rashness than true courage, especially with an Officer who is in the prime of his years and military exercise, as one of your rank in the Army and the station you are going upon must be. I assure you, Sir, I never was afraid of my life, and should by having fewer years to live be less so now, but what formerly might have been both justifiable and incumbent, now I should think ridiculous and rash for an old fellow retired from the world, who cannot even without great fatigue visit his friends, to begin duelling with an Officer of your rank in his prime. At the same time I never was nor ever shall be ashamed to acknowledge myself in the wrong when I really have been so, and even at this age should think I ought to give satisfaction if I had done such injuries to a man as could not be otherwise remedied; but I am sure I never gave you such personal cause.

'I desire you will keep this letter a little time by you, and read it over with patience once or twice; and then if you recollect what it is I am charged with, otherwise than in this letter, I may set right of my having misbehaved to you as a Gentleman and a neighbour. I shall be very ready to give you all the satisfaction in my power; but I believe things even amongst the youngest and warmest Gentlemen are seldom carried to extremity till an explanation is desired. I hope you will read this, though long, and give me an opportunity of explaining myself if you think I have injured you in anything, because at all events I would think myself quite in the right before I persisted in it. As to my intending any rudeness to you, or any particular gentleman in the Militia, in my opposition to the scheme, I declare I meant no such thing, which I hope is satisfactory. If in other matters I have given you any just cause of offence, I shall be very sorry and very much obliged to you to let me know it; for many falsitys are reported and truths set in wrong lights. As for your great warmth against me, I am persuaded it comes from false information, and have such an opinion of your good reason and candour that if you find this is the case you will be sorry for it, as I should be if I really had deserved it. Wherefor as I am too old to commence combatant at this time of life I thought it right to be as explicit as I could, though obliged to be long.

I am, Sir, your most Obedient and Humble Servant

LEICESTER.

With these explanations Townshend professed himself satisfied. His rejoinder began:

My Lord,

Your Lordship having in your letter declared that it was not your intention to insult the Corps of Militia Officers by treating the Militia in the light you have, I apprehend my duty towards my brother Officers discharged by what has now happened; nor is it necessary for me after this to enter into any further discussion unless where some parts of your letter require it absolutely.' He proceeded to comment, a little ungraciously at times but without any trace of his former indignation, upon various passages in Leicester's letter: ending, however, by repeating his satisfaction with the explanations given. 'But my Lord, I will not recur to the subject, and shall conclude with saying that, the publick point answered, I have no resentment remaining on my own; nor shall I ever show any if you do not give me more proofs of your attempts to drive me out of this county—I mean as an inhabitant, not as the Member, for as to the last let every man with freedom follow his inclination in God's name. I do not expect every man's vote; but be he ever so great, common civility I will have, and endeavour to be treated like a Gentleman.'

164

He had not quite finished, all the same. 'I come with concern to another piece of paper'—and the fresh piece of paper was devoted to a long justification of his complaints on the secondary issue of the game. He had complained, at some earlier stage of their disagreements, about Leicester's keeper Palmer. Leicester had called the man 'a good-for-nothing rascal'. Nevertheless 'he continues to this moment destroying every fox in my best hunting country, beyond all the limits I think your Lordship upon Lady Leicester's account declared you should not preserve them. My Lord, as a man of truth and candour, let me ask you where is the difference between suffering your servant to act with impunity in contradiction to really very polite and kind declarations of your own, and the not executing what you yourself have promised?' Suppose one of Townshend's own keepers had taken to snaring the Holkham pheasants—'nay is such a rascal as to carry off even the pyed pheasants Lady Leicester is so fond of'—he himself would have returned a very different answer to the complaints of their owner, and would have discharged the 'poaching incorrigible dog' from his service. 'My Lord I am sorry, really very sorry, to dwell so long upon these matters, which I must repeat are trifles when they do not derive authority from what you yourself have established as the rule of justice and politeness.' He still 'must confess my concern' upon this point; but his tone was now virtually one of jocular remonstrance. He concluded by apologizing 'if I have in this affair given Lady Leicester any alarm or concern'.

With this letter the episode would seem to have been regarded by both parties as closed. There is no reason to suppose that they met or corresponded again, still less that the dispute broke out afresh during the few days that remained before Townshend left England. He sailed for Canada with Wolfe's expedition on the 17th of February. In the months to come he made himself consistently disagreeable to Wolfe, by minor pinpricks in the form of caricatures, and by frequent criticism and a good deal of quiet obstruction. On the other hand he faithfully carried out Wolfe's orders in the various actions, behaved with gallantry in the battle before Quebec, and took command after the death of Wolfe and the disablement by wounds of Monckton, the senior Brigadier. In that capacity he received the surrender of Quebec, and arranged the terms of capitulation.

On the 20th of April of the same year Lord Leicester died at Holkham. There is no word in any contemporary letter, memoir, book, pamphlet, magazine or newspaper to suggest that his death was due to anything but a natural cause; not the remotest hint that he had sustained a fatal wound in a duel fought earlier in the year.

IV

What, then, gave rise to the story? Presumably Townshend's challenge was the basis of some oral tradition of a duel, which persisted through the years and into the twentieth century. So far as I know, it did not appear in print before 1908, when Mrs. Stirling's *Coke of Norfolk and his Friends* was first published. Unless some earlier instance has escaped me, it might be regarded as almost conclusive evidence against the duel that no mention of such an event was made in print until 150 years after its alleged occurrence.

Mrs. Stirling was inclined to give some credit to the story; and she quoted in support of her view some contemporary comments in a letter from the Rev. Edmund Pyle in London to the Rev. Samuel Kerrich at Dersingham in Norfolk. Writing on 20th May 1759, Mr. Pyle remarked: 'Lord L. is dead since you wrote. I wish, with 1,000 more, that his antagonist were in the shades too (provided his family were no sufferers:) for I hold him, and his brother Charles, to be two most dangerous men; as having parts that enable them to do great mischief, and no principles that lead them to do any good. The challenger was (by confession of his friends) drunk when he wrote to Lord L.—of whom, notwithstanding what I have said here, I was never an admirer. But in the case under consideration, how can one help being of his side? He spoke contemptuously of the Militia—very true—and so do thousands. It has been burlesqued in publick papers, over and over again, and treated with the highest scorn and satire. Yet

The Hon.ᵇˡᵉ Colonel Townshend

COL. THE HON. GEORGE TOWNSHEND
*from a mezzotint by James McArdell
after a painting by Thomas Hudson*

because Lord L. was a little severe upon it at his table he is to be challenged, truly!—and by whom—why, by G.T., a man whose licentious tongue spares not the most sacred characters. . . . This is the man, that denounces death to any one that shall dare to scout a silly project that he thinks fit to espouse—and insists on being received seriously by the English nation. In troth, my good friend, things, at this rate, are come to a rare pass. Noble or ignoble, old or young, are all to look with awe and reverence, on whatever this spark shall think fit to declare for, at the peril of their lives.'

Surely there is no justification for interpreting Mr. Pyle's remarks to mean that Townshend had actually killed Lord Leicester, or that a duel had in fact taken place. The writer was shocked by Townshend's challenge to an older man who had merely disagreed with his opinions. If Lord Leicester had been killed in the duel, Pyle's expressions of horror would have been much stronger, his whole tone far more grave. The controversy between these two prominent personages had aroused wide interest in Norfolk; and they could well be described as 'antagonists' without having given up their pens for more dangerous weapons. A clergyman like Mr. Pyle was naturally distressed at an elderly and infirm civilian of sixty-three being challenged to a duel by a hotheaded young officer of thirty-five. He possibly also felt that the worry and agitation of the dispute had contributed to bring about Lord Leicester's death. And this may indeed have been so, although the tone of his reply to the challenge suggests that he was not greatly perturbed by Townshend's menaces.

In any case, the conclusive point against the duel is the entire lack of contemporary evidence. A fatal affray between the head of the Cokes and the heir of the Townshends would have caused an immense sensation, not only in Norfolk, but in London and throughout the country. Yet in the histories, memoirs and letters of the time there is no mention whatever of any such occurrence. Horace Walpole, whose ambition it was to record in his letters and memoirs the entire panorama of contemporary English history, would have written pages on pages about such a duel if it had actually taken place. Nothing escaped those inquisitive eyes, that tireless pen; but he says not a word about it. Nor did Townshend's enemies ever bring the matter up against him. Later in 1759 he came under a fire of criticism for his conduct to Wolfe during the campaign which ended at Quebec. His assailants would have been delighted to add to his misdemeanours the fact that, just before he sailed, he had mortally wounded an elderly and inoffensive nobleman; but they said nothing of the kind. Some while afterwards the Norfolk satirist, Richard Gardiner, fell foul of Townshend, and devoted himself to vilifying him for years. Yet in all Gardiner's writings against Townshend, I have only found one reference to the dispute with Lord Leicester, in a poem entitled *Raynham in the Dumps:*

> *Much injur'd Shade of LE-ST-R, see!*
> *Thy full revenge is taken. . . .*

This is no stronger than Pyle's 'antagonist'. If Gardiner had thought that Townshend had killed Leicester in a duel, his pamphlets and poems would have rung with epithets of which 'murderer' would have been among the mildest.

Finally, there can be no question, as has been suggested, that the duel took place and was hushed up. Considering the high station of the participants, it would have been the sort of occurrence that no influence or power could have hushed up for a single day. And in any case, though it would have been in the Townshend interest to keep the matter dark, there could have been no reason for the Cokes to conceal the monstrous injury done to the head of their house. But Townshend's career remained unsullied by a deed which would have been regarded as little short of murder. He was destined to become a Field-Marshal, a Marquess, a Viceroy of Ireland. He lived on into the nineteenth century, a figure of immense dignity and prestige, with his earlier indiscretions long since forgotten; and among them this quarrel, so typical of many of the quarrels of his age, in which the resort to arms was avoided by common-sense, by an ability to compromise, even by a due perception of the ridiculous.

Part III

★

PLACES AND THINGS

THE TOUR OF NORFOLK

I

When the cult of the Picturesque first spread across England, its devotees were slow to discover the unspectacular beauties of East Anglia. They made their way to the Lakes, the Peak, Dovedale, the Wye Valley, the southern coasts, the more accessible parts of Wales. Their chaises were rarely to be seen crossing our heaths and venturing down our lanes. The poet Gray often stayed during the seventeen-sixties with two of his friends who were clergymen in Suffolk, and visited many of its churches and its ruined castles; but his letters contain no praises of the countryside which Gainsborough had already painted so exquisitely, and which was soon to find its supreme interpreter in Constable. The Reverend William Gilpin, that high priest of the Picturesque, toured Norfolk in 1769, but his commendations of the scenery were seldom more than lukewarm. Perhaps Humphry Repton, writing about 1780, was the first observer to remark upon the vast spreading distances of Norfolk, the rich arable lands, the innumerable hedgerow trees which added 'a prodigious softness to the landskip, that in many parts appears to be one continued grove of many miles extent'. And even he does not seem to have commented upon the marvellous effects of light and cloud, the endless variety of the windy skies.

But long before the county was allowed to contain even the smallest element of the Picturesque, the tour of Norfolk was regularly undertaken for the sake of certain great houses, their architecture, their contents and their associations. Houghton and Holkham, Blickling and Raynham, Wolterton and Narford—these were the magnets which drew travellers from London and the furthest shires. Otherwise, wrote in 1758 the learned Dr. Charles Lyttelton, Dean of Exeter and presently to be Bishop of Carlisle, 'very few strangers would visit a County that has so few natural Beautys to attract them'. Duly averting their eyes from the landscape, the *connoisseurs* of architecture and painting, and many sightseers who were nothing of the kind, presented themselves at these remarkable houses in a steady stream. As the century proceeded, the Tour of Norfolk ceased to be a haphazard affair and developed into a routine progress from one house to the next. This chapter is designed to trace the story of these houses, and to follow some of the travellers upon their journey.

II

At the beginning of the eighteenth century, the largest and most important houses in Norfolk were Raynham, Blickling and Oxnead. Much is said of Oxnead elsewhere in this book, and need not be repeated here. It is sufficient to know that the end of the house, and of the Paston family, was already in sight. The last Earl of Yarmouth was hopelessly entangled in debt. The hospitality of Oxnead, at one time unrivalled in East Anglia, was a distant memory; and its prosperous days were never to return.

Blickling, for so many years past the Puritan and Whig stronghold, the headquarters of opposition to the monarchical and Tory activities of the Pastons in their heyday, was also at this time a house of sadness, a house without a master. In the summer of 1698 its owner, Sir Henry Hobart, had been killed in a duel over an election dispute by a neighbouring squire, Oliver le Neve, and his heir was a child of four. But Blickling was to enjoy the coming sunshine of the Whig supremacy, while Oxnead passed into final eclipse. The Hobarts would rise high in Hanoverian favour, and prosper greatly throughout the century.

Loveliest and most serene of Jacobean houses, Blickling was strangely out of fashion throughout the eighteenth century. Even though its mellow beauty made no appeal to the strict Palladian eye, it might surely have roused the antiquarian enthusiasms which were also cherished by most persons of taste. After all, they were solemnly shown the bedroom in which Anne Boleyn had been born; and only the more historically-minded were aware that in fact the house had not been built until almost a century after her death. But even Dr. Charles Lyttelton, who was soon to become President of the Society of Antiquaries, dismissed Blickling, apart from its gallery, as 'a bad old House'; and the verdict of many other visitors was the same. It may indeed be that the place presented a somewhat unfinished appearance. The west front was still unbuilt, and remained so until the first wife of the second Earl of Buckinghamshire, at her death in 1769, bequeathed her jewels for the express purpose of completing it. But even after that was done, and the commendable alterations by the Ivory family of architects had been carried out, there remained the same note of reservation. It was left to the nineteenth and twentieth centuries to admire Blickling as the place deserves.

No such reservations were expressed about Raynham. The architect of the house, built a decade or so later than Blickling, was universally believed to be Inigo Jones, despite its Flemish gables and other features which were unlikely to have formed part of any design by that master. The name of Jones acted like a talisman to the Palladians, and to everyone else. No fault was ever found with Raynham. And indeed it was, and is, a splendid and historic house—'the noblest Pyle among us' in the eyes of Sir Thomas Browne, writing during the Commonwealth years; the noblest pile still in the reign of King George I.

Its owner, moreover, was the most important Norfolk figure of the day. Charles, second Viscount Townshend, was a young man, one of the rising hopes of the Whig party, and already beginning to play some part in national affairs. His supremacy in all local business was unquestioned. 'The Lord Townshend', wrote Dean Prideaux in 1708, 'florisheth much among us, for the whole countey is absolutely at his beck, and he hath got such an ascendant here over everybody by his courteous carriage that he may doe anything among us what he will.' No one could suppose that this ascendancy was likely to be challenged, in any possible respect, by the ambitious young Member of Parliament for King's Lynn, Robert Walpole.

III

Two decades later the scene had changed. As the years went by, Walpole had gradually drawn level with Townshend. In national politics and in local affairs they had established a partnership of perfect harmony. Their friendship was ratified when Townshend married one of Walpole's sisters as his second wife. At the accession of George I they were both called to high office; and after the South Sea Bubble they virtually directed the Government, Walpole as First Minister and Townshend as Secretary of State. Then in 1730 their long association, which for some considerable time had been subjected to strain, was severed by a violent quarrel. Townshend resigned and withdrew to Raynham, to pass his remaining years in the agricultural developments associated with his name. Walpole remained at the head of affairs, in effect the ruler of Great Britain.

Many observers had attributed the growing coolness between the brothers-in-law to Townshend's jealousy of Walpole's great new house at Houghton, which he had begun to build in 1722. Lord Hervey, for example, spoke of 'this fabric of fraternal discord', and affirmed that Townshend 'considered every stone that augmented the splendour of Houghton as a diminution of the grandeur of Raynham'. Even to an easy-tempered man it might have been a galling situation; and Townshend himself once confessed that 'I know I am extremely warm'. Despite his many years of office, and all the golden opportunities which they presented, he had added nothing to his paternal fortune. Walpole had begun his career as a squire of very moderate estate; yet he was now enabled to raise a palace whose splendour astonished the whole country.

Year after year the structure rose. Where Raynham and all other Norfolk houses had been built of the local bricks, everything at Houghton was of stone brought from afar. Colen Campbell's plan was adjusted and brought to completion by Thomas Ripley, the *protégé* of the Walpole family and the butt of Pope, whose ridicule he did not deserve. The entire decoration and furnishings of the interior were superbly designed by William Kent—ceilings and cornices and door-cases, beds and tables and chairs. The Hall, the Saloon, the Marble Parlour, the State Bedchamber, the Library, the Hunting Parlour, room after room was created. And every room was filled with Sir Robert Walpole's collection of paintings, the like of which had not been seen in England since the men of the Commonwealth dispersed the treasures of King Charles I.

The building and the decoration of Houghton were at last completed in 1735, thirteen years after the laying of the foundation stone. But long before that date it had already become the scene of the Norfolk Congresses, those meetings at which Walpole's political associates and his local supporters used to foregather each summer for some crowded weeks of hunting, feasting, drinking and the transaction of important business. And long before that date, too, designs were being prepared and discussed for yet another great house by which Houghton in its turn was to be rivalled. Thomas Coke of Holkham had determined to give reality to his long-cherished dream of a vast Palladian mansion, filled with all the works of art which he had collected during his protracted sojourn in Italy.

Thomas Coke was born in 1697, and at his parents' early death had come into the inheritance of a great estate. When still a boy he had left England for an unusually prolonged Grand Tour, six years of travel and the pursuit of *virtù*, during which he acquired many of the paintings, sculptures and manuscripts which are the glory of Holkham today. Most of all he had engaged in the study of architecture. On his return to England he joined the group of Palladian enthusiasts whose leaders were the Earls of Burlington and Pembroke, and whose favourite architect William Kent, their admired 'Signior', he had known well in Italy. He engaged actively in politics, and his services to Walpole's government were recognized in 1728 by his elevation to the peerage as Lord Lovell, and later by an advance to the Earldom of Leicester. But his deepest interest was the planning, with Kent and Lord Burlington and his other friends, of the masterpiece of classical architecture which was to replace the cramped old-fashioned home of his ancestors on the windswept coast at Holkham. In 1734, a year before the completion of Houghton, the foundations of the new Holkham were laid.

At Houghton only the interior decoration had been the work of Kent. At Holkham he was responsible for everything —the ground plan, the elevations, all the decoration, all the furniture, the planting of the woods, the layout of the park and the buildings which were to adorn it. His taste was wholly in sympathy with that of his client, and the two men worked together in absolute harmony. Burlington and the other Palladians were consulted at intervals, as the walls of white Norfolk brick steadily rose, their sober correctitude masking an interior of the utmost state and richness. The splendours of the building culminated in the Great Hall, based upon a design of Vitruvius for a Temple of Justice, with its colonnade of alabaster columns and its rich coffered ceiling. This hall is surely Kent's crowning achievement as an architect, even as Holkham is the masterpiece of all his buildings. But he was dead long before the house was completed, and before Coke could place above the entrance to the hall his tablet with the proud inscription: 'This Seat, on an open barren Estate, was planned, planted, built, decorated and inhabited the middle of the XVIIIth Century by Thomas Coke, Earl of Leicester.'

At Raynham, too, the same assiduous hand was to be traced. Lord Townshend had decided, about the time of his retirement in 1730, to remodel much of the interior of the house, and Kent was employed to design the alterations. The entrance hall, with its elaborate plasterwork ceiling and frieze, is a noble example of his work. So is the room on the first floor, known to generations of travellers as the Belisarius Room from the painting by Salvator Rosa of that unfortunate hero in the days of his penury. It is a singular circumstance that these three houses—Houghton, Holkham and Raynham—situated a few miles apart in the north-west of Norfolk, embody the greater part of all Kent's surviving domestic architecture.

During the years when Sir Robert Walpole was building Houghton, his younger brother Horatio was similarly occupied on his newly-acquired estate at Wolterton in the north of the county. Horatio Walpole, afterwards the first Lord Walpole of Wolterton, was an able politician and diplomatist, and his brother's right-hand man in the execution of his foreign policy. In that capacity he spent long periods abroad, twice as Plenipotentiary at The Hague, and from 1723 until 1730 as Ambassador at Paris. It was owing to these absences that Wolterton, although a much smaller house, was even longer in building than Houghton. As befitted the younger brother, it was altogether a less grandiose affair. Instead of Houghton's massy stone, Ripley used at Wolterton a beautiful pale red brick with Portland stone facings. The house was beautifully situated, admirably planned, and decorated with sober richness. Even Horace Walpole, who detested the uncle from whom he derived his name, was obliged to admit that it was 'one of the best houses of its size in England'. On another occasion he wrote: 'I really was charmed with Wolterton, it is all wood and water.'

Far away in the south-west lay Narford, the house built at the beginning of the century by Sir Andrew Fountaine. The creator of Narford was a well-known figure in his day—the familiar friend of Swift, Newton's successor as Master of the Mint, Vice-Chamberlain to Queen Caroline, Pope's victim under the guise of Annius. A lifelong virtuoso, he assembled at Narford a truly remarkable collection of pictures, statuary, objects of antiquity, coins, books, and in particular a wealth of majolica and Limoges enamels. The house, with its hall and staircase frescoed by Pellegrini, was crammed with these treasures; and Fountaine, having withdrawn from his London life about 1732, led a retired and rather solitary existence amongst them until his death twenty years later.

There were other places in Norfolk which were occasionally visited by travellers—Oxburgh, so romantic with its towers and its tranquil moat; Melton Constable, a stately example of seventeenth-century classicism; the lesser Tudor and Jacobean mansions such as Heydon, Barningham, Felbrigg. But the Tour of Norfolk was really undertaken for the sake of the six outstanding houses whose history has now been briefly outlined—Blickling, Raynham, Houghton, Holkham, Wolterton and Narford.

IV

In the summer of 1731 the stream of visitors to Norfolk included two men unusually well qualified to appraise, respectively, the social and the architectural aspects of its great houses. These were John Lord Hervey and Sir Thomas Robinson of Rokeby. Hervey, who had been appointed Vice-Chamberlain to King George II and Queen Caroline in the previous year, was commanded by the Prince of Wales to send him 'a very particular account of this place', and did so in letters full of the same sharpness of wit as his admirable *Memoirs*. Robinson, more interested on the whole in buildings than in people, described what he saw in lengthy dispatches to his father-in-law Lord Carlisle.

The building of Houghton was now nearing completion, and the surrounding landscape was already changed almost beyond recognition. Hervey, the heir to the beautifully diversified park of Ickworth, could only commiserate Sir Robert on the flatness of the Houghton countryside. 'The soil is not fruitful, there is little wood, and no water. . . . These are disadvantages he had to struggle with, when that natural leaning to the paternal field and the scene of his youth, a bias which everybody feels and nobody can account for, determined him to adorn and settle at Houghton. He has already, by the force of manuring and planting, so changed the face of the country, that his park is a pleasant, fertile island of his own creation in the middle of a naked sea of land.'

Hervey disclaimed exact architectural knowledge. 'As to the style of a virtuoso, I own I am not ambitious to learn it, for, by the technical jargon of a true follower of Palladio and Vertuvius [*sic*], one would imagine that a modern architect must have as great a contempt for his mother tongue as his grandfather's taste.' Nevertheless he described the house in considerable detail, most of which need not be reproduced here. Several rooms were not yet finished, but the great house was already throbbing with life and assuming its own character. The ground floor, 'the base or rustic story', was brought into fullest use at the Congresses—'your Royal Highness must perceive that the whole is dedicated to fox-

178

hunters, hospitality, noise, dirt and business'. The *piano nobile*, on the other hand, 'is the floor of taste, expense, state and parade'. The stucco-work of the Great Hall surpassed anything he had seen in any country. The Saloon was completed, and already hung with some of Sir Robert's finest pictures. The furniture designed by Kent would soon be in place. 'The great staircase is the gayest, cheerfullest and prettiest thing I ever saw; some very beautiful heresies in the particulars, and the result of the whole more charming than any bigotry I ever saw.'

The party went over to dine with Lord Lovell, already engrossed in the plans for his future palace, at the old house of the Cokes at Holkham. 'It is at present a most unpleasant place; but he comforts himself with a park in embryo, and a Burlington house with four pavilions on paper.' They went to see Narford, 'which is absolutely the prettiest trinket I ever saw. My Lord Burlington could not make a better ragoust of paintings, statues, gilding and virtù!' And, despite the recent political breach between Sir Robert Walpole and Lord Townshend, they also went to see Raynham. 'It is great, noble and complete. It has all the advantages Nature can bestow in the situation, and all the additions Art can make in the finishing. Wood, lawn and water can produce nothing more beautiful than the park; Kent, gilding and expense can add nothing to the house.' Finally, before Hervey retired to the tranquil glades of Ickworth, 'our company at Houghton swelled at last into so numerous a party that we used to sit down to dinner a little snug party of about thirty odd, up to the chin in beef, venison, geese, turkeys, etc.; and generally over the chin in claret, strong beer and punch. We had Lords spiritual and temporal, besides commoners, parsons and freeholders innumerable. In public we drank loyal healths, talked of the times and cultivated popularity: in private we drew plans and cultivated the country.'

It is not certain whether Sir Thomas Robinson was at Houghton at the same time as Hervey. If so, he would undoubtedly have been prominent on the occasions when plans were being drawn. He was a much travelled young man, a great *connoisseur* of architecture, with a passion for expensive building which he indulged to the serious detriment of his fortunes. He greatly enjoyed his week at Houghton. 'We were generally between twenty and thirty at two tables, and as much cheerfulness and good nature as I ever saw where the company was so numerous. . . . Sir Robert does the honours of his house extremely well, and so as to make it perfectly agreeable to everyone who lives with him.' There was hunting throughout the week, three days with fox-hounds and three with harriers.

His description of the house is evidence of the impression made by its scale and splendour upon the most informed contemporary observers. 'I believe it is the best house in the world for its size, capable of the greatest reception for company, and the most convenient state apartments, very noble, especially the hall and saloon. The finishing of the inside is, I think, a pattern for all great houses that may hereafter be built; the vast quantity of mahogoni, all the doors, window-shutters, best staircase, &c. being entirely of that wood; the finest chimnies of statuary and other fine marbles; the ceilings in the modern taste by Italians, painted by Mr Kent, and finely gilt; the furniture of the richest tapestry; the pictures hung on Genoa velvet and damask; this one article is the price of a good house, for in one drawing-room there are to the value of three thousand pounds; in short, the whole expense of this place must be a prodigious sum, and, I think, all done in a fine taste.'

Robinson had much to say also about the offices, stables, gardens and park. He tried to persuade his host to build his new stables as wings to the east front of the house, but Sir Robert was in favour of a detached quadrangle some considerable distance away; and this was eventually carried out. The landscape gardener Charles Bridgman was engaged in laying out the plantations, and there was much discussion of his designs. There were to be 'plumps and avenues to go quite round the park pale, and to make straight and oblique lines of a mile or two in length, as the situation of the country admits of. This design will be about twelve miles in circumference, and nature has disposed of the country so as these plantations will have a very noble and fine effect; and at every angle there are to be obelisks, or some other building. In short, the out-works at Houghton will be 200 years hence what those at Castle Howard are now, for he has very little full-grown timber, and not a drop of water for ornament; but take all together, it is a seat so perfectly magnificent and agreeable, that I think nothing but envy itself can find fault because there is no more of the one, and I scarce missed the entire want of the other.'

Robinson saw and admired Raynham, being especially im-pressed by the woods and the size of the oaks. He was also taken to see Lord Lovell in his 'exceeding bad old house', and shook his head over the ambitious nature of his projects, with so many disadvantages to overcome, and so much 'to be com-passed only by art, time and expense'. But we must pass to the following year and to a very different traveller, dis-gruntled where Hervey and Robinson were enthusiastic, and politically at odds with Walpole and the other Whig poten-tates of Norfolk. This was Edward Harley, second Earl of Oxford, the son of Queen Anne's Tory minister. He was an indolent and somewhat ineffectual figure, best remembered as the friend of Pope and Prior and many other literary men, and as an insatiable collector of books and prints. It was his frequent custom to make an expedition to some distant part of the country, and to record his experiences in a journal. In Septem-ber 1732 he travelled into the eastern counties, accompanied by his wife and his daughter Lady Margaret Cavendish Harley, who had been commemorated in childhood as 'my noble, lovely, little Peggy' in one of Prior's most charming poems.

Lord Oxford was a good-natured man, but he cherished a particular scorn for the Burlington group of *cognoscenti* and for their favourite Kent. His comments upon them, and upon his other aversions such as bad inns and Whiggish clergymen, impart an agreeably choleric air to his journal. They passed the second night of their tour at Bury St. Edmunds, where they admired the churches, disapproved of the assembly rooms, and noted that the abbey gateway was being used as the lodging of a performing bear. Their own lodging was the Angel, 'one of the worst inns I ever was at. It is kept by one Hannibal Hill, a great sot, being now quite stupid, whatever

181

he might have been. The room we dined in is much decorated (as Mr. Kent's phrase is, and those that follow him) with the paintings or rather daubings of one Bryan Hill, nephew to our landlord. The works of this gentleman's hand are the only proper pieces to decorate the buildings of Mr. Kent or his great patron the Earl of Burlington, and I wish he was their sworn servant, only to attend them and their operations, that he might not fall in the way of any honest gentleman to cheat him of his money.' His opinion of the Scole Inn and of the Swan at Harleston was equally unflattering.

The party was greatly pleased with the neatness, decorum and general prosperity of Yarmouth. The town was so well managed that they did not see a single beggar in the streets; the herrings were the most delicious they had ever tasted; and altogether it was 'the prettiest seaport town that belongs to this island'. As they approached Norwich they were surprised, as so many other travellers have been, by the beauty and variety of this reputedly flat and uninteresting countryside. 'Between Blofield and Norwich is a most noble prospect and extremely beautiful. When you come upon the hill, on the left hand you overlook a fine rich vale, the river Yare running in fine windings, the hills at a proper distance clothed with fine woods, and the other part cultivated, either grass ground or ploughed, and farmhouses scattered up and down, making all together a most beautiful landscape, worthy to have been imitated by the famous landskip painter Gaspar Poussin.' They stayed in comfort at the Maid's Head, where they were offered the choice of thirteen different sorts of liquors, and spent a day in exploring the city. In an outburst of Tory prejudice, Oxford described the Bishop, Dr. William Baker, as 'a most worthless wretch'. In the same vein he noted next day at Fakenham that the rector, Dr. Hackett, whose fine portrait still hangs in the church, was 'an infamous rascal'.

At Fakenham they put up at the Red Lion, 'a sorry house', and went over to Raynham early next day. There they were cordially welcomed by Lord Townshend and his family, dined with him, rode about the park and surveyed the agricultural improvements which were the solace of his last years. The disappointed Whig exchanged confidences with the disappointed

Tory. 'He is resolved never to see London again. It is happy for him that he can live contentedly here and free from the storms and shipwrecks of State. I think he has been a very fortunate man to get himself so well out from the politicians and courtiers and ministers.' Oxford was immensely impressed by the beauty of the place—'it is by much the finest in England that ever I saw'—and likewise admired the house, with the exception of the recent improvements. 'The rooms are fitted up by Mr. Kent, and consequently there is a great deal of gilding; very clumsy over-charged chimney pieces to the great waste of fine marble. Kent has parted the dining-room, to make a sort of buffet, by the arch of Severus; surely a most preposterous thing to introduce a building in a room, which was designed to stand in the street!'

Later in the day they went on to Houghton, where Oxford was obviously determined to approve of nothing. 'This house has made a great deal of noise, but I think it is not deserving of it. Some admire it because it belongs to the first Minister; others envy it because it is his, and consequently rail at it. These gentlemen's praise and blame are not worth anything, because they know nothing of the art of building, or anything about it. I think it is neither magnificent nor beautiful, there is a very great expense without either judgment or taste.' The original architect, Colen Campbell, was 'an ignorant rascal': indeed 'the house as it is now is a composition of the greatest blockheads and most ignorant fellows in architecture that are'. The hanging of the pictures in the Saloon was all wrong; the Great Hall was overcrowded with terms and bustos, and much too dark; Sir Robert's bed was 'shut up in a box, a case made of mahogany with glass, as if it were a cabin'; the quantity of mahogany used in the doors revealed 'the greatest profusion and waste'; the rooms on the ground floor had 'a very ill look'. As for the gardens, 'we did not go into them, we saw enough of them from the windows'. There was really nothing to commend except the kitchen. And so away, through 'a fine moonshiny night', to King's Lynn.[1]

---

[1] Lord Oxford visited Houghton again in 1737. He was hospitably welcomed by Sir Robert Walpole's eldest son, and stayed a couple of nights in the house. The remarks in his journal on this occasion are considerably more cordial.

Places and Things

The last visit of their tour was to Narford, the home of a rival collector and *connoisseur*. 'It is a pretty box, a great deal of gilding and painting, done by very bad hands.' Poor Pellegrini, whose charming frescoes still adorn the house today! 'The library is very smart and beauish, there are round the room the heads of several learned men, but very ill done.' Sir Andrew Fountaine was at pains to show them all his treasures, but there was no pleasing Lord Oxford. He took them to his china room through the kitchen, 'perhaps to show us that meat was dressing there, and more than ordinary because my Lord Lovell was to dine with him, and at the same time to wipe off the scandal that his kitchen was so neat no meat was ever dressed in it'. When they reached the china room it was 'a most wretched place, set out upon shelves like a shop, no old china, a mere baby room'. So much for one of the most justly celebrated collections of the time, which the engraver George Vertue, visiting Narford seven years later, described as 'a most rare cabinet of earthenware, painted, gilded and adorned, with great beauty and variety . . . ranged in the most elegant and delightful order possibly can be imagined'. But there was nothing that the disgruntled peer consented to admire, except a Chinese pheasant and the rivulet running through the garden.

V

Let us move on a couple of decades, into the seventeen-fifties. Roads and vehicles were steadily improving; more people were moving about the country, and with greater ease and comfort. The practice of visiting great houses was growing more widespread, and at the same time more standardized. It was customary for travellers to seek admission, and indeed to expect it almost as a right, at any notable house. At a few places, access was seldom or never granted; at others it was granted only in the absence of the family; in certain cases a special day was set aside for tourists. Towards the end of the century that delightful diarist John Byng, afterwards the fifth Viscount Torrington, who often travelled on horseback alone and unattended, describes with his usual rueful humour more than one occasion when he was refused admission to a house which he had gone a long distance to see. But generally speaking any visitor or party of visitors, if their appearance and equipage were reasonably 'genteel', might expect to be admitted on most days of the week, and shown round the principal rooms by the housekeeper or some upper servant. A substantial gratuity was expected in return. It was not invariably bestowed. Horace Walpole records an occasion when his father's old adversary William Pulteney, Earl of Bath, and his family visited Holkham, forgot to give anything to the servants, and then sent one of his retinue galloping back six miles with half a crown. The travellers on their part expected refreshments to be offered. Again, this courtesy was not always observed. A discontented visitor described his experiences at Houghton and Narford in an indignant epigram:

> *We saw* Sir Andrew's, *but* Lord Walpoole's *first.*
> *At both, we felt a Calenture of Thirst:*
> *At both, we sought in vain our Throats to cool:*
> *Dry was the* Fountain, *and as dry the* Poole.

An ever-swelling stream of travellers undertook the Tour of Norfolk—politicians, clergymen, agriculturists, artists, learned ladies and ladies of fashion, every sort of person. By now Sir Robert Walpole was dead, and Houghton was declining into impoverishment and confusion under his spendthrift grandson. Raynham, Blickling, Narford, Wolterton continued to flourish. But the great wonder of Norfolk was now Holkham, still growing every year in size and splendour. It made the same overwhelming impression upon travellers as Houghton had done twenty years before. 'To a man of your taste no part of England is so well worth a visit as Norfolk,' wrote Sir George Lyttelton to his friend the amateur architect Sanderson Miller. 'Lord Leicester's alone would pay you the trouble and expense of your journey . . . and even Lord Leicester's wants the view of a Gothick Castle to make it compleat, of which he himself is so sensible that he has desired me to make interest with you to come and give him a plan.' A Gothick Castle would have been an unexpected lapse on the part of so

strict a Palladian, and it is not surprising that this adornment
to Holkham was never carried out.

Sir George's younger brother, the Dean of Exeter, took a
much less favourable view of Norfolk. His contempt for its
landscape, and his dismissal of Blickling as 'a bad old house',
have already been quoted. He was a tedious letter-writer, and
there is really nothing worthy of quotation in his conventional
praises of Holkham and Houghton. He did not really enjoy
his tour of Norfolk, and in due course the reason becomes
apparent. 'The Accomodations at the Inns in general are bad,
which would be the less felt, if the gentlemen were more
hospitable; but you will allow me to say that Hospitality does
not remarkably flourish in Norfolk, when I assure you that
except at the Palace at Norwich, where the Bishop does great
honour to himself and to his station by his noble and generous
Hospitality, I was not offered the least refreshment, but a
glass of wine at Lord Leicester's, at any House I visited in the
whole County.'

A much better writer was Miss Caroline Girle, aged
seventeen, who paid a visit in the summer of 1756 to a family
called Jackson who lived at Weasenham Hall. She derived
great entertainment from her stay in Norfolk, and employed
a sharp eye and an active pen to the full. She had much to say
about Houghton and Holkham, although she looked at the
latter house so superficially as to mistake its white brick for
stone. She and her party fared better there than the Dean of
Exeter, since 'we had a breakfast in the genteelest taste, with
all kinds of cakes and fruit, placed undesired in an apartment
we were to go through, which, as the family were from home,
I thought was very clever in the housekeeper, for one is so
often asked by people whether one *chuses* chocolate, which forbidding word puts (as intended) a negative upon the question'.
But her real interest was in people—the household at Weasenham, with its long-established servants in green camblet
gowns; the parson and his wife, 'a good kind of ordinary
couple', whose vicarage was nothing but a poor thatched
cottage; and poor Edward Spelman of Westacre, 'a most
strange old bachelor of vast fortune, but indeed I'll not fall in
love with him', sitting in his library, 'where he seemed deep

in study (for they say he is really clever) in a jockey-cap and white stiff dog's gloves'. Since he produced excellent translations of Xenophon and Dionysius Halicarnassiensis, some degree of cleverness may certainly be allowed to Edward Spelman.[1]

Miss Girle was followed, within a few years, by ladies of greater celebrity—Mrs. Delany, for example, and Miss Hannah More. The latter was inspired by the dining-room at Houghton to classical raptures. It was so exquisite a room, 'with marble recesses, columns, and cisterns, that I fancied myself at the villa of Pliny, or of Lucullus; and though I cannot bear oysters, yet I could have eaten some conchylia of the lake we saw out of the window; and I drank, in idea, a glass of Falernian, of twenty consulships, cooled by the elemental nymph'. She duly admired the curiosities at Narford, the painting of Belisarius at Raynham, the 'state and commodiousness, beauty and elegance' of Holkham. Unlike most of her fellow-travellers in the eighteenth century, she was moved by the serene beauty of Blickling. After all, she was a poet in her fashion, Horace Walpole's 'tenth muse'. 'You admire Houghton, but you wish for Blickling; you look at Houghton with astonishment, at Blickling with desire.' And while Mrs. Delany had tittered at the flatness of Norfolk, and pretended that she could not see a tree or shrub which might shade the turnips, Miss More perceived that 'the charms of nature in this county are of the middling, calm, and pacific sort—she does not put forth her bolder, stronger beauties'.

VI

All the foregoing accounts of the Norfolk Tour are taken from printed sources, some of them obscure enough. But the journals of Lady Beauchamp Proctor have remained entirely unpublished until I was allowed to make use of them through the kindness of their present owner, a descendant of the sister for whose amusement she wrote them. None of these other

---

[1] In 1781 Miss Girle (now Mrs. Lybbe Powys) made a second tour in Norfolk, but nothing in her journal on that occasion calls for quotation.

travellers, it seems to me, have described their experiences so personally, so gaily, and with the same profusion of detail.

Early in the seventeen-sixties Sir William Beauchamp Proctor, of Langley Park in Norfolk, married as his second wife Letitia, daughter of Henry Johnson of Berkhampstead in Hertfordshire. Her father had amassed a large fortune in South America, and gained some reputation in his day as a traveller and writer. Sir William had been for many years one of the Members of Parliament for Middlesex, and is perhaps best remembered now for the violent contest in which he was defeated by Wilkes in 1768. His young wife was a stranger to Norfolk, and her new home was situated rather remotely in the south-eastern corner of the county. From Langley a tour of the great houses in the north and west of Norfolk was something of an adventure, an expedition not to be undertaken lightly. In 1764, soon after her marriage, and again in 1772, she and her husband and some of their friends made such a tour; and on both occasions she described her experiences in journals addressed to her sister Agneta, the wife of the Hon. Charles Yorke, the ill-fated politician who was to become Lord Chancellor in 1770 and to die only three days afterwards.

On the first occasion the party set out from Langley at eleven o'clock on a Sunday morning, the 8th of July 1764. Lady Beauchamp Proctor travelled in the family coach and six, together with two friends, Mrs. Tyson and Mrs. Barton, and her maid. Sir William and Mr. Barton followed in the post-chaise. They dined and drank tea at the King's Head in Norwich, and then set out for Aylsham, where they arrived at the Black Boys at eight in the evening. The road between Norwich and Aylsham was excellent, and they thought the countryside very beautiful, as no doubt it was, with Robert Marsham's plantations in the rich verdure of their early growth. The little town of Aylsham, so charming in our eyes today, merely struck them as 'neat and clean', and they were principally impressed by the fact that it boasted the establishments of two undertakers, who lived just opposite one another. But the charges at the Black Boys were very reasonable, the beds were tolerable, and they set out for Blickling next morning in cheerful spirits.

188

The Tour of Norfolk

Lady Beauchamp Proctor, like most of her contemporaries, was not greatly impressed by Blickling. ''Tis a fine old house,' she wrote, 'but no room remarkable except the library; the ceiling is very antient, and as I am fond of antiquities, pleased me very much. Most of the apartments are hung with India paper . . . the beds are all double under one tester, and curtains let down in the middle to part those who lie in them, an odd fancy. The park is full of young wood, very little timber; there is a good piece of water, no prospects worth mentioning, and I think on the whole but a dull place.'

From Blickling it was only a short drive to Wolterton. Horace Walpole's praises of the house—its size, its planning, the profusion of wood and water around it—have already been quoted; and Lady Beauchamp Proctor took a similar view. 'The house is extremely convenient without being grand, the furniture is all good, and some very fine; beautiful tapestry chairs and hangings, an elegant set of French worked chairs, fine Egyptian marble slabs and chimney pieces, noble glasses, many Japan'd chests, etc. Here is a good picture of the present King of France, when young, and the pictures of all our Royal Family, I mean the last generation, very ill done. There are some fresco paintings over the doors in Lady Walpole's dressing-room, exceedingly well executed. I could not believe they were other than stucco, until I was convinced of the contrary by touching them with a stick. The park is no way remarkable, there is a pretty piece of water, and one may say 'tis a chearfull place. The family were not down, but a very dirty French cook offered us wine.'

From Wolterton they drove to Felbrigg, which belonged to the future statesman William Windham, then a boy of fourteen. ''Tis a very grand looking old house, with three elegant modern rooms added above and below, hung with crimson and India papers, and some good pictures, chiefly landscapes. There are a great number of rooms fitted up very neatly. There is not much garden, but a very good greenhouse, out of which the gardener gave each of us a fine nosegay of orange-flowers, geraniums, etc., which travelled with us the rest of our tour, and are safely arrived at Langley, a little fatigued as you may imagine. The park is walled round,

189

and capable of great improvements; but the owner being a minor, nothing can be yet done. There is a good view of the sea, great variety of ground, and the situation, in my opinion, is as good, if not better than any of the seats in Norfolk.' The greenhouse was the orangery which still stands to the west of the house. The Great Wood, the work of many successive generations of planters, has shut out the good view of the sea. The view must indeed have been very agreeable when the travellers admired it in that far-off July; but no one who inhabits Felbrigg during the winter and early spring could possibly wish for its restoration.

They then went on to Holt, enjoying the spectacle of the sea all the way, since the Sheringham and Weybourne woods were not yet planted. They put up at the Feathers, dined and drank coffee, and walked to the Spout Hills, still a noted local beauty spot. 'It looks very romantic, but seems more to have been the work of art than nature, as there are high knolls and several deep valleys in which stand cottages, that have a most rural effect. It takes its name, as I suppose, from a very fine spring which is walled round, and the water issues from it in three spouts. I saw numbers come from the town to fill their pails, and therefore imagine the water is in high repute, or scarce in the town itself. The chief trade of Holt seems to be spinning, in which young and old are employed.' The beds at the Feathers are 'pretty good', the inn itself 'neat and clean'.

Next morning they set out for Holkham. The road was 'very romantic, with great variety of ground, most of it well cultivated, and interspersed with plantations of firs, etc. We drove for about a quarter of a mile on the brink of a precipice not much inferior to some described by those who have crossed the Alps. At the bottom winds a river, which loses itself behind a high hill on the opposite side, which hill was covered with sheep, and the whole formed a most charming landscape.' Such a passage would indeed have startled those of Lady Beacuhamp Proctor's contemporaries who complained so much of the flatness of Norfolk. Clearly she had only the haziest idea of what an Alpine landscape might be like, and it is difficult to be certain exactly where she encountered this precipice. It might have been supposed that her road lay along

HOLKHAM
from an engraving after a drawing by William Watts

the high ground above Bayfield, which unquestionably pro-
vides some of the finest scenery in Norfolk; yet she definitely
states that Bayfield Hall, then occupied by a Mr. Mitchell,
lay upon her right hand. Towards Holkham the country grew
less interesting; but she was deeply impressed by the enormous house, only recently completed and standing in its
equally vast park, whose surrounding woods, now so splendid
in aspect, were then struggling plantations with 'the cold sea
breeze too visible on the shrivell'd leaves'.

We will not follow her through all the rooms of Holkham.
Her observations on the pictures, here and in other houses,
were amusing no doubt for her sister to read—lively nonsense
not intended to be taken seriously, and not worth reproducing
now. For example, she objected to the paintings in the chapel
at Holkham, because they looked 'so like the Roman Catho-
lick superstition'; and she considered that the best portion of
the magnificent Rubens, the 'Flight into Egypt', was the
head of the donkey. But a few of her descriptions may be
quoted. They first entered, 'through a plain door in the
Rustick', the great Hall. 'It is very superb, I believe the
grandest thing of the sort in England. The sides are wains-
coted with marble, 'tis a sort of yellow and white, and for the
honour of our own country was all brought out of Derbyshire.
Eighteen fluted pillars of the same marble support the roof,
nine on each side, the passage or gallery runs round these
pillars, making a communication to the rooms. Opposite the
door you enter at is a flight of nineteen steps, which lead into
the Salloone. 'Tis the fashion to condemn the Hall, and not
without some reason, for to look down the steps from the
Salloone, it does certainly appear like a cold bath.' At the top
of the steps, the windows of the Saloon 'open into a portico
which keeps the room delightfully pleasant and cool, it being
full south, and is besides a great ornament to the outside of
the building'. The Chapel, despite its papistical pictures, was
'very elegantly fitted up, the Communion table is a slab of
very fine marble; the bannisters before it, the reading desk,
and my Lady's gallery where she sits, are all of cedar, which
sends forth a delightful perfume'. The Gallery was a superb
apartment, 'one of the most pleasing rooms I ever was in,

with niches on each side filled with fine statues. I suppose they were all brought from Rome, but it was impolite to examine them, they were all so slenderly cloath'd. Where there was drapery we ventured to criticise, and some of them were very beautiful'. Outside, the orangery and the menagerie gave her great pleasure. The latter was 'filled chiefly with Indian pheasants, but there was one uncommon bird, which came from Barbary, coal black with a yellow bill and frizzled crown, about the size of a goose. It made such a doleful noise, I can liken it to nothing but the humming of a bass string of a violincelli, and so loud withal that you could not avoid hearing it the whole time you were in the garden.'

They drove round the park, and then set out for Fakenham, stopping on the way at 'a little dirty inn, where we dined in a bedchamber'. They put up for the night at the Red Lion at Fakenham, 'an indifferent inn but a very pretty town'. Next morning they went to Raynham, where Lady Townshend received them with great politeness, but 'my Lord was at Dereham with his Militia, playing at Soldiers'. This Lord Townshend was George, fourth Viscount and later to be created first Marquess, the grandson of the statesman more familiarly known as 'Turnip Townshend'. His martial ardours have already been described in this book. A delightful painting at Raynham shows him reviewing his Militia in the park, or, as Lady Beauchamp Proctor would have it, playing at soldiers.

Despite her friendly welcome from Lady Townshend, she was somewhat critical of Raynham. 'This is a very handsome house built by Inigo Jones, and too much in his heavy style. The principal room is a Salloon, which is grand enough, but the ceiling much too substantial to please me. It is hung with portraits, among others a very fine one of Belisarius by Salvator Rosa. There are many small bedchambers in the atticks, but few on the first floor, and none of those grand, except one in which was a red damask bed put up for Queen Anne who once lay there. In one of the rooms below, hang the portraits of all the officers sent by Queen Elizabeth into the Netherlands, pretty well done. The park is chearfull, and there is a good piece of water, both of which his Lordship intends to improve.'

The Tour of Norfolk

From Raynham they drove the short distance to Houghton, where everything bore traces of the third Lord Orford's negligent rule. Her remarks on the house and its pictures are conventional and need not be given. The environs, she noticed, 'at present wear a very ruinous aspect. The park is noble, full of fine trees, and here, for the first time in Norfolk, I saw some beeches. There is an artificial knoll in the park, which is so ill made and so formal, it looks like a plum cake just drawn out of the oven. Here is no water, except a small bason near the stables, which has swallowed up an immense sum and after all looks like a watering pond, and I believe is used as such. The lodge is in ruins; in short, nothing less than Miss Bowes's fortune or another First Minister's purse can put it in proper order. Lord Orford is very little here; he takes more pleasure in living at inns than in this noble mansion, as it certainly is with all its faults.' And so to dinner at the little inn at the park gates, to Fakenham once more for the night, and home to Langley the following evening. 'So ends our tour, which I assure you gave me great pleasure and more than answered my expectations, and I bore my journey well.'

Eight years afterwards, in September 1772, Lady Beauchamp Proctor made virtually the same tour again, with her husband and three young ladies named Gore. We will not follow them this time in any detail; but their adventures at three of the houses they visited—Blickling, Holkham and Raynham—deserve quotation.

They admired Blickling as little as before, but derived much amusement from the efforts of its owner, the second Earl of Buckinghamshire, and his wife to avoid being seen by them. 'We were afraid of being too soon, but on sending in our names were admitted. We found they had breakfasted, and my Lord's horses stood at the door, though the servant told us he was gone out. We saw no other traces of her Ladyship than two or three workbags and a tambour; I believe we drove her from room to room, but that we could not help. We saw only the old part of the house, over which a very dirty housemaid with a duster in her hand conducted us.' But as they were leaving, Lord Buckinghamshire appeared, and 'made a thousand courtier-like speeches, but they were so

little worth attending to that they went in at one ear and out
at t'other; one thing, however, I could not help remarking—
he said he was mortified beyond expression that he happened
to be out when he came, and you know I have mentioned his
horses being at the door when we went in'. At Wolterton,
their next place of call, 'we met with a very different reception. My Lord and Lady were at home; you know what a
good natured creature he is, and Lady Walpole was in one of
her gracious humours, and walked all over the house with us
herself.'

When they arrived next morning at Holkham, 'the servant
told us we could not see it for an hour at least, as there was a
party going round. As it was but just ten o'clock, we wished
to have filled up the time with a review of the park and buildings, but there was no one disengaged to attend us.' They
were shown into the vestibule under the south portico, then
used as a waiting-room, and furnished with busts and reliefs.
Its most conspicuous adornment was the fine marble head of
Jupiter, which the first Earl of Leicester had bought during
his travels in Italy. Here another large party was awaiting the
guide; and for some considerable time they all underwent the
embarrassment customary in an age when it was highly im-
proper, at least for ladies, to enter into any sort of conversation without a formal introduction. 'We were obliged to submit to be shut up with Jupiter Ammon, and a whole tribe of
people, till the housekeeper was ready to attend us. Nothing
could be more disagreeable than this situation; we all stared
at one another, and not a creature opened their mouths. Some
of the Masters amused themselves with trying to throw their
hats upon the heads of the busts, whilst the Misses scrutinised
one another's dress. Sir William indeed and an old terror did
chat a little, and by this means we found out they were the
whole family of the Swailes, going the Norfolk Tour.' At last
the housekeeper appeared, 'and we rushed on her like a swarm
of bees; we went the usual round, all but the wing my Lord
and Lady used to inhabit themselves, which was new doing
up. I dragged them all into the atticks, for which I believe
none of them thanked me; I wanted to look at the sea, but it
was so hazy we could not distinguish it from a cloud. The

tower library has been put in order, two librarians from London have been at work there ten weeks, and it is but just finished.' When they came downstairs the other sightseers were ushered out, but their own more privileged party 'were conducted a second time to Mr. Jupiter, where we poured libations of chocolate on his altar, that is we had some set out in great form in the Leicester style, and a most elegant little Birmingham vehicle to hold the rusks was placed on the table. I made Mr. Fetch-and-carry [the footman] tell me where it was bought, and am determined to have one. I inquired, you may be sure, after her Ladyship, and left all proper compliments.'

Their visit to Raynham was a sad one, for Lady Townshend, who received them so hospitably in 1764, had since died, and the place seemed almost deserted. 'We went to Raynham, commonly called the Gay. I'm sure it did not appear at all so to me, as in the first place the rain totally excluded all prospects; the house was in disorder, entirely uninhabited except by one old witch and a great dog, that attended us all over the house, and saluted every corner that was convenient for his purposes; and the melancholy reflection that the amiable mistress of the mansion was no more, cast a gloom on every thing. The last time I was there, she was sitting at work in the great room, and received us with that good nature and politeness, so peculiar to herself.' And so home once more to Langley, after 'an agreeable tour considering the weather was not the most favourable; we did not once lose our way, though we travelled 137 miles, nor met with any one accident'.

I know no more of Lady Beauchamp Proctor than her journals have told me. Her husband died just a year after their second Norfolk tour, on the 13th of September 1773. She long outlived him, dying on the 12th of January 1798. To the sterner sort of critic the little narratives of her travels will perhaps appear trivial and insipid; but personally I cannot but feel grateful to her light-hearted and loquacious shade.

VII

During the latter part of the century an increasing number of agriculturists made the Tour of Norfolk, in order to study the farming innovations for which the county had become famous. By now the improvements so strenuously advocated by 'Turnip' Townshend, the root shift and the four-course rotation of crops, were adopted almost everywhere. Raynham was the model of a well-farmed and productive estate, and as such agriculturists were glad to visit it. But the main focus of their interest had shifted to Holkham, where successive Cokes and their agents were grappling with the problems of a less kindly and tractable soil.

The story of Holkham as an agricultural estate is a remarkable one, and its hero is unquestionably 'Coke of Norfolk', Thomas William Coke, who became the first Earl of Leicester of the second creation in 1837. He was the great-nephew and eventual successor of the builder of Holkham, being the grandson of his sister by her marriage with Philip Roberts. But he must not be allowed to assume the entire credit for the agricultural pre-eminence of Holkham. The claim, already quoted, which his predecessor had inscribed upon that tablet above the entrance to the house was not an empty boast. Arthur Young made the Tour of Norfolk in 1767, when the future 'Coke of Norfolk' was a boy of fifteen; and he found that the 'open barren estate' was already vieing with its more fortunately situated neighbours. The entire landscape between Holkham and Houghton was already transformed. 'Instead of boundless wilds, and uncultivated wastes inhabited by scarcely anything but sheep, the country is all cut into enclosures, cultivated in a most husband-like manner, richly manured, well peopled, and yielding an hundred times the produce that it did in its former state.' This revolution had been largely affected by generous applications of marl—'for under the whole country run veins of a very rich kind, which they dig up, and spread upon the old sheep walks, and then by inclosing they throw their farms into a regular course of crops, and gain immensely by the improvement'. Yet some authorities on agricultural history write almost as though 'Coke of Norfolk' himself discovered the process of marling.

Although the purpose of Young's tours was the study of husbandry, he also enjoyed viewing and commenting upon the great houses of England. 'You must accept the medley,' he told his correspondent, 'and not be too criticising on my jumble of heterogeneous parts.' The pages describing his experiences in Norfolk deal mainly with turnips and sainfoin, dung and marl, acreages and farm accounts; but in enormous footnotes he gives his opinions of the architecture, statuary and pictures at Holkham and Houghton, Raynham and Narford. His verdicts on the paintings are admirably terse— '*Jacob and Esau*, dark and disagreeable'; '*Death of Joseph*. Exceeding fine heads'; '*Marriage of Cana*: a striking instance of wretched grouping'; 'Nothing can be finer than the attitude of *Cocles*'. The great *Flight into Egypt* by Rubens at Holkham is thus described: 'A good picture; but the figures disagreeable, especially *Mary's*, who is a female mountain. The drawing appears to be indifferent.' He also derived much aesthetic pleasure from Mrs. Henley's hermitage at Docking, in which the hermit's bedroom was walled with oyster-shells and his parlour frescoed 'with scrolls and festoons of sea-weed, deal-shavings, and painted ropes, in a gothic, but neat taste'. Almost equally to his liking was the grotto which Mrs. Styleman of Snettisham had contrived out of the halves of a boat. 'It is stuck full of spar, shells, sea-weed, coral, glass, ore &c., all disposed with taste. The front pretty, but too regular, and not rustic enough; composed of the same materials on a ground of powdered sea-shells stuck in cement.'

During the ensuing years Young's many writings on agriculture brought him a celebrity which extended beyond these shores. In 1784 one of his admirers, the duc de Liancourt, sent his two sons and their Polish tutor on a prolonged visit to England, largely in order to study farming methods in the eastern counties. They established themselves at Bury St. Edmunds, not far from Young's home at Bradfield Hall; and one of the young men, Comte François de la Rochefoucauld, produced a journal of their experiences. Written with great intelligence and good humour, and with a foreigner's observation of details which a native would have passed over, it forms a most valuable description of East Anglian life in the eighteenth century.

At this time François de la Rochefoucauld was eighteen years of age. Like his father he was a liberal, a *philosophe*, an admirer of the laws and institutions of England; and he took easily, on the whole, to the English habit of life. His journal is a miscellany of impressions—travel and hospitality, Suffolk farming, an election dinner, the boredom of English Sundays, the ungainliness of the English when dancing, the cleanliness of their houses, their prodigious consumption of tea and beer. He describes racing at Newmarket, hunting with the Duke of Grafton's hounds, the splendid Suffolk punches and the consideration they received from their owners—'they always look clean and shiny, and never have sore places such as one too often sees in France'. English manners sometimes perplexed him, with their singular contrasts of refinement and grossness—the rigid etiquette of dinner at Euston, the loose talk afterwards and the row of chamber-pots in full view under the sideboard. He was disconcerted at first, but only at first, by their reception by Sir Gerard Vanneck at Heveningham. 'He received us very coldly and, with his hat still on, invited us to enter. No notice should be taken of this sort of thing in England. The goodwill is there; it is merely the form that is lacking. We retired to put on our own hats and then entered. Sir Gerard's sister was at breakfast; we took tea with her and the conversation became less chilly every minute. Sir Gerard talked a little, and we realised how friendly he was towards us and how his first greeting had given us an entirely wrong impression of him.'

In September they set out to make the Tour of Norfolk. De la Rochefoucauld particularly liked the little town of Swaffham, even today so little altered from its eighteenth-century aspect. A few miles further on, Castleacre provided a regrettable contrast in the eyes of this *anglomane*—'the village houses were dirty and badly built, fit only for France'. Harvest was almost completed, but they were struck with the excellence of the turnips and the clover leys on the barley stubbles. Armed with Young's introductions they inspected several notable farms, particularly one at Rougham which was rented at £1,660, and where everything was on an immense scale—fields, buildings, animals, even the Norfolk dumplings in the kitchen, 'puddings in linen bags quite as large as those which in France are used for cement'. But de la Rochefoucauld was growing weary of his journal, and few of his Norfolk entries compare with his vivid records of Suffolk. The party visited Houghton and Raynham, and spent a night at the house of Mr. Styleman at Snettisham. 'We found our host to be a real character—typically English, full of good-nature and entirely lacking in polite manners.' Then they went on to Lynn, where Young joined them, and attended the dinner and ball given by the newly-elected Mayor. At the ball they met Mr. and Mrs. Coke, who invited them to stay at Holkham. At this point the journal peters out altogether. 'This account of our Norfolk tour was left unfinished because we enjoyed ourselves too much at Holkham to have time for writing.' So de la Rochefoucauld fades from the landscape of East Anglia. It is agreeable to know that he and his brother survived the coming Revolution, and served France with distinction both under the Empire and the restored Monarchy.

VIII

It was remarked at the outset of this chapter that Norfolk found little favour with the earlier devotees of the Picturesque. The commendations of the Rev. William Gilpin, during the brief tour which he made in 1769, were remarkably tepid, seldom rising above 'not unpleasant' or 'not disagreeable'. The first consistent and informed appreciations of Norfolk landscape came from Humphry Repton. While living in idle seclusion at Sustead, some years before he embarked upon the career of a landscape gardener which brought him wealth and fame, he had passed the time in sketching and writing about the surrounding countryside. In his contributions to Armstrong's *History of Norfolk* which appeared in 1781, and still more in the Red Books which he prepared for the owners of various houses and parks in later years, he revealed a most sensitive perception of the Norfolk scene.[1]

He was followed by others; and as the eighteenth century drew to its close, the scope of the Norfolk Tour steadily widened. The great houses were visited as much as ever. The agriculture of Holkham, and especially the annual Sheep Shearings with their festivities and speeches, drew sightseers from all over the country. But tourists also began to penetrate into areas hitherto neglected, and above all to discover the beauties of the cliffs and the sea.

All through the centuries the waves of 'this majestic element', as it was now respectfully called, had broken unregarded against deserted beaches. The people of the coastal villages drew from it their dangerous livelihood. Everyone else ignored it entirely. There was no notion whatsoever of bathing or swimming for pleasure. I can only recall a single instance, until late in the reign of King George III, of anyone deliberately entering the sea; and that was when a young man, the future planter Robert Marsham, was bitten by a dog supposed to be mad, and was told by his doctor that the only remedy was to bathe in the sea at Runton. But in due course sea-bathing came to be advised for maladies other than suspected hydrophobia, and the virtues of sea-air were widely extolled. Invalids took courage and plunged into the surf. Those in health contemplated the German Ocean from beach or cliff, admired its clouds and sunsets, listened to the romantic surging of its waves at nightfall. Little fishing-towns such as Cromer came suddenly into fashion, and their merits were discussed in many households besides that of Mr. Woodhouse at Hartfield. 'You should have gone to Cromer, my dear, if you went anywhere. Perry was a week at Cromer once, and he holds it to be the best of all the sea-bathing places. A fine open sea, he says, and very fine air. . . .'

People no longer travelled solely in quest of spectacular landscapes or vast Palladian houses. Gentler scenes began to attract their eyes—a secluded farmhouse; a group of cottages

---

[1] The reader is referred to the chapter 'Humphry Repton in Norfolk' in *A Norfolk Gallery* for a more detailed discussion of this subject.

beside a wood; a gnarled and solitary oak; the play of sun and cloud over an expanse of heath. A tourist of this kind was Samuel Jackson Pratt, whose wanderings in 1798, embodied in his *Gleanings in England,* covered the northern part of Norfolk with unusual thoroughness. Pratt was an indifferent actor and a scarcely more successful writer, who played and often published under the imposing name of Courtney Melmoth. Despite the pretentiousness of his reflective passages, and the tedium of his dialogues with imaginary rustics, he described the Norfolk scene—'the unambitious beauties of nature in which this county abounds'—with an agreeable freshness of appreciation. He noted, as he made his way from Fakenham towards Walsingham, how 'the country now begins to lift itself into superior beauty', and admired the long rich prospects that met the eye on every rising ground. When he explored that delectable tract of countryside around Bayfield and Letheringsett, with its hills, its woods, its little river, at times he stood 'charm-bound'. So one may stand in that unravaged valley, and upon those secluded hills, even today. And the whole description of his journey from Holt to Cromer is full of vivid touches—the sea constantly in view, with its fishing-boats and its fleets of colliers on their voyage between Newcastle and London; the yet unplanted heaths of Sheringham; the ruins of Beeston Priory and the prosperous farm-house nearby; the wooded hills of Beeston and Runton; and finally Cromer high on its cliffs, facing the ever-changing sea, 'the marine picture moving on the face of the water, its colouring, its quietude, its menace of a storm'.

Here, at the very turn of the century, it is time to take leave of the Tour of Norfolk. The tourists continued to wander, to admire, to appraise and describe; but we have reached a moment when the Norfolk scene was already being recorded, not in the journals of casual visitors from afar, but by a group of painters with a most intimate understanding of their native countryside. The flowering of the Norwich School, so sudden, so unexpected and so far-reaching, had begun. 'O rare and beautiful Norfolk!' wrote Cotman, in the letter which described his last day in his own county, before he returned to London to sicken and to die. 'O rare and beautiful Norfolk!' In that spirit he and Crome, their followers and their friends, depicted the things they knew and loved—meadow and cornfield, tree and heath, river and broad and sea, sunlight and moonlight, the clouds and the cold pure air.

THE GUNTON
HOUSEHOLD BOOK

It is a fine folio volume bound in red morocco, with gilt tooling on the covers and gilt edges to the leaves. The binding is somewhat worn, the result of almost daily consultation over a long stretch of years. For this is a specimen, and a particularly fine one, of the manuscript books which were carefully compiled and diligently used, during the seventeenth and eighteenth centuries, by the ladies of every large household throughout the land.

John Harbord, the younger brother of the Charles Harbord whose story was told in an earlier chapter of this book, purchased the Gunton estate from the Jermy family in 1676. His collateral heirs have been there ever since, and so has this volume. There is nothing to show which of the Harbord ladies actually compiled it; but three distinct handwritings can be traced in its pages, and it appears to cover the last few decades of the seventeenth century and to extend a little way into the eighteenth. Starting from one end, the writers have filled 154 closely packed pages with medical prescriptions. From the other end they have filled almost as many pages with culinary recipes, and with directions for preserving, distilling and such minor arts as 'to recover stinking venison'.

The affairs of kitchen and larder, still-room and brewhouse were conducted by the Harbords, and by their neighbours who supplied many of the recipes, in the generous fashion of that age. Every dish was prepared from varied and lavish ingredients, and of the dishes themselves there was no end—beef à la mode and oyster pies, tansies and sheeps' head puddings, whipt syllabub and clouted cream, jumbles and cracknells, Westminster wiggs and Italian biskets, cherry marmalade and violet cakes and pickled samphire and candied pippins. Every sort of liquor was brewed, distilled or compounded—mead and shrub and punch, sack possett and ratafia and aquamirabilis. And there was an impressive range of home-made wines—cowslip, gooseberry, raspberry, birch, raisin, sage, apricot, orange, currant, elder, primrose, black cherry and clove gillyflower.

But the most remarkable feature of the volume is the medical section. There can hardly exist a more striking picture of the oddities and horrors of the art of physic as practised in a country household in the later seventeenth century. It opens promisingly with 'A Wound Drink', a blend of twenty-four different kinds of herb, root and leaf, all of which had to be gathered in May and carefully dried. They were then boiled in white wine and honey; and the patient was to drink six spoonfuls every morning and fast afterwards for two hours. It cured every kind of wound, cut or sore. The compiler even goes so far as to claim that this innocent herbal preparation 'hath driven out Bullets of a Soldier's body that hath lain 6 or 7 years within him'. The same touching confidence is displayed, a couple of pages on, in 'Doctor Burghes' Receipt for the Plague'. For this it was necessary to boil red sage, rue, pepper, ginger and nutmegs in malmsey wine, and add mithradate, treacle and angelica-water. 'Keep this as your life above all earthly treasures', the compiler urges her family. 'Take it warme always morning and evening, a spoonfull at a time, or two if you be infected; if you be not, a spoonfull a day is enough, half a spoonfull at morning and as much at evening all the Plague time. Under God trust to this, for there was never Man, Woman or Child that this deceiv'd.' Besides being a matchless antidote for the plague, the mixture was an effective cure for small-pox, measles and surfeits.

All through the book there is a noticeable contrast between the herbal remedies, harmless and no doubt often beneficial, and the remedies of other kinds which must have been perfectly useless and are often altogether horrible. The very names of the herbs are beautiful—betony, bugloss, melilot, tormentil, pellitory of the wall, marjoram, vervain, centaury. The medicines, too, are full of delicious ingredients—syrup of mulberries, marmalade of quinces, conserve of red roses, lily of the valley water. And there are directions for their preparation which suddenly bring Shakespeare and Herrick to mind. A remedy for the stone begins 'Take herb grace in May when the sun is an hour high'; and a lotion for the eyes, 'In the month of May take a fine linnen Cloth and gather a Pint of early dew in a morning before the sun be up.'

But these gentle pastoral distillations of herbs and dew are interspersed with remedies of a very different kind. There is a surprising number of cures suggestive of white magic. If a bone got stuck in your throat, you swallowed a thimbleful of gunpowder in a spoonful of beer. For a sore throat, you dropped heated black flints into milk until half of it had boiled away, and then drank what was left. For the gout, you anointed the grieved part with the fat of young herons. For the stone it was often helpful to boil a mixture of herbs and roots in the new milk of a red cow: it was, of course, essential that the cow should be red. Conserve of rosemary, eaten fasting every morning, would restore one's failing memory. For a looseness, 'take a Good Friday Bun and grate some into Milk and boyle it and take it as often as occasion requires'. This was what we know as a hot cross bun, and it must have grown disagreeably stale if the looseness occurred several months after Good Friday. For the bite of a mad dog, 'Take a quart of Ale and 2 spoonfulls of Honey, 2 Onyons sliced, as much Alom as a Hen's Egg, boyle them till the Onyons be tender, then wash the Place with the Ale very well: that done, lay the Onyons upon the Sore and roll it up, doe this 3 or 4 times: if you can get the dog that bit the Patient, take some of his hair and lay it next the Sore and lay the Onyons upon it. This has bin proved upon severall that have bin bitten.'

Besides these eccentric and semi-magical cures, there are many whose ingredients might fittingly have been stirred into their cauldron by the witches in *Macbeth*. The faith reposed in them was in fact a kind of hangover from the days of witchcraft.

> *Eye of newt and toe of frog,*
> *Wool of bat and tongue of dog,*
> *Adder's fork and blindworm's sting,*
> *Lizard's leg and owlet's wing. . . .*

Places and Things

Late in the seventeenth century, the ladies of this opulent country household were giving their patients jelly of snake-skin, syrup of snails, the powdered eyes and claws of crabs, the juice of young swallows pounded in a mortar. They pre-scribed grey slugs for sciatica, toad-spawn for bleeding at the nose, sheep's dung in beer for jaundice, horse's dung in white wine for pleurisy. Powdered earthworms were thought to be a most reliable cure for consumption, and were also very effective in cases of gunshot wounds. If none of their herbal remedies could alleviate the pain of the stone, there was always this alternative: 'Take the bladder of a badger and put out the water, and put therein the blood of a kid, dry it and make powder thereof and drink of the powder with old ale or white wine, and it will cure the patient.' Thinning of the hair might be arrested by a horrid mixture of honey and roasted moles; and for convulsion fits in children there was a remedy involving the blood of a cat, obtained by a ghastly method which might well have been devised by the black and mid-night hags on the blasted heath.

So the entries go on, page after page, dealing with aches and ague, colic and flux and falling sickness, gripes and hickock, King's evil and melancholy and passion of the heart, all the maladies that afflicted our seventeenth-century for-bears. The mild, the magical and the horrific remedies are all jumbled together. Some must have been drawn from the life-long experience of the book's compilers, others are attributed to various neighbours, and others again are noted as having emanated from doctors in London or in Norfolk. Of all Nor-folk doctors the *doyen* was Sir Thomas Browne, who is known to have been on intimate terms with the Harbords, both pro-fessionally and as a personal friend. It is not surprising, there-fore, that seven of the prescriptions are marked with his name —a drink for the stone in the kidneys, a drink for whooping-cough, a poultice for the gout, a receipt for a cough and rheume, another for the ague, a honey drink and a purge of damask roses. They are short, and in comparison with many others in the book they are simple. They are soothing and cooling remedies, based on honey and barley water, and confected with such pleasant things as marshmallow roots,

206

SIR THOMAS BROWNE
from a painting by an unknown artist,
in the possession of the Hon. Doris Harbord

marigold and cowslip flowers, raisins of the sun, syrup of violets, oil of lilies. Those bizarre and alarming ingredients, in which the Harbord ladies sometimes indulged, had no place whatever in the prescriptions supplied to them by Sir Thomas Browne.

II

When he gave these prescriptions to the Gunton household, Browne had probably entered the final decade of his life. He had achieved European celebrity; his works were already translated into French and German, Dutch and Latin; his name was honoured, by scholars and physicians alike, at Montpellier and Leyden and Padua. But he was still living in Norwich as a practising doctor, visiting his patients in the city and all over the Norfolk countryside, experimenting, dissecting, gathering the herbs for his medicines in the fields and marshes. People came from afar to visit the author of *Religio Medici* and *Pseudodoxia Epidemica*; his house and garden were renowned, in the words of Evelyn, as 'a Paradise and cabinet of rarities'; but he pursued his happy family life, and the daily course of visits and consultations, serenely indifferent to his fame.

The closing years of Browne's life are brought before us with exceptional clarity in his correspondence with his son Edward in London; and the greater part of his notes and memoranda, with their wealth of personal detail, belong to the same period. We come to know all the family—Lady Browne, with her household cares and the loving ill-spelt postscripts which she dashed off so hurriedly; the daughters, Frank with her skill in drawing, Betty who read to her father from one formidable folio or another every night of his life; the little grandson Tommy whom they all idolized and spoiled. In his letters Browne was no longer a master of sonorous prose, but an old provincial doctor gossiping contentedly of his neighbours, and his patients, and the forthcoming elections, and the extravagance of women's clothes, and the best way of pickling oysters, and the new figures which Tommy wanted for his puppet-show.

The house was crammed with books and pictures, coins and medals and relics of antiquity, stuffed birds and dried fishes and bottled spiders, and always something new on the dissecting table—a dolphin or a bustard or some strange creature taken in the nets off Yarmouth. The spacious garden was the admiration even of that city of gardens, with its profusion of flowers and herbs. The visitor never knew what unexpected denizens he would encounter among the flower beds—the eagle, perhaps, which Browne kept for years, feeding it with whelps and cats; the bittern, whose diet was fish and mice; the stork, which Betty described as 'the tamest stately thing you ever saw'. Any rare bird, any inexplicable fish, any freak of nature would inevitably be sent to Browne. With his lively interest in all natural phenomena, he was always delighted to receive them; even such peculiar objects as the fragments of the hat of a woman killed by lightning near Bungay, and the teeth discovered in Earsham churchyard, which the finders supposed to have belonged to a giant but which proved in fact to be those of an ox.

Sir Philip Wodehouse of Kimberley once presented Browne with an anagram on his name: Doctor Thomas Brouneus— *Ter bonus, cordatus homo.* No anagram could have been more apt: and nowhere is there more abundant evidence of Browne's wisdom and virtue, and his unfailing goodness of heart, than in his letters. As he discusses with his son, a doctor like himself, the symptoms of his patients—Norwich aldermen, invalid dowagers out in the countryside, the poor of his own parish of Mancroft—he is never once tempted into an intolerant or harsh remark about any of them; nor indeed about any human being. He was able to carry out, in his daily life in Norwich, his own exacting precept: 'Tread softly and circumspectly in this funambulatory Track and narrow Path of Goodness.'

It was with these words that he opened *Christian Morals*, the principal literary work of his last years. He was engaged upon it throughout the period during which he must have supplied his prescriptions to the Harbords; and it is pleasant to think that when he had visited them in their distant manor-house, and his coach was jolting him back to Norwich over the ill-made roads, the cadences of his final masterpiece may have shared his thoughts with the roots of marshmallows and the purge of damask roses.

APPENDIX

The following are the seven prescriptions, printed exactly as they are given in the Gunton Household Book.

DOCTER BROWNS PURGE OF DAMASK ROSES

Take 30 Roses and infuse them all night in a wine pint of claryfied Whey, put in 4 Spoonfulls of White Wine and a half a Spoonfull of Carraway Seeds, in the morning make it ready to boyle and strain it and put in 3 Spoonfulls of Sirrop of Violetts.

Sʳ THO: BROWN'S DRINK FOR THE STONE IN Yᵉ KIDNEYS & BLOODY URINE

Take of Marsh Mallow roots 4 ounces, Eringo Roots and Asparagus of each 3 ounces, Liquorish 2 ounces, Red Sanders an ounce and half, french barly 3 ounces, sweet fennell seed an ounce, quince seed half an ounce, honey 4 pints: boyle all these in 5 gallons & a half of water to 4 gallons, often scumming it, then strein yᵉ Liquor & work it up with Yeast like beer and tun it, & after it's ten dayes old draw it out into bottles well stoped & drink thereof as of beer, at & out of Meals.

Sʳ THO: BROWNS DRINK FOR A HOOPING COUGH

Take of Raysons of yᵉ Sunne ston'd an ounce, Currance a Spoonfull, 5 or 6 figgs, 8 or 9 Coltsfoot leaves, marrygold & cowslip flowers of each a few, Liqorice half a quarter of an ounce, Anniseeds a thimble full, China roots a quarter of an ounce: boyle all these in a Pint & a half of Barly water to a Pint, then strein it & give it 2 or 3 Spoonfulls at a time warme when you see occasion, adding to it a little Syrrup of Violets or Sugar Candy: it's good without either.

FOR Yᵉ AGUE THO' EVERY DAY BY SIR T: B:

For a Child of 6 years old 9 graines of Gascoigne Powder or Lady Kent's, & soe more or less according to yᵉ age &

o   209

strength of yᵉ Person, 3 houres before yᵉ fit cometh, and marygold Posset drink with harts horn in yᵉ fit it's very proper, & to take of Confection of Alkermes for a Child yᵉ quantity of a small Nut, at any time fasting an houre before yᵉ fit cometh and an houre after it.

A POULTES FOR THE GOUT BY Sʳ THO: BROWNS DIRECTIONS

Take Mallows, Camomile, Elder leaves, of each one handfull, boyle these in running water until they be tender, then strein them from the Liquor and beat the herbs into a pulp, then put them into a Skillet with the Liquor that was streined, and add to them 4 ounces of flax seed powdered and as much barly flower to make them into a Poultes, adding 2 or 3 ounces of Oyle of Lillies.

Sʳ THOMAS BROWNS HONEY DRINK

Take 2 ounces of the roots of Marshmallows, 2 ounces of Eringoes, 3 ounces of Licorish, an ounce & half of China root, Comfrey, Fennell, Tormentill of each an ounce, Bettony and Plaintain of each a handfull, Seeds of Quinces 2 drams, Raysons one pound, Currance 3 ounces, Jubibs one ounce, of the best honey 2 pound and a half, of water 3 gallons and a half, mix them and boyle it to 3 gallons, and after it's wrought put in 2 Oranges.

Sʳ THOMAS BROWNS RECEIPT FOR A COUGH AND RHUME

Take of frensh barly, and hartshorne, 3 ounces, of China root one ounce, Coltsfoot a good handfull, Eringo roots 4 ounces, one ounce of Liquorish, Rosemary 3 sprigs, Cowslip flowers a handfull, sweet fennell seeds half an ounce, Raysons sliced but not stoned a pound, Currance a quarter of a pound, honey 3 pints: boyle all these in 5 gallons of water and a pint over, boyle it to 4 gallons, then work it up with yeast, like beer, when it's boyled tunne it and after it's tenn days old bottle it up.

At the other end of the book, in the culinary section, is a recipe ascribed to Lady Browne; and as she was famous for her skill in cookery, and on one occasion prepared the flesh of a dolphin, sent to her husband for dissection, for the table of King Charles II at Newmarket, it seems fitting to include here:

HOW TO BROYLE A TENCH, L: BROWN

Take of large Tench, scoure y^m & wash y^m clean in warm water, y^n slit y^m down ye belly all ye way, y^n take a pretty deal of winter savory & parsly, wash & shred y^m fine w^t an onyon, y^n mix it w^t a good peice of butter & some salt & turn ye Tench ye inside outward & sew it up w^t ye butter & herbs in it, & broyle it upon a gridiron till it be brown enough on all sides, y^n take a good peice of butter & melt it w^t an anchovy, y^n take ye herbs out of ye belly & put into ye butter, dish it & poure ye sauce over it.

THE TREASURE OF OXNEAD

I

The end of Oxnead must have echoed through Norfolk like the fall of an ancient oak. The tree had long been in decay, the vast trunk hollow and tottering, the branches torn away by the storms of many years, and hardly a trace remaining of the once luxuriant foliage. Yet its final collapse removed a landmark which for centuries had been familiar to Norfolk eyes, and the scene would never again be quite the same.

The life of Sir William Paston, who assembled most of the treasure of Oxnead, has been described earlier in this book. The decline of the family fortunes under his son and grandson, the first and second Earls of Yarmouth, was the theme of a chapter in *Norfolk Portraits*. It is sufficient to say here that the Pastons upheld the Stuart cause, and remained faithful to their Tory principles, both before and after the Revolution of 1688. In East Anglia the tide was with the Whigs, more completely perhaps than in any other quarter of the kingdom. Nor were the later Pastons fitted in character to withstand it. There had been some mysterious weakening of their ancient and once vigorous stock. Extravagance, love of display, a taste for the expensive cult of alchemy, recklessness and incompetence in their business undertakings—many factors contributed to their undoing. They lost their local power and prestige. They drifted hopelessly and irrevocably into debt. The great days of Oxnead were already little more than a memory when William Paston, second Earl of Yarmouth, died on the Christmas Day of 1732—a disconsolate and embittered man, with his three sons dead before him, the last of all his line.

There are those who are saddened by the dispersal of a great collection of works of art. There are those also—and theirs is perhaps the more generous view—who take pleasure

212

THE TREASURE OF OXNEAD
from a painting by an unknown artist,
in the Strangers' Hall Museum, Norwich

in the thought of the precious objects setting out on their
travels once again, to adorn other houses and delight the
hearts of other owners. But however one may feel upon this
issue, it is always fascinating to encounter some relic of
Cannons or Fonthill, Strawberry Hill or Stowe. The Oxnead
collection was, of course, not to be compared with these. But
it contained many beautiful, curious and unexpected things,
now widely dispersed, but still occasionally to be identified in
their new and oddly diverse resting-places.

There hangs in the Stranger's Hall at Norwich a large
painting, by an unknown artist, of a selection from the
treasures of Oxnead. It was presumably executed to the order
of the first Earl of Yarmouth, during that deceptive heyday
of the family fortunes in the reign of Charles II. Here are
heaped together, in reckless and uncritical profusion, the
objects which delighted the hearts of the later Pastons—cups
and tankards richly embossed, nautilus shells elaborately
mounted in gold, goblets of agate and crystal, splendid hangings, instruments of music. Dishes are piled high with fruit,
grapes and nuts bestrew the table, and in the centre of the
composition sprawls an enormous lobster. Almost submerged
in this welter of still-life are a few animate figures—a girl
with a music book, a negro page, a marmoset and a cockatoo.
But in the background the painter has also depicted a candle
guttering towards its end, an hourglass with its sand fast
running out, a clock with its hands at half-past eleven. The
picture is by no means one of the well-known *Vanitas Vani-
tatum* group. The emphasis is entirely on riches and prosperity and success. Nevertheless it is significant to find, in an
inconspicuous corner, this group of references to the transi-
toriness of all earthly splendour. For Lord Yarmouth and his
family, as they struggled to rally the supporters of the Crown
and to maintain their own ascendancy in Norfolk, such sym-
bols must have held a meaning of which they were too well
aware.

II

After the death of the second Earl of Yarmouth in 1732, the
contents of Oxnead were sold to pay some fraction of his

debts, and the house itself soon became derelict. The antiquary Tom Martin was there in 1744, and set down the appropriate reflections in his notebook. 'The Hall, now in the utmost Ruins, is a deplorable sight. *Heu! Quantum Mutata!* In its prosperity it must have been a noble, and delightful Seat.' Soon afterwards the Oxnead estate was bought by Admiral George Anson, newly returned from his voyage round the world and fabulously enriched by the prize-money from the Spanish treasure-galleon which he had captured off the Philippines. He regarded his new property solely as an investment, and had no thoughts of living in Norfolk. The park and its surroundings were converted into farm-land and the house was demolished, except for a subsidiary or office wing which was left as a residence for the farmer.[1] And a very handsome farm-house it made, with its mullioned windows set in mellow red brickwork, its immense chimney-stacks, its panelled rooms and marble fireplaces. The elaborate garden, stretching down to the waters of the Bure, mostly reverted to meadow; but even now it is possible to trace the ghosts of the terraces along which Sir William Paston used to walk in philosophic converse with Dr. Thomas Browne.

We shall never know the exact appearance of Oxnead, despite the ingenious conjectural reconstructions of the architect John Adey Repton, who lived in the surviving wing for several years. But some idea of the house in its great days can be obtained from an inventory of 1687, now in the British Museum. The most impressive room was no doubt the Great Hall, its walls decorated with the heads of more than fifty stags and other beasts of the chase. It also contained a large landscape over the chimney-piece, two stands with gilt statues, six pedestals with gilt heads, fourteen carved heads, 'one antic standing in the window', and '2 crocodiles, 2 creatures stuft hanging over the Stone Table'. In Elizabethan days this would have been the dining apartment and general place of resort for the entire household; but by 1687 there was also a Great Dining Room, more politely furnished and

---

[1] It is possible that these alterations had been already made when Anson acquired the estate. The evidence on the point is scanty and somewhat contradictory.

adorned. It contained a painting of the King and a considerable number of family portraits, together with more statues and gilt heads.

Seventy-nine rooms are mentioned in this inventory. These included a Chapel, a Great and a Little Parlour, a Withdrawing Room, a Billiard Room, and several Galleries. There were two Friscateen Rooms, hung with gilt leather. (It has been suggested that these were vaulted rooms or grottoes, *freschetti*, designed for the summer months.) There were a Court Yard and a Venice Court, containing great stone flower-pots and new gilded flower-pots. There were a Buttery, a Preserving Room, a Spice Room and a Hog Room. There were countless Chambers—the Fountain Chamber, Lady Beck's Chamber, Mr. Peckover's, John Davy's, the Chaplain's, the Butler's, the Cook's. Unluckily there are few details of what any of the lesser rooms contained. One is tantalized by such entries as '36 large pictures' in the Lower Gallery, and '10 midling and 40 small pictures' in the Withdrawing Room, without the smallest inkling of the painter or the subject of any of them.

A more elaborate inventory, but one which covers only a small portion of the house, has also survived from 1670 or thereabouts. Again, all too few pictures are mentioned. There were 'a great picture of Magdalen, in a great carved frame', and 'a fine limd picture of Andromeda, chained to a rock'. These may well have been acquired by Sir William Paston during his travels in Italy; and one wonders if the last-named was a contemporary copy of Titian's famous *Perseus and Andromeda* now in the Wallace Collection. Portraits of the family by Lely, Wright and Cooper are also mentioned. But most of the inventory describes, shelf by shelf, the Pastons' accumulation of jewels and ornamental plate, 'Cheiny potts' and 'Indian Kans' and other curious objects from the east. It might be a translation into words of the painting in the Stranger's Hall, and undoubtedly includes some of the objects there depicted. The list extends for pages—gold and silver and crystal, agate and ivory and coral and mother-of-pearl: 'a shell, engraven with the story of Atalanta, standing upon an eagle's foot of silver'; 'a shell standing upon a dolphin,

silver and gilt, with a silver and gilt figure upon the top';
'a paire of coaker-shell cups with covers, in the middle of the
covers agate-stones sett in enamell, with a gold knob of the
top'; 'a crystall tankard with a cristall cover, set in a silver
and gilt frame with two handles, a flying horse on the top';
'a white agat dish in fashion of a heart with a white rose in it';
'a mother of pearle shell, the fashion of a boat, standing upon
a silver and gilt foote upheld with two anchors, with two
spoones in it, one christall and one amber'.

The dispersal of the collections at Oxnead must have taken
place quite soon after the last Earl's death, and several years
before Anson bought the estate. No sale catalogue or similar
document exists, so far as I know, except for the collection of
books. In fact it remains uncertain whether there was a sale
in the modern sense at all, or whether the contents of the
house were disposed of privately and over a considerable
period. Substantial purchases were undoubtedly made by
Norfolk neighbours, anxious to preserve some relics of the
vanished family: and some of these I have been able to trace.
By far the greater number of the Paston treasures have of
course disappeared; but it seems desirable to place on record
those which can still be identified.

III

For generations there had been hostility between the
houses of Oxnead and Blickling—between the Pastons, representing the Royalist and Tory interest in Norfolk, and the
Hobarts, traditionally Puritan, Parliamentarian and Whig.
The last Earl of Yarmouth had hardly been in a position,
impoverished and disheartened as he was, to play much part
in local politics during recent years. The Wodehouses and the
Bacons had assumed the Tory leadership in his stead. But
ancient rivalries die hard; and it was perhaps with some faint
feeling of triumph that Lord Hobart bought the statues and
garden ornaments from Oxnead and transferred them to
Blickling. To this day the Oxnead fountain throws up its
graceful jet of water among the flower-beds of the Blickling
parterre; and the remains of a second fountain may be seen in

another part of the garden. The statues commissioned by Sir William Paston from Nicholas Stone a hundred years before—Jupiter and Mercury, Diana and Flora and the rest—were also transferred to Blickling. All but one have disappeared; they are supposed to have fallen into decay after three centuries of Norfolk weather, and to have been used to fill up a pond. Hercules alone survives, in a somewhat battered state, and has been given shelter among the camellias and passion-flowers of the orangery.

Lord Hobart also acquired a piece of beautifully carved stonework which was originally at Caister, and must have been removed by the Pastons to Oxnead. It consists of a pair of angels—those luxuriantly feathered angels which appear, in stone or in glass, in so many East Anglian churches—supporting the arms and the garter emblems of Sir John Fastolf, the builder of Caister Castle, together with the arms of his wife Millicent Tiptoft. This was re-erected as a chimney-piece in one of the ground-floor rooms at Blickling, with the addition of the Hobart coat of arms. Another relic of the furnishings of Oxnead, a long refectory table now in the Castle Museum at Norwich, found its way to the Black Lion in the neighbouring village of Buxton, where it was used for the game of shovel-board by many generations of the inn's frequenters.

The finest picture at Oxnead was almost certainly the *Last Supper* by Raphael, which had been in the collection of the Earl of Arundel. This passed into the possession of Sir John Holland, who had married Lord Yarmouth's daughter Lady Rebecca Paston—the 'Lady Beck' whose chamber at Oxnead was mentioned in the 1687 inventory. It was soon acquired from him by Sir Robert Walpole, who had just completed Houghton and was assembling his own great collection of pictures there. Later in the century it was bought with the rest of the collection by the Empress Catherine of Russia, and is still at the Hermitage. Walpole's son Horace was too young at this time to be a collector in his own right; but two objects from Houghton were in due course to take their place among the treasures of Strawberry Hill. He recorded them in his own catalogue as 'a nautilus mounted in silver gilt, with satyrs and the arms of Paston', and 'a crystal tankard and cover, mounted in silver gilt'. When the contents of Strawberry Hill were sold in 1842, the famous auctioneer George Robins described these pieces—and indeed everything else— in more grandiose terms. The first was 'a Nautilus shell, richly mounted in silver gilt, representing *Neptune Riding on a Dolphin*, the Arms of Paston supported by Satyrs on a turtle pedestal with Sea Monsters, of very rare workmanship'. It was bought by J. Morrison, Esq., M.P., for £37 16s. The other appears as 'a crystal tankard and cover, mounted in silver gilt, richly worked, representing Cariatic Figures supporting the mounting, the cover and foot bordered with fruit and flowers, and a serpent handle'. This fell to the Baroness Anselm de Rothschild for £50 8s.

The portrait of Sir William Paston, reproduced as the frontispiece of this book, was bought by Ashe Windham of Felbrigg, where it still remains. It was one of a series of family portraits which hung in the Great Dining Room. Several others of the series were acquired by the Buxtons, a long-established Norfolk family unconnected with that distinguished and philanthropic house whose members have figured so prominently in the county since the early nineteenth century. These Buxtons had lived for several generations at Channonz Hall in Tibenham. They had lately moved to Shadwell Lodge in Rushford, a house designed by one of their number, an able amateur architect named John Buxton, who was also responsible for Earsham Hall and Bixley Hall. I do not know whether they had any personal associations with the Pastons, but they certainly acquired a considerable number of paintings and other objects from Oxnead.

Foremost among these was the portrait of Charles II by Michael Wright, which was given to the first Earl of Yarmouth after the King's visit to Oxnead in 1671. There were also portraits by an unknown painter of the second Earl as a young man, and of his first wife, Charlotte Jemima Henrietta Maria, the King's daughter by Viscountess Shannon.[1] All

[1] These are the traditional subjects of the two portraits. On grounds of style and costume, however, I cannot help suspecting that they may in fact represent the first Earl of Yarmouth and his wife Rebecca Clayton.

three are in fine contemporary frames, and remain in the possession of the present representatives of the Buxton family at their house in Wiltshire. The Buxtons also bought an excellent half-length portrait of Sir John Holland. For generations he was a notable figure in Norfolk politics; and when he died in 1701, in his hundredth year, he was the last survivor of all the members of the Long Parliament. It was his grandson of the same name who married Lady Rebecca Paston. This portrait now hangs in Norwich Castle Museum, to which it was presented by the late Mrs. Buxton.

The remarkable painting of the treasures of Oxnead, described at the beginning of this chapter, was also acquired by the Buxtons, as was at least one of the objects depicted in it, a great strombus shell mounted as a cup in gold and enamel. They likewise bought a whole group of standing cups of Swiss and South German workmanship. The picture and all these cups were presented by Mrs. Buxton to Norwich Museum. So was another curious picture which may once have been at Oxnead—its subject and treatment would not have been alien to the Paston taste. It is a Flemish 'mannerist' painting of the sixteenth century, in which a naked Venus, reclining with her lapdogs in a voluptuous chamber, receives from Cupid the unaccustomed offering of a skull.

The collection at Oxnead included a number of early paintings on a panel of royal and courtly personages. Six of these passed into the possession of Robert French, the son of Sir Robert Walpole's chaplain and a Fellow of Caius College, Cambridge. In 1787 these were given by French to the Rev. Thomas Kerrich, the eminent collector and Librarian of the University of Cambridge. They represent King Ferdinand of Aragon, Louis XII and Francis I of France, Richard III of England, and two less easily identifiable figures whose frames are respectively inscribed Monsour de Nassou and Monsour de Ravestein. All six were subsequently bequeathed by Kerrich, together with several other paintings of great historical interest, to the Society of Antiquaries, whose rooms at Burlington House they now adorn.

At the Paston Grammar School at North Walsham there hangs an excellent portrait of the early seventeenth century, representing the founder of the school, the Sir William Paston who died in 1610. This may have been there since the foundation, four years before Sir William's death; but tradition relates that it was acquired at the time of the break-up of Oxnead. A good still-life painting by Edward Collier, with most of his usual properties—watches and clocks, glasses and goblets, a globe, a violin, writing-materials and an open book, a furled banner and so forth—is supposed to have come to the school from Oxnead at the same time.

Lord Yarmouth's library was dispersed in 1734, two years after his death. A catalogue was printed by the bookseller who had bought the collection, Olive (not Oliver) Payne. He drew particular attention to the 'great Number of scarce and curious Books in Chymistry, Alchemy, on the Philosopher's Stone, and several curious Manuscripts on those Subjects, wrote by the Earl.' The books, he declared, were in excellent condition, and many of them finely bound.

The library must largely have represented the taste and erudition of Sir William Paston and his son Robert, first Earl of Yarmouth. Fine editions of the classics abounded; there were quantities of French and Italian works; history and antiquities were well represented, with poetry, divinity, travel, medical and scientific treatises, English black-letter tracts, and volumes of seventeenth-century pamphlets and plays. Nor does the second Earl appear to have been a less enthusiastic book-buyer than his predecessors. In spite of his declining fortunes, he acquired many expensive new books— Campbell's *Vitruvius Britannicus* is an example—and bound them in yellow turkey, or morocco with gilt leaves, or 'red Calf with a Pane of Gold'.

The most striking feature of the library was, however, the accumulation of works dealing with alchemy, astrology and magic. The two Earls of Yarmouth never abandoned the hope of restoring their fortunes by the transmutation of metals, or the discovery of the philosopher's stone; and their shelves, crammed with Paracelsus and Raymond Lully and countless minor practitioners of the art, bear witness to their optimism. It is unfortunate that Olive Payne, when compiling his catalogue, did not specify which of the alchemical manuscripts were actually written by the last Earl. He only mentions that he had copiously annotated Geberus *De Alchimistae*, and another work entitled *Sanguis Naturae, or a manifest Declaration of the Sanguine and Solor congealed Liquor of Nature*.

But the most important of all the contents of Oxnead, strange though such an estimate would have seemed to the Pastons themselves, was the private correspondence of their medieval forefathers. The achievements of the family in its prime, its wealth and power, offices and dignities, were to weigh as nothing in the scales of history against these records of its early struggles in the fifteenth century. According to Sir John Fenn, the first editor of the *Paston Letters*, the manuscripts 'became the property of that great collector and antiquary Peter le Neve, Norroy', and thence passed to Tom Martin, who married le Neve's widow. If this account is correct, the last Earl must himself have transferred the papers to le Neve, whom he outlived by three years. It may have been so; but when in 1735, three years after the Earl's death, the Norfolk historian Francis Blomefield spent a fortnight at Oxnead, there was still a quantity of documents of all descriptions piled high in the 'evidence-room'. Blomefield reported on what he found in a letter to Major Weldon, one of the Earl's sons-in-law. There were trunks and chests and boxes crammed with title-deeds, court-rolls, surveys, extent-books, account-rolls, muster-rolls, freedoms, charters, even a manuscript history of Great Yarmouth. It is hard to believe that the orignals of the *Paston Letters* had somehow been extricated from this chaos and sold or given to le Neve. Moreover, Blomefield expressly told Major Weldon that 'there are innumerable letters of good consequence in history still lying among the loose papers, all of which I laid up in a corner of the room on a heap, which contains several sacks full; but as they seemed to have some family affairs of one nature or other intermixed in them, I did not offer to touch any of them, but have left them to your consideration whether, when I go to that part of the country, I shall separate and preserve them, or whether you will have them burnt, though I must own 'tis pity they should; except it be those (of which there are many) that relate to family affairs only. I have placed everything so that, now, the good and bad are distinguished, and preserved from the weather. A great number have perished entirely.'

In any case, whether they left Oxnead before or after the last Earl's death, the *Paston Letters* eventually reached the trustworthy hands of John Fenn; and after a further series of vicissitudes the entire collection now reposes in the British Museum.

IV

Houses, like human beings, have their allotted span, and without exception will vanish during the unimaginable succession of the years which lie ahead. Their accumulated relics of our civilization—painted canvases, carved and gilded wood, the moulded plaster of ceilings, the woven thread of tapestries —how shall such fragile things stand up to the passage of a hundred centuries? Even the monumental buildings of Vanbrugh and Gibbs—will anything remain of them when a thousand centuries have gone by? But such speculations are idle indeed, at a time when it is difficult to believe, in view of the social and political temper of our age, that the great country houses of England will survive, in any recognizable form, even for one single century.

So at Oxnead, though the place is heavy with the sense of departed grandeur, there is no need for sadness. Its treasures have been dispersed, and adorn public collections or have become the cherished possessions of other men. The house has vanished; its galleries and gables, its terraces and fountains are only a memory. All is peace, and verdure, and the clear East Anglian light. In the garden martins are circling, fly-catchers dart out from the spreading rose-bushes, the blackbirds sing at evening; and down on the Bure the swans are pallid shapes in the twilight, as they were three hundred years ago.

VENTA ICENORUM

It is only a great square field, fringed here and there with wind-blown ashes and oaks. Across its forty acres the crops pass year after year in their accustomed rotation. I have seen it under wheat, barley, oats, grass, sugar beet. I have watched it being ploughed, harrowed, drilled, harvested, and mucked again for the next ploughing. Except for the steep banks on north and south, and the immense ditch and rampart on the east, nothing remains to tell the passer-by that during the Roman centuries this was the principal town of easternmost Britain.

Closer investigation reveals a little more. There are broken stretches of tremendously solid wall-core, deeply overgrown, fissured by the roots of trees; and even a few surviving courses of the fine squared flints with which all the walls must once have been faced. The position of the southern entrance-gate may still be traced; and the outlines of the streets are perceptible in aerial photographs when the corn is ripe. Fragments of heavy Roman tiles, *tegulae* and *imbrices*, are always to be seen among the stones removed from the surface of the field and heaped along its edge. And the red of Roman bricks is mingled with the grey flint of the little square-towered church, half hidden in its ring of trees beside the great rampart.

Past excavations have revealed much of what lies beneath the soil. They have uncovered the forum, the pair of squat provincial temples, a few of the scattered houses—bases and foundations, nothing more. Like all but a few of the towns of Roman Britain, the growth of Venta Icenorum never fulfilled the expectations of those who first laid out its ground-plan. At no time, during the three centuries of its existence, were there enough dwellings to fill the space within its imposing walls. Houses straggled at irregular intervals along the streets. In any case the territory of the Iceni was never one of the more prosperous regions of Britain. The atrocities of Boudicca's rising led to reprisals—massacres certainly, and perhaps large-scale deportations to a lifetime of forced labour —which must have depopulated the area and may have led to its permanent impoverishment. The opulent villas of the south and west, with all their culture and refinement, had few counterparts here. Only a dozen or so villas, mostly of an unpretentious kind, have been recorded in the whole of Norfolk.

Nevertheless, three hundred years of continuous occupation have left their memory, their intangible but most definite impress, upon these acres. All over the field, stirred to and fro for centuries by the plough, lie sherds and fragments of Roman Britain. Brick and tile, amphora and dish and wine-cup, kitchen-ware of coarse grey and black, elegant Samian vessels of polished sealing-wax red, their remnants are everywhere. The rim of a Samian bowl will shine from the depression where a partridge has been dusting. A great segment of a quern, worn down by ages of use, will lie among the gnarled thorn-roots of the surrounding hedge. There are oyster-shells innumerable, mostly shells of those big coarse oysters from the beds off Burnham and Brancaster, which have been eaten and enjoyed all through Norfolk history. And on a memorable day I picked up a cornelian intaglio, deeply cut with a Roman galley being rowed towards a light-house, a *pharos* with its streaming flame, once set in a ring worn by someone at Venta Icenorum nearly two thousand years ago.

The living soil has been replaced above the excavations, and the remains of temples and houses are far below the surface, 'ashes under Uricon'. May it always be so. Further diggings will no doubt be undertaken in years to come, and deeply interesting they will prove; but may the poor foundations never lie permanently exposed, with barbed-wire fencing, and little informative notice-boards, and fragments of mosaic pavement under dilapidated wooden sheds. For the whole expanse, so calm and so beautiful under the changing Norfolk skies, is symbolic of the continuity of English life. In spring the Roman sherds gleam amongst the rows of sprouting barley. In autumn the huge combine-harvester throbs above the lines of the ancient streets. There is always a cawing of rooks in the distance, and the calling of partridges, and larks singing overhead, as there must have been in the days of the Iceni; and somewhere a tractor, and usually an aeroplane, the characteristic sounds of our own age. Snipe drum above the stream in the meadows beyond; and the wind strains, day after day, across the grassy banks of the town which is only a great square field.

BIBLIOGRAPHY

GENERAL

As in *Norfolk Portraits* and *A Norfolk Gallery*, I have made use of certain indispensable local works of reference throughout this book. They include:

Francis Blomefield and Charles Parkin. *History of Norfolk.* (In the eleven-volume edition of 1805.)

M. J. Armstrong. *History of Norfolk.* (This compilation, issued in parts, and reissued in ten volumes in 1781, is usually known by the name of Armstrong, one of the several writers who took part in it.)

R. H. Mason. *History of Norfolk.* 1884.

Transactions of the Norfolk and Norwich Archaeological Society (*Norfolk Archaeology*). From 1847 to the present time.

The East Anglian. Ed. Samuel Tymms. 4 vols. 1864–6. Ed. C. H. Evelyn White. 12 vols. 1885–1908.

Walter Rye. *Norfolk Families.* 1911.

Prince F. Duleep Singh. *Portraits in Norfolk Houses.* 2 vols. 1928.

Hamon le Strange. *Norfolk Official Lists.* 1890.

When quoting old letters and other documents, I have retained the original spelling in almost every instance. But contracted words (including the inevitable 'y^e' and similar formations) have been given at their full length; and I have in some places adjusted the punctuation, and made a few other concessions to the reader's convenience.

SIR WILLIAM PASTON

The letters between Sir William and Lady Paston, the Earl of Manchester and Sir John Potts, which deal with Sir William's troubles during the Civil War, are in the Bodleian

Bibliography

Library (*Tanner MSS.* 62, ff. 423, 431–2, 471–2, 489, 543–4; 64, ff. 8, 9, 30–2; 133, f. 166). Such details as I have found of his sequestration and other payments are in the Public Record Office, *State Papers* 19/4, 67, 69: 23/247: 28/238; in the British Museum, *Add. MS.* 5508; and *Commons' Journals*, iii, 434. Ralph Knevet's unpublished poems are in the British Museum, *Add. MS.* 27,447.

The letters between Sir William Paston and his mother are printed in *The Correspondence of Lady (Katherine) Paston*, ed. Ruth Hughey (Norfolk Record Society, 1941).

Other sources:

The Knyvett Letters. Ed. Bertram Schofield. 1949.

The Note-book and Account Book of Nicholas Stone. Ed. W. L. Spiers. Walpole Society, 1919.

Clarendon. *History of the Great Rebellion.* 1702.

Thomas Fuller. *History of the University of Cambridge.* 1655. *History of the Worthies of England.* 1662.

Sir Nicholas L'Estrange. *Merry Passages and Jests.* In *Anecdotes and Traditions* (ed. W. J. Thoms). Camden Society, 1839.

Ralph Knevet. *Funerall Elegies; Consecrated to the immortall memory of . . . the Lady Katherine Paston.* 1637.

Thomas Browne. *Pseudodoxia Epidemica.* 1646.

John Greaves. *Pyramidographia.* 1646.

Thomas Carlyle. *Letters and Speeches of Oliver Cromwell.* Ed. S. C. Lomas. 3 vols. 1904.

Edward Husband. *Collection of Orders, Ordinances and Declarations.* 1646.

John Hildeyard. *Sermon Preached . . . at the Funeral of the Earl of Yarmouth.* 1683.

Edward Phillips. *The New World of English Words.* 1658.

William Coles. *Adam in Eden.* 1657.

Robert May. *The Accomplisht Cook.* 1660.

Dawson Turner. *History of Caister Castle.* 1842.

CHARLES HARBORD

This chapter is based on the unpublished letters of Charles Harbord to his brother John, and those written to John by

Bibliography

their father Sir Charles Harbord. They are in the possession
of the Hon. Doris Harbord at Gunton Park. Reference has
also been made to a letter from Charles Harbord to his father,
in the Bodleian Library (*Tanner MS.* 49, f. 139). *MS.* 49, f. 139
Other sources:

The Diary of John Evelyn. Ed. E. S. de Beer. 6 vols. 1955.

The Diary of Samuel Pepys. Ed. H. B. Wheatley. 8 vols. 1926.

Arthur Bryant. *Pepys: the Man in the Making.* 1933. *Pepys: the Years of Peril.* 1935.

F. R. Harris. *The Life of Edward Montagu, K.G., first Earl of Sandwich.* 1912.

Journals and Narratives of the Third Dutch War. Ed. R. C. Anderson. Navy Records Society, 1946.

The Letters of Sir Thomas Browne. Ed. Geoffrey Keynes. 1931.

HUMPHREY PRIDEAUX

The basis of this study is *The Life of the Reverend Humphrey Prideaux, D.D., Dean of Norwich,* 1748. This anonymous work is ascribed to Thomas Birch, who is stated to have compiled it from materials supplied by Prideaux's son Edmund. The other principal source is *Letters of Humphrey Prideaux to John Ellis,* ed. Edward Maunde Thompson (Camden Society, 1875). The originals of these letters are in the British Museum, *Add. MS.* 28,929. His letters to his brother-in-law and sister, Mr. and Mrs. Coffin, are in *H.M.C.* 5th Report (MSS. of J. R. Pine Coffin).

For the years during which Prideaux was Dean of Norwich, I have drawn heavily on the two later volumes of the unpublished *Diarium* now in the possession of the Dean and Chapter of Norwich. The first volume is unfortunately missing.

The Account of Affairs in Norwich and Norfolk, mentioned on p. 70, is printed in Mason's *History of Norfolk,* pp. 367-8. I have given in *Norfolk Archaeology,* xxviii, 76-7, my reasons for assuming that this document was the work of Prideaux.

The letter about the "jaws of Hell," quoted on p. 70, is printed in *Original Letters of Eminent Literary Men,* ed. Sir Henry Ellis (Camden Society, 1843).

Bibliography

ACTON CREMER

The sources for this study are:

Thomas Hearne. *Collections.* Ed. C. E. Doble. Vol. iii. 1889.

John Nichols. *Illustrations of the Literary History of the Eighteenth Century.* Vol. iii. 1818.

Humphrey Prideaux. *Letters to John Ellis.* Ed. E. Maunde Thompson. 1875.

Falconer Madan. *Oxford Books.* Vol. iii. (*Oxford Literature, 1651–80*). 1931.

THE RECTOR OF FERSFIELD

There is a memoir of Francis Blomefield by S. W. Rix in *Norfolk Archaeology*, ii, 201–24. There are also accounts of him by Walter Rye in the *Norfolk Antiquarian Miscellany* (1887) iii, 177–84, and in the *Dictionary of National Biography*.

For this short essay I have consulted his manuscript Letter-Book in the Norwich Public Library, and (more especially) the parish registers and accounts at Fersfield.

ALEC PENROSE

It should perhaps be mentioned that Penrose did not publish any of his poetry. The passage quoted on p. 109 is the opening of a series of poems entitled *Wings of the Years*, which he printed privately in 1943.

THE COMING OF THE STRANGERS

The principal sources for this chapter are:

William Hudson and J. C. Tingey. *The Records of the City of Norwich*, vol. ii (1910). I have made much use of the admirable introduction to this volume, which was the work of Tingey, and of the extracts later in the volume from the *Book of Dutch and Walloon Strangers* in the City archives. I would re-emphasize here my view of the importance and interest of the material contained in the *Book of Dutch and Walloon Strangers*, and my hope that a complete transcription and edition of it will one day be undertaken.

Bibliography

Walter Rye. *The Dutch Refugees in Norwich.* A valuable article in *Norfolk Antiquarian Miscellany*, vol. iii (1887), pp. 185–248.

W. J. C. Moens. *The Walloons and their Church at Norwich: their History and Registers, 1565–1832.* (Huguenot Society's Publications, 1887–8.) This volume contains most useful material relating both to the Walloons and the Dutch, including the letters from the refugees in Norwich to their friends at Ypres.

Some of the details about Antony de Solempne are taken from the edition of his *Perpetual Calendar* by E. M. Beloe (King's Lynn, *circa* 1910). The inscription about the 'dyke reeve' in Haddiscoe church is discussed in *Norfolk Archaeology,* xxv, 161–2, 449–50.

Other sources:

W. Cunningham. *Alien Immigrants to England.* 1897.

Stanley Edwards. *Strangers at Lynn in 1572.* (*Norfolk Antiquarian Miscellany*, i, 195–8.)

Lucy Toulmin Smith. *The Walloon Church in Norwich.* (*Norfolk Antiquarian Miscellany*, ii, 91–148.)

E. A. Kent. *Notes on the Blackfriars' Hall or Dutch Church, Norwich.* (*Norfolk Archaeology*, xxii, 86–108.)

John Nichols. *The Progresses and Public Processions of Queen Elizabeth.* 2 vols. 1788.

Thomas Fuller. *History of the Worthies of England.* 1662.

John Gage. *History and Antiquities of Hengrave.* 1822.

C. B. Jewson. *Three Registers of Passengers from Great Yarmouth to Holland and New England, 1637–1639.* (Norfolk Record Society, 1954.)

THE GREAT BLOWE

The depositions of persons concerned in, or witnesses of, the riot described in this chapter are in the City archives of Norwich. They were used extensively by Walter Rye in an appendix to his *History of the Bethel Hospital at Norwich* (1906), which contains a lengthy account of the episode. Although I do not agree with his account in all particulars, I am greatly indebted to it as a whole.

Bibliography

Blomefield also described the riot at some length in the third volume of his *History of Norfolk* (1805 ed.). I think he undoubtedly made use of these depositions; but he seems also to have had access to some other contemporary account, unknown to Rye or to myself.

The letters from eye-witnesses which I have quoted are in the Bodleian Library, *Tanner MSS.* 57, f. 35, and 311, ff. 36, 38.

The sermons of the Rev. John Carter were published in 1647 in a volume entitled THE NAIL AND THE WHEEL. *The Nail fastned by a Hand from Heaven. The Wheel turned by a Voyce from the Throne of Glory. Both Described in Two Several Sermons in the Green-yard at Norwich. By John Carter, Pastor of Great St. Peters.*

The account of Charles Porter's part in the affair occurs in Roger North's *Lives of the Norths* (ed. Augustus Jessopp, 1890), i, 381–2.

THE PHANTOM DUEL

This story is an expansion of a section of the chapter 'Norfolk and the Threat of Invasion' in my *Norfolk Portraits* (1944). Certain passages have been reproduced *verbatim* from the earlier book. The letters between the contestants were taken from contemporary copies at Felbrigg.

Other sources:

Edward Spelman. Dedication of *The Expedition of Cyrus into Persia . . . translated from Xenophon.* 2 vols. 1749.

Horace Walpole. *Letters.* Ed. Mrs. Paget Toynbee. 1903–5.

C. W. James. *Lord Justice Coke: his Family and Descendants at Holkham.* 1929.

A. M. W. Stirling. *Coke of Norfolk and his Friends.* 1908.

Albert Hartshorne. *Memoirs of a Royal Chaplain, 1729–1763.* 1905.

Memoirs of Richard Gardiner, alias Dick Merry-fellow. 1782.

THE TOUR OF NORFOLK

The letters from Lady Beauchamp Proctor, describing her tours to her sister Mrs. Charles Yorke, have not been
231

Bibliography

previously published. They were kindly lent to me by Mr. Gerald Yorke.

Other sources:

An Eighteenth-Century Correspondence. Eds. Lilian Dickins and Mary Stanton. 1910 (for George and Charles Lyttelton).

Lord Hervey and his Friends. Ed. the Earl of Ilchester. 1952.

H.M.C. Report on the MSS. of the Earl of Carlisle. 1897 (for Sir Thomas Robinson). *Report on the MSS. of the Duke of Portland.* Vol. vi. 1901 (for Lord Oxford).

George Vertue. *Note Books.* Vol. v. (Walpole Society, 1938.)

The Foundling Hospital for Wit. 1743.

Passages from the Diaries of Mrs. Philip Lybbe Powys. Ed. Emily J. Climenson. 1899 (for Miss Caroline Girle).

Memoirs of the Life and Correspondence of Mrs. Hannah More. Ed. William Roberts. 4 vols. 1834.

A Frenchman in England. Being the Melanges sur l'Angleterre of François de la Rochefoucauld. Ed. Jean Marchand, translated with notes by S. C. Roberts. 1933

Arthur Young. *A Six Weeks Tour, through the Southern Counties of England and Wales.* 1772.

William Gilpin. *Observations on . . . Cambridge, Norfolk, Suffolk and Essex.* 1809.

Jane Austen. *Emma.* 1816.

Samuel Jackson Pratt. *Gleanings in England.* 3 vols. 1804.

Sydney D. Kitson. *The Life of John Sell Cotman.* 1937.

The Torrington Diaries. Ed. C. Bruyn Andrews. 1954.

THE GUNTON HOUSEHOLD BOOK

The Household Book described here is still at Gunton Park. I have reproduced certain passages from a broadcast talk which I gave in the Third Programme in June 1950. Sir Thomas Browne's prescriptions were printed in the *Times Literary Supplement* of 2nd November 1951.

I have made use of the *Letters* and the *Miscellaneous Writings* of Browne, ed. Geoffrey Keynes (1931).

Bibliography

THE TREASURE OF OXNEAD

A description of Oxnead, together with the inventory of a portion of the contents of the house, was printed by John Adey Repton in the *Gentleman's Magazine*, 1844, pt. i, pp. 21–4. The inventory which covers all the rooms of the house, though with a regrettable meagreness as to their contents, is in B.M. *Add. MS.* 36,988 ff. 254v–255. I am indebted to the researches of Dr. Pamela Tudor-Craig for further illumination on the subject of Oxnead. Tom Martin's note-books, from which I have quoted, are in the Norwich Public Library. The copy of the sale-catalogue of the Oxnead library is in the British Museum, and is, I believe, unique.

INDEX

Acton, Anne, 92
Acton, Thomas, S. J., 74
Adams, William, 50
Albemarle, George Monk, Duke of, 55
Alcock, Aaron, 86
Aldrich, Henry, 65, 93, 95–6
Alexander, Rev. Thomas, 77
Alva, Duke of, 113, 116, 121
Anne, Queen, 177, 181, 192
Anson, Admiral George, 214, 216
Arundel, Thomas Howard, Earl of, 67, 217
Ashmanhaugh, 102
Ashwell, Thomas, 133–6, 145
Ashwellthorpe, 18, 20
Atkyns, Sir Edward, 79
Austen, Jane, 200
Aylsham, 30, 115, 188

Bacon, Capt. Robert, 22
Bacon family 216
Baker, William, Bishop of Norwich, 182
Baret, Christopher, 134, 146–7
Barker, Rev. John, 99–100
Barningham, 177
Bath, William Pulteney, Earl of, 185
Bathurst, Dr. Ralph, 94
Bayfield, 190, 201
Beauchamp Proctor, Lady (*née* Letitia Johnson), 187–95 *passim*
Beauchamp Proctor, Sir William, 187–195 *passim*
Beeston Regis, 201
Bensly, Richard, 144–5
Bergen, attack on, 48, 56
Besthorpe, 43
Bidwell, Thomas and John, 150
Blackstone, Sir William, 151
Blickling, 38, 69, 171–3, 187–9, 193–194, 216–17

Blofield, 182
Blomefield, Rev. Francis, 97–104 *passim*, 221–2
Blomefield family, 98–9 102–3
Boleyn, Queen Anne, 173
Bokenham, Anthony, 72
Boscawen, Admiral Edward, 153
Braconash, 84
Bradenham, 105–7
Brancaster, 224
Bridge, Rev. William, 130, 147–8
Bridgman, Charles, 180
Bromholme Priory, 18
Brooke, Thomas, 122–3
Browne, Sir Thomas, 26, 36, 45, 50, 173, 206–11, 214; prescriptions by him, 209–11
Browne, Lady (*née* Dorothy Mileham), 207, 211
Browne, Thomas, 42, 48
Buckinghamshire, John Hobart 2nd Earl of, 173, 193–4
Bungay, 208
Burlington, Richard Boyle 3rd Earl of, 175, 179, 181–2
Burman, Edward, 147
Burnham, 224
Busby, Dr. Richard, 64, 70, 93
Buxton, John, 218
Buxton family, 218–19

Caister Castle, 17, 39, 217
Caister-by-Yarmouth, 39, 99
Caistor St. Edmund, 223–5
Campbell, Colen, 174, 183
Caroline, Queen, 178
Carter, Rev. John, 132–3, 148
Castleacre, 198
Castle Rising, 28, 40
Catelyn, Richard, 28
Charles I, 18, 21, 27–9, 31, 35, 42, 131, 136, 147, 175

235

Index

Charles II, 33, 39, 40, 42–3, 54–5, 61, 71, 211, 213, 218
Cleveland, Duchess of, 66
Cley, 41
Coke (*see under* Leicester)
Coldham, James, 161
Coles, William, 36–7
Collinges, Rev. John, 132, 148
Corbet, Miles, 34, 130
Cornwallis family, 17
Costessey, 125
Cotman, John Sell, 210–2
Cotterell, Sir Charles, 53, 59,
Cotterell, Clement, 53–6, 58–62
Cranmer, 156, 159, 162
Cremer, Acton, 92–6 *passim*
Cremer, Henry, 96
Cremer, John, 92
Cringleford, 122
Crome, John, 202
Cromer, 200–1
Crostwight, 24, 50
Crowe, William, 39
Cumberland, William, Duke of, 154
Cuttinges, Captain, 46

Danckerts, Henry, 52
de Grey, Sir Robert, 30, 34
Delany, Mrs. 187
Dereham, East, 106, 136, 192
Dersingham, 166
Diss, 97
Docking, 197
Drayton, Michael, 127
Dryden, John, quoted, 41, 156

Earle, Erasmus, 79
Earsham, 198
Elison, Pastor Joannes, 128
Elizabeth I, Queen, 17, 92, 116–17, 124–6, 192
Elizabeth, H.M. the Queen Mother, 110
Ellis, John, 65–87 *passim*, 95
Emerson, Charles, 150
Euston, 198
Evelyn, John, 31, 42, 55–6, 59, 67

Fairfax, Henry, Dean of Norwich, 77–80, 83
Faithorne, William, 38
Fakenham, 182, 192, 201

Fanshawe, Sir Richard, 49
Fastolf, Sir John, 17, 217
Felbrigg, 139, 157, 189–90, 218
Fell, Dr. John, 64–7, 70–2, 93–6
Fenn, Sir John, 221–2
Fenne, Captain, 42
Fersfield, 97–104 *passim*
Finch, Hon. Charles, 67
Fleetwood, Colonel Charles, 136, 148
Florists' Feasts, 124, 131
Foulden, 139
Fountaine, Sir Andrew, 177, 184–5
Frederick, Prince of Wales, 178
French, Robert, 219
Fring, 92
Fuller, Thomas, 19, 36, 124

Gardiner, Alderman Francis, 85
Gardiner, Richard, 168
Gawdy, Framlingham, 28
George I, 173–4
George II, 178
George III, 200
Gibbs, John, 46
Gilpin, Rev. William, 171, 199
Girle, Caroline (Mrs. Lybbe Powys), 186–7
Godolphin, Sir William, 49, 53
Goldingham, Bernard, 125
Gostlin, William, 134
Goward, Henry, 138, 141, 150
Gray, Edward, 150
Greaves, John, 26
Greeve, James, 41
Grove, Robert, Bishop of Chichester, 86
Gunton, 44, 203–8

Hackett, Rev. John, 182
Haddiscoe, 115
Haddock, Captain Richard, 57–8
Hanbury Williams, Sir Charles, 153
Harbord, Sir Charles, 42–62 *passim*; letters of, 59–62
Harbord, Charles, 42–62 *passim*, 130, 203; at Tangier, 44–7, 51–2; in Spain, 49–51; association with Lord Sandwich, 43–62; knighted, 48; in England, 51–4; death at battle of Solebay, 56–8; uncertainty as to his fate, 59–61; will and monument, 61–2

Index

Index

Index

Index

True, William, 150

Utting, John, 132–49 *passim*

Valevin, — , 56–7
Van Brakel, Captain, 57
Van de Velde, Willem, 41
Van Dyck, Sir Anthony, 21
Van Ghent, Admiral, 57–8
Vanneck, Sir Gerard, 198
Van Tromp, Admiral, 66
Vertue, George, 184

Walker, Obadiah, 73
Walpole, Horatio 1st Lord Walpole of Wolterton, 176–7
Walpole, Horatio 2nd Lord Walpole of Wolterton, 194
Walpole, Hon. Horatio (Horace), 38, 153, 155, 167, 177, 185, 187, 189, 217–18
Walpole, Sir Robert (afterwards 1st Earl of Orford), 173–85 *passim*, 217, 219
Walpole (*see also* Orford, Earl of)
Walsall, Dr. Samuel, 19
Walsham, North, 17, 219
Walsingham, 30, 201
Warwick, Robert Rich 2nd Earl of, 29
Weasenham, 186
Weldon, Thomas, 221

Westacre, 186
Whall, Thomas, 121
Wighton, 85
William III, 60, 75–6
Williamson, Sir Joseph, 60
Wilson, Anthony, 150
Winch, West, 92
Windham, Ashe, 218
Windham, William, 157
Windham, Rt. Hon. William, 189
Wisbech, 105, 109
Wodehouse family, 216
Wodehouse, Sir Armine, 157
Wodehouse, Sir Philip, 208
Wodehouse, Sir Thomas, 28
Womack family, 98–9
Wolfe, General James, 156, 165–6, 168
Wood, Anthony À, 66
Wood, Mrs. 84–5
Wootton, 85
Worstead, 115
Wren, Matthew, Bishop of Norwich and Ely, 28
Wright, Thomas, 52

Yarmouth, Great, 28, 39, 41, 68, 75, 114–15, 129, 142, 154, 182
Yarmouth, Earls of (*see under* Paston)
York, Duke of (*see under* James II)
Yorke, Hon. Charles, 188
Young, Arthur, 196–9